UMBI

Landscapes of the Imagination

The Alps by Andrew Beattie
Provence by Martin Garrett
Flanders by André de Vries
The Thames by Mick Sinclair
Catalonia by Michael Eaude
The Basque Country by Paddy Woodworth
Andalucía by John Gill
Patagonia by Chris Moss
The French Riviera by Julian Hale
The Andes by Jason Wilson
The West Country by John Payne
The Ionian Islands and Epirus by Jim Potts
The Cotswolds by Jane Bingham
The Danube by Andrew Beattie
Siberia by A. J. Haywood
The Loire by Martin Garrett
The Sahara by Eamonn Gearon
The Isle of Wight, Portsmouth and the Solent by Mark Bardell
The Peak District by John Bull

Landscapes

UMBRIA
A Cultural History

JONATHAN BOARDMAN

Signal Books
Oxford

First published in 2012 by
Signal Books Limited
36 Minster Road
Oxford OX4 1LY
www.signalbooks.co.uk

A catalogue record for this book is available from the British Library

ISBN 978-1-904955-94-8 Paper

Cover Design: Devdan Sen
Design and Production: Devdan Sen
Cover Images: Claudio Colombo/istockphoto
Illustrations: all images courtesy Wikipedia Commons except: istockphoto i, 11, 28, 60, 88,
151, 160, 170, 210; ibew.org.uk 195; Laura Valerio 85
Printed in India

Contents

Introduction and Acknowledgements
BECOMING UMBRIAN   vii

Chapter One
A RIVER AND A ROAD: LANDSCAPES   1
   The Via Flaminia (5); Umbrian Identity (7)

Chapter Two
UNDERGROUND UMBRIA: PREHISTORY TO ROMAN ERA   15
   Caves, Catacombs and Crypts (17); Perugia: the Whiff of
   Sulphur (23)

Chapter Three
THEATRE: THE ROMAN ERA   29
   Golden Age (36); Modern Theatrics (42)

Chapter Four
TEMPLE TO CHURCH: A PERIOD OF INVASIONS   45
   Early Christianity (50)

Chapter Five
THE CASTLE: MIDDLE AGES I   61
   Feudal Umbria (62); Good Friday Processions (69)

Chapter Six
THE TOWN HALL: MIDDLE AGES II   75
   The Urban Ideal (77); The Day of the Mad (83)

Chapter Seven
THE CHURCH: MIDDLE AGES III   89
   Holy Umbria (100)

Chapter Eight
THE CONVENT: UMBRIAN SANCTITY   105
   The Basilica di San Francesco (111); Franciscans and
   Dominicans (115); Relics (119)

Chapter Nine
THE FRESCO: UMBRIAN ART   121
   Il Perugino (122); Masters and Mysteries (128); Serious about
   Art (133)

Chapter Ten
THE PALACE: THE AGE OF THE *SIGNORI*   137
   Gubbio (140); Noblesse Oblige (143)

Chapter Eleven
THE CASA COLONICA: FARMING AND THE AGE OF THE PAPAL
STATE   149
   Love of the Soil (153)

Chapter Twelve
FOOD: TIMELESS UMBRIA   163
   Culture of Eating (169)

Chapter Thirteen
THE FACTORY: THE NINETEENTH AND TWENTIETH
CENTURIES   173
   Industrial Landscape (176); Taming the Falls (178); Chocolate, Water
   and Wine (182)

Chapter Fourteen
THE MUSIC FESTIVAL: CONTEMPORARY UMBRIA I   187
   Umbria Jazz (190); Musical Culture (192)

Chapter Fifteen
MODERNITY AND TRADITION: CONTEMPORARY UMBRIA II   197
   A Modern Saint (203); Managing the Past (205)

EPILOGUE   209

FURTHER READING   213

INDEX OF LITERARY, ARTISTIC & HISTRORICAL NAMES   215

INDEX OF PLACES & LANDMARKS   220

Introduction and Acknowledgements

BECOMING UMBRIAN

So why Umbria? During the preparation for this book I have often asked myself this same question, especially when faced with relatively little written in English on the subject. My former excursion into travel writing, a cultural and literary guide to Rome, could draw on such a deep well of material in almost every conceivable language which had then been translated into English that the task sometimes seemed more like editing than composing. In fact, I was able to write the book while living in London, making only relatively short trips to confirm and expand information. Ironically, I have since lived ten years in Rome, and might even now be ready again to tackle that inexhaustible source of reflection and excitement from a rather more immediate perspective.

Yet the fact of working in Rome and the way it has improved my understanding of the Italian language has also clearly made Umbria more accessible in various ways. I live only half an hour's drive or so from the southern border and no more than three hours away from the most far-flung corner. My car almost seems to know the road unguided. And much of my research has been from the naturally more substantial corpus of Italian writing on the region, from standard modern texts of general interest such as the excellent Touring Club *Guida*, through collections of original documents such as the correspondence of Federico Cesi, to some of the numerous locally produced monographs of highly specialized interest. Of course, there are recent and not so recent writers in English who have mentioned or even focused on Umbria in both fact and fiction: the seventeenth- and eighteenth-century tourists, Lord Byron, Henry James, Barry Unsworth and Lisa de St. Aubin de Terán. Then again superb general guides, gazetteers and tours of the region have been provided by the likes of the pleasantly exhaustive Ian Campbell Ross and the consummately elegant Jonathan Keates. To all of these I owe a huge debt both of direct information and of setting me off on trails that caught my interest. I have tried to acknowledge this with direct citation of their material.

But the real answer to my opening question remains a personal one.

Umbria is the only landscape I feel capable of writing about, since from first acquaintance with the region I have felt reassuringly at home here. So what is it about the place that cast the spell? Some (or do I mean all?) of it is undoubtedly autobiographical—so back to me!

Earlier in my Italian slice of life I had experienced similar instantaneous attractions both to Rome and to the east coast of Sicily, one leading to an abiding relationship with the Mother of European cities and the other still exerting a strong sense of nostalgic attachment. But twenty-five year's acquaintance has revealed the truth that I will never be a Roman and now I doubt I will ever see Catania, Syracuse or the Aci coastal towns again for anything more than a delightful, occasional visit. But what has crept up on me is that I have aspirations of *being*, or at least *becoming*, Umbrian. Now this naturally presupposes that there is both something definable as "Umbrian", a claim that for example Chapter One will strongly contest, and that a foreign-born settler might aspire to this perhaps non-existent condition. In later chapters my musings on the nature of Umbrian spirituality and art will get me closer to what "feels like kin" to me in this place—and surely art and religion should be open to all? There is also the incontestable fact that property ownership is freighted with investment—emotional as well as financial. My own home, the only house that I own, is in Umbria, making a big difference to how I view the place, how my proprietary sense exerts itself, however exaggeratedly or even inappropriately.

For as will become pretty clear my point of view is not just/even Umbrian, it is north-Umbrian (not to be confused with Northumbrian. Not long after I bought the house in the upper Valley of the Tiber a friend drew my attention to the strange coincidence of place-names in central Italy and north-east England. It makes no sense even to note it except for oracular or occult affect, but when have I ever let that stop me?). Further, I have no intention of making apologies for the fact that direct, anecdotal evidence of how Umbria is, how its people operate and think, will almost always be drawn from this marginal district, for I have also striven to expose all parts of Umbria for your delight. I have been inevitably rewarded in so doing by getting to know the whole a good deal better than I did before.

Relative permanence and time to reflect have also provided me with the opportunity to build up friendships in the region and to get to know (and develop a critique for understanding) some of the inside workings of what might otherwise be just thought to be a rather seamlessly managed, internationally acclaimed and nationally treasured floor-show. For a "spectacle" Umbria undoubtedly is, and that is what I mean to demonstrate in this book. But let me immediately qualify the assertion, and further explain why it is this particular show in a nation of performance that is so appealing. I, and I guess others, find Umbria comfortably manageable. What do I mean by this? Let me try to explain.

Its varied and interesting landscape lacks the unremitting ruggedness of Le Marche, Abruzzo or Basilicata among the peninsular, and all of the Alpine, regions, only very occasionally venturing into the territory of the "sublime". I have never wanted to live in a corridor, the impression I got from a visit to the Val d'Aosta, and not even the Hollywood glamour emanating from George Clooney's sojourn by Lake Como would tempt me to settle by these heavily shadowed, mountain-hung shores. Nor is Umbria as intimidating as Tuscany or Sicily in social, culinary or artistic terms. (I truly have detected something snobbish about Florence, Siena and even Lucca and their hinterlands, even if only resulting from their inhabitants' standardization of Italian pronunciation, something I have never managed to acquire in any language, speaking English with what someone once termed "my unmistakably northern brogue" and with a dash of *romanaccio* to my Italian. And, well, the respect due to Sicily and the impossibility of becoming a part of its "cultural structure" to avoid any more pejorative terms for how things work there, are simply insurmountable, as we all know.) The region takes its name from the indigenous tribes (Umbri) which the Etruscans and Romans encountered there in antiquity, which itself seems not to be connected with the modern Italian word *ombra,* designating "shade". For the most part we are in the sun here even when traversing the valleys.

Yes, Umbria provides sufficiently different landscapes and cultural contexts to tower above the Cities of the (Po) Plain over in Emilia Romagna and Lombardy. Its status as a former province of the Papal States also has the advantage for me of assuring its inclusion in southern, or adopting the modern distinction, central Italy. No Italian Umbrian would be clamouring to include his or her region in those territories termed *meridionale,* southern, since it is a matter of honour always to eschew its negative, poverty-stricken connotations. Indeed, social historians have noted that Italians always describe "the South" as starting in the town, or region, just further south than their own—even when they are living in Puglia… But my wishing to place Umbria in this half of the peninsula is personal once again. I simply do not want to have to negotiate the confusion caused by finding a statue to a Hapsburg prince in the piazza and having to imagine myself suddenly beyond the Alps. From Umbria's medium heights we look only south to Rome, following the Tiber, and then beyond in an inevitable progress to the "Land where the Lemon Trees Bloom", as Goethe would have it. This may, these days, be only "a comfort" temperamentally, since crossing the regional border from Tuscany to Umbria also usually spells a decline in the quality of the road surface. Maybe it always has. Tobias Smollett, leaving eighteenth-century Umbria for the north, noted that the road was "so unequal and stony, that we were jolted even to the danger of our lives".

Umbria gets hot in the summer and cold in the winter, recommendations to my limited range of seasonal expectation. One has to be careful that potted citrus trees are taken inside against the burning winter frost and yet one must be assiduous in watering them during July's scalding blast. Lisa St. Aubin de Terán expresses her surprise in *A Valley in Italy* when, delighting in her refurbishment of an Umbrian historic house, her failure to have installed the windows by the start of the cold weather proves something of a trial to her family: "Rain, wind and the icy cold could not be excluded with the plastic sheeting hastily erected by the workmen. By the end of October the need for windows had been transformed from an aesthetic *desideratum* into a means of survival."

She had recently transferred from Venice, memorably chilly, so how it could have slipped her mind that Italy can become cold (and in *La Serenissima*'s case, uniquely damp) is beyond me. In Umbria there are also recognizable springs and autumns, with wild flowers and fruits of wood and field appropriate to each. All seems right under heaven, then, in this intelligible ordering of the year's turn, provided you have windows fitted in your house.

Umbria's intelligibility is part of its distinction, its modestly challenging vistas the root of its charm. It is not that the unexpected never happens here, nor that a puzzle cannot be found to intrigue—it is simply that a state of secure well-being seems to be the place's genius, her abiding spirit. And this in the face of lively seismic activity, a special religious wealth, an occasionally violent history and an innovative present. It could just be that the accrued human living which has been banked in the region leaves the place feeling deeply human and humane.

If it is humane, then what about the humans? Unsurprisingly, land-locked Umbria can inspire a certain insularity in its natives. For example, about five years ago I accompanied a retired *carabiniere* officer from Città di Castello on his first flight and first trip outside Italy. The highlight of his jaunt, if volubility was the standard for enjoyment, was his catching sight of Lago Trasimeno (Lake Trasimene) beneath us, as we made our aerial way north from Rome towards the Alps. He also stuck firmly to Italian food, I noticed, during his stay in England. On the flight home a good deal of his conversation centred on what his wife might have prepared for supper. But against this interiority can be set a spirit of adventure typified by the figure of St. Francis of Assisi; called in his own imagination to be a knight errant, he finished off becoming a hugely travelled holy man whose name has been given to a metropolis on the Pacific shore of North America, among other towns almost too many to count.

Eccentricity, too, finds a home here: we will meet it in my chapter on the clergy and Church of Umbria in particular, and it crops up with pleas-ing regularity in expatriate settlers. I was once invited to supper at the home of an elderly friend who had retired to Umbria after crowning his legal career with the town clerkship of a Lakeland borough. On entering his elegant apartment within a dignified town *palazzo* he donned a velvet smoking jacket and tassled hat, both of which provided sartorial comple-ments to his monocled eye. Perhaps you can imagine that my expectations were considerably raised about what we might be going to have to eat. I had not predicted soup made from a packet and warmed up meat from the Sunday roast. He made up for it years later (he is now nearing ninety) with a full English cream tea, including home-made scones.

Women, it seems, are of two types in Umbria—tall, leggy, dark-haired beauties taking after the actress Monica Bellucci, the local girl made super, sexy good, or little old countrywomen wearing flowered housecoats brush-ing the steps on brisk late winter mornings or gossiping with friends in the cool of a summer evening. How the two types are connected, that is, exactly when the one turns in to the other, I simply do not know. My closest woman friend from Umbria is definitely in the first category, even achieving more Bellucci-esque standing by being a fellow townswoman of the super star. Elena Lenari, thirty something and recently married to a successful accountant, continues to work as the accounts clerk in a small local business. She has a rather personal but highly successful dress sense. No useless snow-white ball gown for her "walk down the aisle", but a serviceable, fashionable two-piece in cream. Though we seem for ever to be eating hyper-caloric treats together she remains pencil-thin, and her smile and laughter underwrite a good humour that is contagious. She is close to her family as all Italians are (her mother a former small *restaurateuse*, and her brother a *geometra* or surveyor), but not to the extent that can characterize the more extreme forms of Italian familial relations. She balances well, too, the expectations of a young matron in relation to her in-laws. Ready to lend a hand to them when in need she is also prepared to get away to her own space. Vivacious without being tiringly so, she is remarkably unstuffy and natural. Beginning to wonder why I didn't marry her myself? Well, I was already taken.

And Umbrian men? Characteristically stocky and strong, they seem generally to be able to put their hands to anything. Neat gardens, productive vegetable plots, DIY projects abound. "Boys' toys"—nice cars, fancy bikes and other machinery—are much in evidence. Local football teams swarm across the region, and other country sports attract their followings. The arts are also far from neglected in even the most masculine of portfolios; proficiency in a musical instrument is common, assisted by the persistence of local town bands and the well-known music festivals. And in a city, for example, as industrially modern as Terni, the attention and opportunities given to local modern artists is exemplary.

Well, I am pretty sure that you must by now think that I have become at least sufficiently Umbrian to display a high level of unreconstructed sexism, a trait more noticeable still in Italian society than in the United Kingdom and States—women appraised for their looks, men for all this shiny kit and their manly activities. It is as hard here as it is anywhere in Italy for women to break into the world of politics and business, despite the odd exception such as Città di Castello's smooth left-wing former mayor, and men have an unquestioned predominance in public life, backed up by the family, the Church and other cultural structures. Younger Umbrians are undoubtedly questioning this, and so they should. The changes which have happened elsewhere will undoubtedly follow here. In the meantime, give me a break, and permit me my clichéd last gasp of broad-stroke generalizations about the sexes. Let me talk about "my" football team.

It is mine, since I am its chaplain. There is no tradition of local clergy assuming this position in Italy, unlike countries dominated by an Anglo-Saxon culture. And so I had to tread carefully not to offend the local parish priest, Don Giuseppe, by my presumption when I was invited to take on the duty for Tigrotti Morra, the "Morra Leopards", during the 2008/9 season. We are named not for some whimsy about how the fauna of Umbria might be yet further and frighteningly enhanced (see Chapter Four), but in honour of a 1960s TV show, *Sandokan*, in which the bandit clan surrounding the eponymous hero were so called. Equipped with a bright red Tigrotti tracksuit and interviewed by local TV and radio, I found my duties did not extend far beyond attending the odd match, eating at their seasonal dinners and promising them my prayers. Even the players' attempts not to employ any of the plethora of religiously themed curses when I stood on the touchline, would normally give way by the beginning of the second half. I cannot help thinking they would have done better getting to know my namesake, Jon Boardman, born 1981 (as opposed to JB vintage '63), the professional footballer formerly of Crystal Palace and now of Woking Town. However, supported by my intercession, they did at least go up last year in the league.

And so it looks like I might in some small way have finally become what I have wanted to be these ten years: an Umbrian local. After the football team, who knows, other characteristic activities might follow—a desire to start hunting small birds, develop an *orto* or vegetable garden, take part in planning village celebrations, don Renaissance costume for a *corteo storico*, take up painting or a brass musical instrument. The possibilities seem endless. And as what I hope will be something like an honourable retirement edges just that little bit nearer, my dreams of truly belonging in this landscape of the imagination seem that much closer to becoming reality.

಄

Where can I begin my thanks that have led to the slow gestation and relatively effortful delivery of this book? Certainly with my mother, Yvonne Boardman, who was first to commit to my dream of a land where sunflowers bloom, and without whose love and kindness the life I have lived in Umbria could never even have begun let alone flowered. Then once again my publisher James Ferguson, who trusted me a second time to deliver a manuscript on time and this time was severely tested in his faith. The Chaplaincy Council of All Saints' Anglican Church, Rome, permitted me a two-month study leave in order to get the ball rolling, and many individuals from that community, particularly the Rev'd Sara MacVane and its lay leadership were instrumental then and have continued to be supportive and patient.

There are many Italians, mainly Umbrians, who have also shared the adventure with me. Special thanks go to Giancarlo Vicchi, Andrea Marchesani, Lamberto and Elena Lanari, Fabio Lelli, Tomasso Carbone and Francesco Scoppola. Msgrs. Vincenzo Paglia, Giuseppe Chiaretti and Domenico Cancian have been gracious in their ecclesiastical welcome to me, as have a wide variety of expatriate settlers in the region: Peter Hurd, Colin Baldy, Brian Reed and Jill and Jim Powrie in particular. Old UK-based friends Dr. Clive Marsland, and Atticus and Hilda Hainsworth together put up with a great deal of my obsessing about the region in the run-up to buying property there, and other friends have been equally tolerant and subtly supportive more recently. Paul Butler and Lindsey Barker have been a constant feature for nearly fifteen years of a fortuitously shared interest in the upper Valley of the Tiber. I would not still be anything of an Umbrian resident (or indeed anything of a writer, Umbrian or anything else) without the support and constant friendship of Philippe de Poliakoff and his mother Françoise Cousteau. I am extremely grateful to Professor Ingrid Rowland for having read the first draft and for making the sort of suggestions for improvement only she could. But most of my gratitude goes to Alessandro Gentili who literally has forced me into finishing this book which often I thought un-finishable, despite my continued love affair with its subject. I needed to be bullied and hope that my dedication of this work to him might mean he gives me a bit of a break.

a Alessandro GENTILI

foederis heu taciti Sextus Propertius, Elegies IV, 7

UMBRIA PROVINCE

MARCHES

Città di Castello

Upper
Tiber
Valley

TUSCANY

Gubbio

Umbertide

Gualdo Tadino

Tiber

Lake
Trasimeno

Nocera Umbra

Castiglione
del Lago

Perugia

Assisi

Clitumno

Spello

Topino

Deruta

Città della Pieve

Bevagna

Foligno

Montefalco

Trevi

★ *Fonte di*
Clitumno

Todi

Norcia

Lake
Corbara

Santuario di
Dio Misericordioso

Spoleto

Nera

Cascia

Orvieto

San Pietro in Valle

Terni

Cascate delle
Marmore

Narni

LAZIO

N

| 0 | km | 25 |
| 0 | miles | 15 |

Chapter One

A RIVER AND A ROAD

LANDSCAPES

Everybody seems to start off describing Umbria by saying that it is difficult to be precise about its boundaries. So when have I ever neglected to use a cliché? Let's follow the trend. The region as we find it today is an undoubted innovation. The Romans would have classed everything west of the Tiber as Etruria; the communes of medieval central Italy had no regional identity and the individual prefectures of the Papal State were locally based around their Episcopal cities without any sense of belonging to a larger geographical designation. "Umbria" was, it is true, the name of the 6th Region in the Augustan reorganization of Italia (27 BC-14 AD), but it stretched to include parts of modern Le Marche as far as the Adriatic. A later imperial reformer, Diocletian (280-290s AD), created new divisions and descriptions for his Italian dominions, four of which (Picenum, Umbria, Tuscia and Flaminia) included parts of our region. In the Middle Ages the term Umbria was generally used to define the area around Spoleto but excluded Perugia and her territories. Even more confusingly, until the twentieth century Gubbio was always included in Le Marche, as a former part of the Duchy of Urbino. When we reach the Renaissance, parts of what we now call Umbria feature in no fewer than six of the maps in the Vatican's sumptuous cartographical gallery, cataloguing the entire Italian peninsula and beyond, painted between 1580 and 1583 by Ignazio Danti for Pope Gregory XIII, based upon the groundbreaking scientific geographical researches of his brother Antonio. And even in relatively modern times at least three independent states (the Republic of Cospaia, the Marquisate of the Bourbons del Monte, and the Duchy of the della Corgna) survived to maintain a degree of political diversity amidst the bloc of the central section of the Papal State. Umbria as we now know it is not even a Risorgimento or Fascist creation, taking final form only in the post-war republican reorganization of Italy.

Beyond the definitions of these various successive authorities intellectual commentators such as Bruno Toscano, the well-known historian from Spoleto, have claimed that Umbria is really a "Byzantine corridor" stretching from Ravenna, perhaps even taking in Bologna, finally reaching Rome. But such attempts for political and geographical accuracy or flights of intellectual imagination ignore two important defining factors which lend a unity to this seemingly protean region, one natural and the other the product of human engineering: the first, the River Tiber (*il fiume Tevere*) and the Roman road, the Via Flaminia, the Flaminian Way.

The Tiber meets the sea in Lazio and rises in Emilia-Romagna, but by far the majority of its 252-mile course forms the main natural artery of Umbria. It was navigable by small boats from ancient Rome to the most northern tip of our region, as Pliny the Younger recounts in his description of the area around his country house near the modern village of Lama. And Livy tells us that tree-trunks were floated down the river to build the ships for the invasion of North Africa during the preparations for the Third Punic War (140s BC). To this day enterprising canoeists take to the head waters for an annual race to the nation's capital. Of course, there are other rivers and valleys and these need visiting, but it is the Tiber's course which most fully gives us a sense of Umbria's extent. From Città di Castello in the north to Otricoli in the south the river passes through gorges, forms lakes, waters plains and gives life to trees, the lungs of Italy's oft-cited "green heart".

Henry James in *Italian Hours* epitomizes the thought admirably as he looks down the Tiber Valley from the heights of Perugia:

> For it is such a wondrous mixture of blooming plain and gleaming river and wavily-multitudinous mountain vaguely dotted with pale grey cities, that, placed as you are, roughly speaking, in the centre of Italy, you all but span the divine peninsula from sea to sea. Up the long vista of the Tiber you look—almost to Rome; past Assisi, Spello, Foligno, Spoleto, all perched on their respective heights and shining through the violet haze. To the north, to the east, to the west, you see a hundred variations of the prospect, of which I have kept no record.

Technically James' glimpses of the cities of the Vale of Umbria should be ranked as perched above or on the banks of the Tiber's tributaries, the

Topino and Clitunno, rather than of the mighty river itself, but the spirit of the thought is accurate enough. As we will see in Chapter Three he makes a habit of this "Tiberization" of all the region's rivers.

The term "green heart of Italy" was coined by the nineteenth-century Perugian poet and Nobel laureate Giosuè Carducci, and the expression is both descriptive and memorable. The only gloss that it might warrant is the reflection that there is not a single "Umbrian green" but an entire palette of that colour's every conceivable shade. Any visitor to Umbria notes how much more verdant it is than its neighbours, and it is undeniably central, the only region of peninsular Italy without a coastline. I have heard it claimed that there is a bar in Foligno in which there is a pool table, the centre of which, it is said, marks the precise centre point of the peninsula. This flies in the face of the counter-claim of Rieti, the city in northern Lazio which boasts an ugly but elaborate monument known as l'Ombelico d'Italia—Italy's belly-button. Both claims owe more to local pride and innate fancifulness than geographical precision, I would suggest, but the approximate centrality of the region, notwithstanding my claims for it being a *regione meridionale* (part of the Italian south), is no less established. And the arterial Tiber, in a leisurely double zigzag, unevenly divides it in two.

Yet the river would make no impression without its geologically necessary and companion hills. While it is true that Umbria's elevation ranges from 130 to 7,221 feet above sea-level, only 6 per cent is classified as "plain" against 43 per cent "hills" and 51 per cent "mountains". So it is from these moderate-to-steep heights that the river's defining form is to be discerned. Imagining a sketch map of the region on which lines indicate the ranges of hills, we find four distinct almost parallel verticals which partition the total area. To travel from Orvieto in the west to Norcia in the east by the most direct route you would in effect have to cross all four (Colli Amerini, Monti Martani, the Subasio Range and the hills beyond the Nera Valley).

In prehistoric times the Tiber Valley was a vast lake, and even in the more recent past the river was much broader than its present course might suggest, Ian Campbell Ross noting in his excellent modern *Umbrian Gazetteer* that "now it is perhaps hard to imagine how much of the region was made up of marsh and swamp until even comparatively recently in human history..." This explains in part why Umbrians have tended to settle higher up the slopes, avoiding the malarial standing water as well as creating the all-important defensive lookout posts necessary throughout violent centuries. If any proof were needed of the Tiber's tendency to break its modern banks when left to itself, this was amply provided late in 2010 when part of the dam above Borgo di San Sepolcro broke on the night of 29 December. The artificially enhanced Lago di Montedoglio emptied at a faster rate than planned and the flooding and risk to bridges and riverside properties along the entire length of the Upper Tiber were considerable. From my hillside home I was looking out over a new Umbrian water-world with the low cloud and atmospheric mist complementing the novelty. Heavy rain or melting snow had occasionally caused the fields to flood in the previous years that I had spent here; but this was a true inundation recalling the original character of this valley.

And it is from these same slopes that we will note that all the rivers of Umbria are tributaries of Father Tiber. From the shady Nera with its own spectacular valley and illustrious waterfall beloved of all romantically minded tourists including the most romantically minded of all, Lord Byron, to the classically hymned Clitunno; from the Paglia, which skirts the acropolis of Orvieto, to the Puglia, which waters the robustly named Bastardo; from the Chiasco overlooked by the Lungarotti family's vineyards, source of the most marketed of regional wines, to the countless *torenti*, seasonal streams, overlooked by the tiny family vineyards of unsung Umbri: they all make their way to the Tiber, and so to the Tyrennian (Etruscan) sea. Even the Chienti, unrelated to the Tiber system at the far north east of the Colfiorito Plain's National Park, proves the rule, rising just across the border with Le Marche before making its way past Tolentino and Macerata to the Adriatic. Today it is beside the Tiber and its many tributaries that the typical modern crops of tobacco, sunflowers and maize thrive, often watered directly from the nearby stream. Woods of weeping willow, cypress and poplars follow and then spread out from the river's course. The Tiber's waters are dammed to form the Lago di Corbara, Lake Corbara, and the tributary Nera generates industrial Terni's power from the massive hydroelectric plant just below the Cascata delle Marmore, the Marbled Cascades.

Further up the slopes of the valleys come the olives and the vines. And finally on the remote high plains gripped with frost throughout long, hard winters grow the lentils and potatoes for which Casteluccio and Colfiorito are famed. In the late spring on these same plains the *fioritura* of millions of crocus flowers supply a harvest of the saffron which is worth far more than its weight in gold. In the ilex, aleppo pine and chestnut woods of the gentler hills the myriad forms of both benign and poisonous fungi are to be hunted out or avoided, including the most highly prized truffles and porcini. And it is across these forested hills that wild boar, porcupine, polecats, deer, martens, wild goat and even wolves and bears roam and sometimes are pursued, both in and out of the permitted hunting seasons. Umbrians (almost exclusively in their masculine version) are inveterate hunters—more hunting licences are issued per head of population than in any other Italian region, in a recent census 60,000 permits granted amidst an entire population of 800,000 souls.

The Tiber may not be Italy's longest river, beaten by the sluggish Po, but it is surely her most romantic. This is how a simple tourist guide (*Il Cuore Verde della Romagna*) introduces it to the rambler (my translation):

> The Tiber's source has been marked since the 1930s with a marble column topped by a Golden Eagle. You can reach it by means of the provincial highroad coming either from Balze or Alfero, two tourist villages, belonging to the Town Council of Verghereto. Depending upon which area it is crossing, the river has been given a variety of names during the centuries, amongst them Albula, Serra, Tarentum, Coluber, Rumon, the probable origin of the names Romulus and Remus. According to an old Roman tradition the Tiber gets its name from Tiberino, a descendant of Aeneas, who drowned in his waters. The Tiber has always been awarded the status of a historic waterway, a river-museum.

THE VIA FLAMINIA

So much then for a natural axis upon which Umbria may turn, but what of that engineered for human movement, the Via Flaminia?

It has its origins in the consulate of Gaius Flaminius, the Roman general who later suffered the Republic's greatest defeat fighting Hannibal at the Battle of Lake Trasimene (see Chapter Three). In 220 BC Flaminius began a project to construct a road which would unite Rome with the Adriatic coast of northern Italy, utilizing lengths of existing road crossing the territories of Veii, Capena and Falerii. It was later modified under the emperors Augustus and Hadrian. Running to the north of the ages-old

Ruins of Carsulae

salt route Via Salaria, it cut a similar diagonal across the peninsula, and in so doing bisected (more or less, see below) the region. The resulting trade and passage of goods led to a vibrant growth of the cities through which it passed during the Republican and Imperial Roman eras.

Starting out from the Roman forum it ran the length of the city's medieval and modern Via del Corso, crossing the Tiber at the Mulvian Bridge, scene of Constantine's (much later) victory over his rival for the imperial purple, Maxentius. Thereafter it followed the course of the Tiber Valley as far as Otriculum (modern Otricoli) and then followed the Nera to Narnia (modern Narni) where it divided just out of town across the famed Augustan-age Roman bridge to form distinct *diverticula*, one (to the west of the Martani hills) which passed via the now ruined Carsulae with its excellently preserved length of the original Roman paving, Massa Martana and Bevagna (Mevania), the other via Terni (Interamnia Nahars) and Spoleto (Spoletum) to reunite at Foligno. Thence, slowly climbing past Nocera Umbra (Nuceria) and Gualdo Tadino (Tadinum) it left modern Umbrian territory via the Passa della Scheggia (2,073 feet).

Descending the Metauro Valley it finally reached the sea at Fano (Fanum Fortunae). One of the medieval names for the road, Ravennina, stresses the importance in Late Antiquity and the Dark Ages for traffic between Ravenna, the Gothic capital of Italy, and the city of the popes. And not only traffic; the repeated passage of armies up and down the road—Goths, Byzantines, Langobards (Lombards)—led to a considerable decline in the fortunes of Umbria. Despoiled and ravaged by war (Belisarius and Witges fought it out in the 540s, only to be followed by Narses and Totila ten years later) the affluence of its towns, with the exception of Spoleto, the Langobard capital, was smashed, not to recover substantially until the coming of the communes in the twelfth century.

Choosing to ignore river or road as potential boundaries, modern Italian bureaucracy has decided that Umbria, like Caesar's Gaul, might still be said to be divided into two parts. Thus as the post-war Republic was formed, politically distinct provinces centred on Perugia and Terni were created, inevitably continuing to pay respect to groupings and boundaries set in past epochs, most observable in the diocesan structure of the Catholic Church. But a fascinating 1994 newspaper poll revealed surprisingly different attitudes to identity among north (Perugian) and south (Terniani) Umbrians when suggestions to reorganize the Italian regions were yet again on the table. Showing that Perugians remained firmly against any proposal that their province should be part of a Greater Tuscany with Umbria as such disappearing, it was equally clear in disclosing an active desire on behalf of Terniani to join with Lazio to create a new maxi-region centred on Rome. So it seems that north-Umbrians are the most loyal to a distinctive identity. And what might that identity be?

Umbrian Identity

Henry James described Umbria as "the most beautiful garden in all the world", but can it really be that Umbrians think of themselves as inhabitants of a kind of modified Eden? In conversation with those who are no longer permanent residents of their home region I have noticed that the majority will begin by rhapsodizing over Umbrian cuisine rather than recalling a particular view or the extraordinary way in which the light just before sunset seems to pulse from the fields and hillsides or the experience of walking through chestnut woods in early autumn. Rarely do they appeal to the pious example of their local saints, or the genius of their home grown artists. Perhaps it is inevitable that it takes visitors, tourists of all sorts, of whom there are annually two million, to reflect on and celebrate the countryside, and cherish religious and artistic significance, whereas it is simply taken for granted by the locals. Where beauty is the norm, natural, moral or artistic, it calls for little comment. Easier then to praise what to a degree is enjoyable even away from home—the way your mother prepares *torta al testa*, a kind of flaky flat-bread, or the taste of your uncle's full-bodied *rosso di tavola*. And certainly while searching for a distinctive Umbrian identity we will not be able to ignore the culinary or alcoholic. In fact it is a commonplace to include in guidebooks "routes" for visitors to follow concentrating on points of gastronomic or bibulous interest. For example in the excellent recent volume produced by the Milanese daily newspaper *Corriere della Sera* for a series which will include all of Italy's regions, you will find a startling variety of *itinerari enogastronomici* which threaten to crowd out itineraries which focus on the artistic, historical or panoramic aspects of the zone. And just in case you cannot read a map or follow instructions in a book the region's civil engineers and tourist officers have created roads which are identified as the wine/oil route with signs to match, keeping you on the (relatively) straight and narrow between *cantine*, wineries.

But if food and wine are defining features of the present day Italian's attitude to Umbria, it would be wrong to ignore the characterizations noted in previous centuries. In the rather "muscular" atmosphere of Fascist Italy it was Corrado Ricci who coined in 1927 the myth of "Umbria Santa", a home for heroes of the soil as well as birthplace of more than its fair share of canonized saints. This sanctity was extended into the artistic field—following Ricci's socio-demographic theorizing, a special spirituality was also awarded to the Umbrian school of painters, so called *santi pittori*. This rather flies in the face of documented evidence for Pietro Vannucci, aka Perugino, whose atheism was surprisingly robust and most definitely counter-cultural for its age. Popular focus on the life and works of St. Francis, encouraged by the writing of Renan and Sabatier, declared Umbria to be the Galilee of Italy, an abiding if somewhat conflated conceit since today Assisi boasts Bethlehem among its twinned cities. What happened to Nazareth? And certainly with its sanctuaries of the founder of the Franciscan movement, with Norcia birthplace of St. Benedict and Cascia home of Santa Rita ("Saint of the

Impossible"), and with Terni under the protection of St. Valentine, patron of lovers the world over, Umbria in religious terms, from the sublime to the faintly ridiculous, punches far above its weight. A surprisingly large proportion of the annual flood of visitors is motivated to make the trip at least partly as pilgrimage.

Northern European and therefore largely Protestant visitors to Umbria in the epoch of the Grand Tour (or Il Giro d'Italia as it was more properly termed for places visited south of the Alps) remained unimpressed by what they thought of as the vestiges of a medieval and superstitious piety. The writings of Addison, Goethe, Smollett, Boswell and Lady Morgan are positive mainly in their considerations of the countryside—although less as an extensive garden than as a wild region making a contribution to the sublime, chiefly the Marbled Cascades (see Chapter Thirteen). Joseph Addison calls these "the famous cascade" and rather incongruously rates them higher than the "water-works at Versailles" (*Remarks on Several Parts of Italy*, 1705). Maybe he was more aware of their dependence upon human engineering than most contemporary visitors. Goethe admired the position of Perugia and the fine views of Lake Trasimene, but his and other commentators' principal preoccupation was with some of the Roman ruins, particularly the Bridge of Augustus at Narni; Addison again: "one of the stateliest ruins in Italy" (see Chapter Three). Eighteenth- and nineteenth-century Umbria in its purest most immediate form was not much more than an inconvenience.

And indeed the economic position of Umbria in the pre-industrial period, with its scattered homesteads (*case sparse*) tied into the subsistence farming system called *mezzandria*, did not lend itself to an orderly landscape. A virtually medieval attitude to agriculture seems to have been a corollary of the Papal Government of the Church State, considered among the most benighted in post-Napoleonic Europe. Tobias Smollett (*Travels through France and Italy*, 1766) captures the intolerant and uneducated spirit of the region in his typically deadpan account of an inn at Foligno:

> In choosing our beds at the inn, I perceived one chamber locked, and desired it might be opened; upon which the cameriere declared with some reluctance, "Bisogna dire a Su eccellenza; poco fa, che una bestia è morta in questa camera, e non è ancora lustrate." "Your excellency must know that a filthy beast died lately in that chamber, and it is not

yet purified and put in order." When I enquired what beast it was, he replied, "Un eretico Inglese." An English Heretick.

Prosperity increased considerably after Italian unification with the steady industrialization of Terni and the suburbs of Perugia throughout the second half of the nineteenth century, and it is from this development that yet another facet of the region reveals itself: the modern, industrious, affluent Umbria; the Umbria which technologically is the second most developed part of Italy, after the Turin/Milan corridor; the Umbria which was bombed heavily by the Allies in the Second World War to reduce the Italian war effort; Umbria home of Perugino chocolate and one of the world's most important jazz festivals. Whatever it was, Umbria is nothing if not sophisticated today.

So how am I to describe this region rich with contrast and paradox, how am I to transmit some of my enthusiasm for this complex place? I am not going to be able to list everything of interest, and I will deliberately make a choice when it comes to suggestions about what to see, where to go and do, what to eat and drink. I will outline the region's history which never lies far beneath the surface, describe its art and culture, tell stories of its inhabitants, explain how to prepare dishes particular to the region and encourage you to drink its wines. I will take you with me on journeys and to special events. I will show you things that are hidden and things well known, reveal secrets about the everyday and perhaps expose the banal in what is over-estimated. Each chapter will focus on a specific feature of the region, examples of which have abided through time or aspects of which are found in all periods, but the progression of chapters itself will broadly describe a chronological consideration, starting in prehistoric Umbria and ending with the twenty-first century. Whether ultimately you enjoy Umbria by visiting, settling there or simply reading about it in the proverbial comfort of your own home I want to share with you what I have gradually over twenty years come to treasure as unique to this region.

And so I end this introductory chapter with a taster, by describing something which, despite being beyond the physical capacities of some of my potential readers, is not beyond the imagination of anyone. Drive to Spello on a late spring afternoon and marvel at the way in which the sun as it dips to the west seems to generate an inner light within the rose-pink Subasio stone of which the town is built. Once inside the ring of extraor-

The stones of Spello

dinarily well preserved Augustan-age walls passing one or other of its majestic gates, book into the Hotel Palazzo Bocci, an elegant sixteenth-century town house. Once settled in, take your time to stroll round the town, savouring its architectural synthesis of Roman origins with medieval elaborations to create the vibrant and lived-in homes and places of business of modern men and women. Visit the dark tunnel-like Church of Santa Maria Maggiore founded in the twelfth century but notable principally for the decoration of its Baglioni family chapel. In 1501, at the height of that family's bloody political stranglehold of metropolitan Perugia, its *contada* (hinterland) and nearby dependent towns such as Spello itself, Bernadino Betti, known as Pinturicchio, the Pocket Painter, created this miracle of his art. In the vault four sibyls enthroned, on the left wall an annunciation, behind the altar an adoration of the shepherds with arrival of the magi, to the right the Christ Child found in the Temple. We see the artist's self portrait and signature framed within the cornice of the left hand wall and on the right wall written upon a scroll held by one of the figures attendant on St. Joseph, his sobriquet. If after this rich feast you still have artistic appetite visit the civic art gallery filled with gems from masters of

Pinturicchio's magi, with horse

the Umbrian school and the town hall (Palazzo Comunale) dating from the end of the thirteenth century. Have a snack at Pasticceria Tullia, shop for local goodies at Il Tartuffo di Paolo, have an aperitif at the fabulously stocked Enoteca Properzio and enjoy an early dinner in the panoramic restaurant La Bastiglia. It has got to be early because you are going to bed early to be up early tomorrow morning.

Up before dawn (not forgetting the *panini*, filled rolls, which the hotel has prepared in lieu of breakfast) set off up the hill passing the old site of the Rocca (fortress) which now contains the oldest of Spello's churches, San Lorenzo, with its origins perhaps reaching back to the sixth century. Outside the second ring of the town's walls constructed in the thirteenth century to take in a new (!) suburb you start your real climb. Up through the ilex woods which clothe the lower slopes of Mount Subasio you glimpse from time to time the thick blanket of mist which fills the whole of the Vale of Umbria. As it gets light the sun, rising out of the cloud as from the sea, begins to warm the landscape and slowly burns off the mist. By now you are up beyond the tree line and the view stretches from the peaks of the Sibiline mountain and Spoleto nestling in the arms of Montelupo to the south, and then northwards to Perugia and far off beyond the Alpi della Luna, the Mountains of the Moon, where Umbria meets Tuscany, Le Marche and Emilia Romagna near the source of the Tiber.

Simply hiking over the hillside or following the winding road will eventually (four hours or so later) bring you to the Eremo delle Carceri (The Prison Hermitage), among the most atmospheric of the pilgrimage sites associated with St. Francis. Originally nothing more than a rocky gorge sprinkled with caves, a tiny monastery was built a few years after Francis' death to commemorate the saint's frequent visits. Wandering the rocky paths one comes across each of the caves in which Francis and his companions spent time of retreat, or at the mouths of which they might simply spend the night in conversation watching the stars, as celebrated in an attractive bronze figure group set up there in the woods. From the Carceri it is only an hour's walk down to Assisi itself. Here there is enough to keep you occupied throughout the day especially if you arrive during the first ten days of May, the period of the May Kalends (Calendimaggio) when the city's regions engage in playful contests of skill, physical prowess and chance. There is a fairground atmosphere throughout the town; open air theatre, many people in Renaissance costume and musical performances in piazza and churches. We will be coming back to visit Assisi again in the course of this book, so I shall hold back my detailed comments for now. After lunch and a wander round town take the bus back to Spello from Piazza Matteotti. You will be tired but it will have been worth it. Twenty-four hours in heaven—or at least in an earthly paradise.

Chapter Two

UNDERGROUND UMBRIA

PREHISTORY TO ROMAN ERA

Passing directly from heaven, let's proceed to hell, or at least to the proprietor of the infernal regions, Old Nick himself. The Umbrian legends tell us that even so great a local saint as Francis was subject to diabolical temptations. The devil, angered by the fabled chastity of the young ascetic from Assisi, would regularly torment him with images of beautiful women during times of retreat. The forty-day fast of Lent, spent a couple of times by the saint on the Isola Maggiore of Lake Trasimene, was just such a time of extra prayer and therefore a re-doubling of devilish efforts. Unimpressed, we are told, by the powers of the Evil One, Francis would fling himself into the thorn bushes and briars to mortify the flesh and dowse the flames of lust common to all humanity but controlled only by the most saintly. He was instantly rewarded by a manifestation of the miraculous power of the one he followed. The bushes which previously had carried such stings were transformed into thorn-less rose trees, a variety of which still flourishes within the famous *rosetto* to be found in the cloisters of the Church of Santa Maria degli Angeli on the plain below his home town. This was the place where the saint would die. This story in a very similar form is told also of St. Benedict, a holy man of the Dark Ages upon whom Francis modelled himself—and if these stories originate in a tradition from Lazio (Subiaco above the Aniene river, to be precise, a place actually visited by Francis out of respect for his saintly predecessor) they lose none of their entertainment value or shock effect from crossing the regional boundary.

> From Rome Francis went to visit the Grotto of Saint Benedict. He considered with great attention the bush covered with thorns, into which the great Patriarch of the monastic life had the courage to throw himself, in order to overcome a temptation of the flesh. In admiration of such extraordinary fervor, he touched this bush as a sacred relic; he kissed it, and made on it the sign of the cross. God, in order to honor his two servants,

Jack-in-the-box demons, School of Giotto

changed it immediately into a beautiful rose-tree, the flowers of which have served in many cases for the cure of the sick; the place has since been held in greater respect. In a chapel which is near it, and which was consecrated by Gregory IX, we see that Pope, with Francis on his left hand, who holds a scroll of paper, on which these words, taken from the Gospel of Saint Luke, are written, "Peace be to this house," words which he constantly used as a salutation. (*The Life and Legends of St. Francis of Assisi* by Father Candide Chalippe, OFM)

The saintly legends which accumulated around Francis' person also tell of him delivering the city of Arezzo on the Tuscan side of the border with Umbria from demons—we see the episode graphically depicted in the frescoes of the upper church in Assisi; red, green and blue fiends explode like so many jack-in-the-boxes from a cubic representation of the town as the saint raises his hand in rebuke.

Perhaps the demons, finding themselves homeless, headed off east over the hills to Umbria's upper Tiber Valley to settle at the tiny town called Casa del Diavolo, Devil's House. For centuries local maps refused, from fear of attracting ill luck, even to acknowledge the name of this ribbon settlement on the road from Perugia to Città di Castello. Only the (slightly) less superstitious climate of the twenty-first century has at last allowed the village to take its proper cartographical place. This otherwise sleepy place comes decisively, and perhaps also somewhat demonically, alive on Friday and Saturday nights and in holiday periods, since it is where Umbria's largest rave night club, Red Zone, is located. Not that I would know much about that.

If Casa del Diavolo was hard to find for Arezzo's dispossessed demons (demons, like men, being particularly loath to ask directions and Red Zone being some 750 years in the future) they might have made due south to another infernally named feature of Umbrian geography: le Tane del Diavolo (the Devil's Lair) caves.

CAVES, CATACOMBS AND CRYPTS

Parrano, a tiny community of only 604 souls north of Orvieto in the Val di Chiana, is where these caves are situated, and it is unique in Umbria not only for the exceptional geological formation of a *fossa* or canyon but also its Palaeolithic archaeological finds. The fossa formed (apparently) in the Miocene period runs for about half a mile between chalk walls which rise between fifty and sixty-five feet, though at its narrowest point it is no more than 27 inches wide. At the bottom, a stream of waters rich in mineral salts and sometimes with a temperature of 23°C underlines the volcanic and seismic nature of Umbria and indeed all of central Italy. The steam rising from the canyon on cold autumn and winter days must also have led to the association of this place with a diabolical presence, and much earlier must also have attracted the attention of the Stone Age settlers to the more than twenty caves which give off the main course of the fossa. Three of the caves in the system, Tana Minore, Tana del Rospo Superiore and the Grotta Grande, were extensively explored in the twentieth century by a team from the Archaeological Museum in Perugia led by its then director, Umberto Calzoni. A "workshop" for the production of flint blades was found in the first cave and in the other two the foundations of huts, some ceramics and a large burial ground.

But undoubtedly the most spectacular and rare find from here was the so-called "Green Venus" (appropriate for "Green Umbria"), a statuette carved from green oolite (egg stone) representing a pregnant female figure with her head bound in a cloth, unearthed in the nineteenth century. This, together with the more recent discovery of large amounts of burnt grain suggesting simple sacrificial practices, indicates that the Devil's Lair caves were the centre of religious activity for the Old Stone Age peoples of the region. Exhibits can be found in Perugia's National Museum, which supported the project.

"Underground Umbria", as a specific topic, is as it happens by no means negligible, especially when we consider that the National Institute for Caving is to be found just outside Perugia at Bosco. In fact, visits underground can be made in quite a number of Umbrian locations, both urban and rural. Guided tours of both Orvieto and Narni "beneath the streets" reveal excavations and amplification of natural geological features dating from the Etruscan origins of these two towns, whereas the Grotta di Monte Cucco near Gubbio in the far north-east of the region reaching a depth of 3,025 feet is the fifth deepest cave to have been discovered anywhere in the world. Known since the 1500s and explored systematically from the 1890s onwards it is reached by a six-mile panoramic road stretching from Sigilo climbing 3,412 feet up the south side of the mountain. The true entrance to the cave is 1,040 feet higher up the cliffs of the so-called Cold Water Canyon (Fossa dell'Aqua Fredda) but that is not how visitors enter the system, typified by an enormous diagonal well (eighty feet long and ten in diameter) which connects a series of caverns stepping down through the chalk for over a mile. Non-specialist visitors can make a descent of about a hundred feet (but even then only with official guides) to view the Sala Margherita, a veritable spectacle of stalactites and stalagmites. The rest of the cave system is given over to expert cavers.

The upper Chiascio Valley, which runs north from Gualdo Tadino in the shadow of Monte Cucco, and shelters the Via Flaminia communities of Fossata di Vico, Sigilo, Costacciaro and Scheggia, was perhaps the original homeland of the Umbri. These were the supposed natives who gave their name to the entire region, though they would have been peripheral as far as modern Umbria is concerned. This part of Italy had, however, known settlement for centuries before the emergence of such historical naming, as we have seen from our visit to the Devil's Lair. In prehistory the Chiascio Valley was the site of just one of three major lakes which would eventually, through millennia, carve plain-like valleys out of the mountainous spine of the region. The others more or less followed the courses of the modern rivers Tiber and Chiana—the fossil forest of sequoias near Dunaroba, south of Todi, is evidence of the largest of these lakes.

Our most distant ancestors of the type *homo erectus* are thought to have crossed over into Italy from Africa, at that time linked to the peninsula by Sicily, and pebble-culture tools as well as those associated with Neanderthal technology have been found at Abeto near Norcia. The culture of *homo sapiens* emerging about 30,000 BC would eventually produce substantial remains such as the ditch tomb at Poggio Aquilone (c. 20,000 BC) near Marsciano. The culture represented by the tomb's finds was that of shepherds moving from plains to heights depending on the season.

Evidence for Bronze Age settlement in the region comes largely from a series of excavations near to Gualdo Tadino, the finds from which are now housed in the Perugia Archaeological Museum, whereas early Iron Age artefacts are commonplace in local collections throughout Umbria. Antiquarianism predates true archaeology by a couple of centuries and many well-to-do Umbrians of the sixteenth and seventeenth centuries gathered together groups of impasto cremation urns typical of the Villanovan culture which proliferated in central and northern Europe after 10,000 BC and clearly penetrated the Italian peninsula, so commonplace is this form of burial.

Historical speculation has generally attributed the emergence of a significant and distinct local culture in north central Italy, that of the Etruscans, to the meeting of the Iron Age Villanovan peoples with Greek colonists further south. What place do the mysterious Etruscans have in a work dedicated to Umbria? After all, they give the name to even more celebrated Tuscany, which flanks our region to the west. Even if we leave aside the hotly debated issue of whether a distinct tribe of Umbri ever existed, being properly only a subset of the Etruscans, the built evidence of Etruscan culture throughout large expanses of modern Umbria give them a special place in her history.

Speaking and writing a non-Indo-European language (unlike Latin and Greek) and with distinctive features to their social practices and art, ancient accounts of the Etruscans emphasized their uniqueness with flights of fancy. Claims were made that they were descended from the Trojans (though of course the same would be claimed for the Romans) or from the inhabitants of Atlantis. It is much simpler to accept that they represent the earliest example of a fully developed indigenous culture in Italy, emerging as a "high" culture at the end of the Mediterranean Dark Age (c. 750 BC), which also marks the peak of Greek colonization of the "wild west". Thucydides notes their presence amongst the allies of Syracuse against the Athenian invasion of Sicily in the mid-fifth century, and this would coincide with the development of a centralized political identity for what had previously been a loose confederacy of city states. Their domination of Rome towards the end of that city's monarchy, and their subsequent expulsion at the foundation of the Republic in 520 BC (mythologized in the account of Lucretia's rape) locates their influence as a good deal further south than our area of interest. However, by 400 BC Perugia (originally founded from Chamars, the Etruscan name for Chiusi) had emerged as the capital of the Dodecapolis (the Twelve Towns) or Etrurian League, which included Rome's neighbour, Veii. Perhaps the only other city in the league which might have contested the leadership in terms of scale and grandeur is Orvieto, then known as Volsinii (Pliny the Elder's *Volsinii oppidum Tuscorum opulentissimum*), and it has recently been shown archaeologically to have been the firm location of the *Fanum Voltumnae*, the national shrine—hosting the League's gatherings for such sacred political functions as the election of magistrates, thus balancing in religious terms Perugia's political pre-eminence. For a taste of what the language sounded like, here is an inscription from Orvieto transliterated into Latin script:

ita.tmia.icac.he
ramasva.vatieKe
unial.astres.ðemia
sa.meK.ðuta.ðefa
riei.velianas.sal
cluvenias.turu
ce.munistas.ðuvas
tameresca.ilacve.
tulerase.nac.ci.avi
l.Kurvar.tesiameit
ale.ilacve.alsase
nac.atranes.zilac
al.seleitala.acnasv
ers.itanim.heram

ve.avil.eniaca.pul
umKva.

Roughly translated:

This temple and (this) statue have been dedicated to Uni/Astarte. Thefariei Velianas, head of the community, donated it for the worship of our peoples. This gift of this temple and sanctuary and the consecration of its boundaries during his three year term in the month of Xurvar [June?] in this way, and in Alsase [July?] this record together with the divinity/statue shall thus be buried by order of the Zilach that the years may outlast the stars.

A visit to an Etruscan tomb is ironically far from a gloomy experience. In the complexes of block tombs on the northern slope of Orvieto's acropolis, known as the *Crocifisso del Tufo*, or at the *Pallazone* necropolis, we find hints of the highly sociable burial practices which have survived into contemporary Italian culture, cemetery design having evolved little in the intervening twenty-five centuries. These ancient cities of the dead have streets, family "homes" and dining spaces. Often decorated with scenes of feasting, dancing and love-making, the bond between husband and wife seems to express something much closer to our concept of romantic love than one has come to expect from the neighbouring Greek civilization. Painting and sculpture shows influence from imported Hellenic art (known from the vast number of Attic black-and-red figure vases found in Etruscan graves). Yet they exhibit a greater degree of freedom from stylization or an established tradition, in short being more "naïve", and so for me as for many other commentators the Etruscans' art is more sensual, gutsy and touching. By the mid-third century BC, works of considerable power and sophistication were being produced in bronze, terracotta and stone; the figure groups of reclining spouses from numerous tombs, the so-called Apollo of Veii or the superb bronze of Mars found near Todi, now in the Vatican collection, eloquently attest to this master-craft becoming true high art.

Among our priorities for underground Umbria, then, ought to be a social call on one of the leading Etruscan clans. Perugia boasts two such major family burial sites: the *Ipogeo dei Volumni* (the Burial Chamber of the Volumni Family) and that of the rival Cutu clan. The tomb of the Velimni family (Latinized as Volumni) is reached by following the road from the city centre of Perugia to Ponte San Giovanni. Its entrance is just before the level-crossing of the local railway. (A tourist sign on the main E45 highway for the site is not particularly helpful in finding it.) It was discovered in 1842 and dates from the late third century BC. That of the Cutu is near to the Policlinico, the main public hospital, out of town on the Gubbio road. Both exhibit a descending *dromos* entrance, a runway flanked by high excavated walls, an entrance portal in carved stone giving on to a chambered hall cut from the rock and decorated to resemble domestic architecture. In each case only the founder of the tomb is interred (in the first case Arnth Velimnia); the rest of the family were cremated and their ashes housed in urns which are smaller versions of the life-sized sculpted sarcophagus of the founder. Such calm sophistication, even or perhaps especially in death, speaks well of a culture which too often can be cast in a chilly shade by the imposing bulk of the succeeding full-blown Roman age, and argues for a cultural hegemony in our region during the flowering of Etruscan political power.

So what about the Umbri? Were they in any way distinct from the Etruscans? We will consider more fully the single most important piece of evidence for their existence in the next chapter: the Fugubine Tablets. But if we are to believe the most influential ancient writer who most certainly

The Velimni family "at home"

believed in them, Pliny the Elder, they founded Todi (known in Etruscan as Tuder, a derivative of the word for boundary) as well as Amelia, famed for its full circuit of pre-Roman town walls. Counter to the independence/distinction argument is the finding of the Orvietan- (and therefore Etruscan-) made statue of Mars at Todi. Perhaps more decisive in the argument would be the choice of Perugia as the Etruscan capital; only a day's walk from Gubbio it surely seems strange as the centre of Etruscan activity if areas which might be called Umbrian were in any real sense independent or beyond Etruscan influence. The so-called Umbrian language could well have been a variant of Etruscan; the only reason we generally think of it as a separate language is that the tiny amounts of it claimed to have been found are expressed in Latin characters. In the long run the argument is of small account. The most important Etruscan city was in Umbria and that city has remained the most important settlement in the region ever since.

PERUGIA: THE WHIFF OF SULPHUR

Visitors to Perugia rarely fail to be impressed by its position. Almost 1,650 feet above the Tiber Valley and built on three spurs of a craggy ridge, it boasts what must be one of the most successfully pedestrianized centres of any Italian city. Corso Vannucci slopes in expansive grandeur from the steps of the Cathedral of San Lorenzo for over half a mile to the extraordinary vantage point of the Carducci gardens, which reveals what seems to be the majority of Umbria in all her greenness. The Corso follows the route of the Etrusco-Roman *cardo*, or main street. Even in this rather inhospitable site with such sudden variation of elevation the town plan attempted a grid, with the present-day Via dei Priori following the route of the secondary street (*decumans*) which meets the cardo at a right angle. And yet despite this triumphant crowning townscape Perugia maintains, even revels in, a reputation for gloom, bloody feuds and dark doings.

"What a town for assassinations," says H. V. Morton, the cultivated 1950s travel writer. And indeed once you have left the urbane breadth of the Corso most of the other streets resemble the most clichéd set for a thriller or horror film. Passages, narrow and dark, wind their way along the steep contours only relieved by occasional plunging staircases. The overhanging medieval palaces generally blot out the light of the sun and the wind is famously chill. Henry James catches it well:

Some of the little streets in out-of-the-way corners are so rugged and brown and silent that you may imagine them passages long since hewn by the pick-axe in a deserted stone-quarry. The battered black houses, of the colour of buried things—things buried, that is, in accumulations of time, closer packed, even as such are, than spadefuls of earth—resemble exposed sections of natural rock; none the less so when, beyond some narrow gap, you catch the blue and silver of the sublime circle of landscape.

It is here that in 1265 was founded the extremist Christian sect of Flagellants, who would publicly beat themselves with whips and chains in order to atone for their own sins and inspire contrition in the minds of their observers. This gruesome religious demonstration might have been one of the town's chief entertainments. Another was the local version of football entered into by huge teams from rival districts of the city, and it was equally bloody. *La Battaglia dei Sassi* consisted in the teams hurling stones at one another until one team had dislodged their opponents from their position on the field/piazza. Deaths often resulted. The Renaissance feuds which raged between the Guidalotti and the Baglioni (and even within the two families) for the lordship of the city are not only subject of legend but even the anachronistic material which informs Barry Unsworth's 1990s novel, *After Hannibal.* Italian Renaissance scholar, and one of the melancholic sufferers of small personal tragedies within the novel, Professor Monti is an expert on the Baglioni family: its arrival with the city's first sole ruler the famous general Fortebraccio, its internecine fracturing, its commitment to violence. Monti feels morbidly connected to the family, and searches out every trace they may have left on the territory:

> In the days of their power, the Baglioni had produced no artists, no patrons of art, no thinkers. None of them had ever said or written anything memorable. They had been men of blood, all of them, arrogant, violent and treacherous. It was not only the habit of research, of leaving no stone unturned, that led him to follow up these dubious leads. There had grown him a kind of superstition, a feeling that something would be vouchsafed to his senses or understanding, some clue, in the end, that would help him understand the present, as well as the past, help

him to see—and so accept—through links infinitely small, some vital connection with his own sense of violation and loss. If the history of Perugia was a record of crime—and it was—then the Baglioni were its true representatives, not a dark exception or an unusually virulent strain, but the quintessential stock.

Attentive readers will here note that Unsworth, or his character Monti, has at least in one particular over-emphasized the Baglioni's violent sterility. Pinturicchio's superb frescoes in Spello were commissioned for their chapel and were in fact created during the height of their bloody tyranny.

Even Perugian local tradition and civic pride have a tendency to glory in the macabre; its citizens claim that the busts representing an entire family which decorate the Porta Marzia memorialize victims of clan rivalry, an entire household wiped out by eating poisoned mushrooms.

And if you think that, carried away by the bloodthirsty chronicles of Perugia, I have forgotten this chapter's guiding theme—Umbria underground—it is to one of the town's most everyday and yet atmospheric features that I am leading. From the bustling *passeggiata* of Corso Vannucci, only a step from the wonderful view from the Carducci gardens, one descends by means of escalators to a series of medieval streets which have been literally entombed. This was achieved by the architect Antonio

Poisoned busts

di Sangallo the Younger when in 1540 he constructed the papal fortress, the Rocca Paolina, on an artificially constructed platform above. This symbol of the city's subjection to the government of the pope was raised at the conclusion of the so-called Salt War fought by the Perugians against Paul III. The pope might have been victorious in maintaining his tight monopoly of the supply of salt to the city, but the citizens discovered a novel way of continuing resistance. The most common local bread (*pane sciapo*) even to this day is still baked without salt. When the war came to an end and the Baglioni were finally subdued, the wily pope and his strategists hit on a plan to humble the city's dominant families. The Baglioni quarter near San Domenico in which their palaces and towers were positioned was simply built over, the old foundations and streets becoming subterranean support for the massive terrace upon which the fortress and seat of papal government could be placed. And so for three centuries the Rocca Paolina dominated the Perugian skyline just as the fourteenth-century fortresses of an earlier papal clampdown under Cardinal Albornorz still belittle Spoleto, Narni and Assisi.

So how did the Perugians free themselves from this hated symbol of tyranny? In 1848, when the pope took flight from Rome and Perugia allied itself with the Roman Republic of Garibaldi and Mazzini, the ecstatic populace burst into the fort and began its demolition, emulating the Parisian treatment of the Bastille sixty years before. Yet with the status quo quickly re-imposed by the French and Austrian allies of the papacy, the final dismantling of the Rocca Paolina had to wait another twelve years and for the secession of Umbria from the Papal State and its incorporation within the Kingdom of Italy. On the cleared terracing rose a new headquarters for the Province of Perugia and the public gardens which form such a breathtaking "balcony" over the Vale of Umbria. The entombed streets of the sixteenth century, for so long the fortress's dungeons, became once more accessible to law-abiding citizens simply taking advantage of a short cut to the lower levels of the town.

A neat and ironic coda to the papal contributions to the theme of underground Umbria is the very recent excavation and exhibition of the chamber in which the four medieval conclaves conducted in Perugia took place. Located beneath the present Cathedral of San Lorenzo, which was the church attached to the papal residence—the cathedral then being today's San Domenico—decisive history was made here as it was the location for the election of Boniface VIII because of whose actions the relocation of the papacy in Avignon was an inevitability.

Perugia was not the most common stop-over for tourists of the eighteenth and nineteenth centuries. When they did come, like Lady Morgan, they tended to be underwhelmed by the beauties of the place and to focus largely on the prevailing air of decay and gloom with "no society worth pursuing in these dismal palaces".

> Under the late French regime, the city of Perugia was governed by a military prefect, who introduced much of the order and discipline of his profession into its society. He gave gay entertainments, held assemblies, and obliged the old murky, time-worn nobles, to throw off their dusty great coats... Perugia is now under the jurisdiction of a priest, the Prelato Spinola, with the title of Governor. There are, of course, no balls—no assemblies, and the nobles are at liberty to resume their great coats, in which by the way we saw some of them perform that weary pilgrimage, the *corso,* in coaches which seemed to have existed since the time of Forte Braccio. We left Perugia as the dawn broke upon the towers of its horrible fortress; but yet not so early but misery was awake; and the same cries which ushered us into its gloomy walks, now followed us out.

Today Perugia attracts vast numbers of foreign visitors and temporary residents first as a result of its internationally renowned Università degli stranieri (University for Foreigners) with more than 30,000 students and then for its globally celebrated jazz festival. That it has never yet entirely escaped from its sombre reputation was horribly illustrated in autumn 2007 with the brutal murder of a young English Erasmus programme student. The occasion of the murder being connected with a Halloween party further led to a flurry of newspaper and TV reports tracing the city's reputation as capital of all that is macabre if not down-right diabolical. Despite a notorious and seemingly endless trial in which two of the victim's best friends stood accused, were convicted and imprisoned, only to be released after appeal, the student population has been far from deterred from coming here. In fact, applications have increased, perhaps fuelled by the lurid descriptions of undergraduate drug-use which have accompanied the judicial process, and the final condemnation and imprisonment of the chief suspects of the crime.

St. Patrick's Well

One last stop underground in Umbria awaits us—itself another extraordinary feat of Renaissance engineering by Sangallo the Younger and at the same time an example of the futility of human effort. It is even flavoured with just a hint of the sulphur which has scented the whole of this chapter. The Pozzo di San Patrizio in Orvieto, St. Patrick's Well, was constructed for Pope Clement VII to supply the town's fort with an unlimited supply of water. In 1527 Clement withdrew here from Rome in the wake of its sack by Imperial forces, and he fully expected to have to withstand a prolonged siege. The architect, who would go on to entomb Perugia's Baglioni quarter for the succeeding Pope Paul III, excavated a cylinder 203 feet deep and 42 feet in diameter in the *tufo* rock in the time of the emergency. The project was completed, however, from 1532 after the peril had passed with the brick lining, the double helix staircase enabling mules both to descend and ascend simultaneously, and the 72 openings to let in the light. And the name? A pious legend has it that St. Patrick, patron of Ireland, had a vision of descending to hell via purgatory—*pace* St. Patrick's Purgatory, the island in Lough Doug. Though never used in times of war, the well with its endless donkey machinery provided Orvieto's Rocca with its water till its dismantling in the nineteenth century. A hell of a lot of effort for precious little—but yet another extraordinary example of the riches which lie beneath Umbria's surface.

Chapter Three

THEATRE

THE ROMAN ERA

Umbria is as theatrical as any other Italian region, and in some senses more so. The survival of ancient folk customs with elements of performance, such as the *Befana* New Year's pantomime in the homesteads of the Norcia region, where young men dress up as ugly old women begging from door to door and then leaving gifts of produce, and the myriad Holy Week processions, more than outweigh the absence of an abiding high theatrical culture. Yes, it is true that Perugia produced an early nineteenth-century opera composer of distinction, Francesco Morlacchi (1784-1841) after whom the city's *teatro stabile* (state-funded repertory house) is named, but his triumphs were far from Umbria, in Bologna and then Dresden. And no less a critic than Henry James recounts what might be seen at the theatre in 1870s Perugia whilst sitting "in an orchestra-chair at twenty-two soldi", enjoying "the curious didacticism of 'Amore senza Stima', 'Severita e Debolezza', 'La Societa Equivoca'." It does not sound scintillating, as indeed the Master meant it not to. A number of opera singers celebrated in the late eighteenth and early nineteenth centuries were born in the region but they trained and performed exclusively beyond its boundaries.

The absence of a resident court, or indeed any substantial upper middle class, amplified by the restrictive censorship of the Papal State, meant that no real centre for theatrical performances emerged in the early modern era. Yet few Italians have ever been shy of performance and display, it seems, and the regular Umbrian exhibition of the *passegiata*, the stroll through town to show off new clothes, new hairstyle, new partner or child, is a tradition as cutting-edge as it is antique. Umbrian behaviour on a daily basis can also provide entertainment where it might least be expected, generally verbal rather than physical. Slow of movement as a people, their sharpness of wit more than makes up for it. I remember the sigh of disapproval which issued from an elderly electrician opening an overcrowded junction-box and then his laconic comment: "the Lord God made the world so big and we go and choose to put on narrow shoes."

Now neither this "natural theatre of the ordinary" nor the provincial character of the region cited above means that Umbria does not have theatres; it just means that its many theatres are local concerns and typically tiny—in fact a number of them compete in the claim to be the smallest eighteenth- and nineteenth-century auditoria in the world. How one could prove (or indeed disprove) these claims remains one of the conundrums of Umbria's surely exaggerated self-esteem. Even so, a visit to such a gem-like theatre as that in Monteleone d'Orvieto or Montecastello di Vibio is a truly charming experience. Influenced by trips to La Scala in Milan or Naples' San Carlo theatre, the petty nobility of eighteenth-century Umbria had to have their gilded boxes, their swags of red velvet and their cupolas rich with frescoes, even if as at Montecastello the entire house seats only ninety, at Monteleone ninety-six. These theatres still often receive small touring companies (Il Teatro dei Illuminati in Città di Castello recently hosting a Milan-based performance of Aristophanes' *Ecclesiazusae*) as well as welcoming local amateur groups—an English-style Christmas pantomime even becoming part of the annual programme at Umbertide's classic theatre, a centre for recent British settlement. Sadly, the theatre at Montleone is virtually disused and the key has to be requested from a retired British couple living in the *borgo*.

In this small-scale sophistication Umbria's eighteenth-century aristocrats proved to be only distant descendants of their classical predecessors. If Umbria is to boast of a really world-class dramatist then it has to be Plautus (Titus Maccius Plautus), born in the small Umbrian town of Sarsina around 250 BC. Even he gained his popularity and wealth exhibiting his adaptations of Greek New Comedy to Latin language and taste in the great city south of our region, Rome. Steven Saylor's recent epic historical novel, *Roma,* gives him a walk-on part:

> Plautus rolled his eyes heavenward. "And to think I was raised a poor country boy in Umbria. Had to make my living as a baker when I first came to Roma; thought I'd never get the flour out of my hair. For years I was just a starry eyed, would-be actor with a funny stage-name—yes, they called me Plautus on account of my flat feet, but I figured it was a name no one would forget. But Fortuna's wheel turns

round and round, and Plautus the clown is the best playwright in town."

The archaeological evidence, however, makes it clear that the region of Plautus' birth was eventually, certainly by the end of the first century AD, more than equipped to put on the plays of its scion. The surviving Roman theatres of Umbria are substantial and they suggest a thriving theatrical tradition, on the most lavish scale, for the provincial Italians of the Augustan age. One only has to glimpse the partially ruined auditorium at Gubbio to get a sense of the scale and magnificence of these structures. Originally able to seat 6,000 spectators (and some scholars estimate many more), the theatre was excavated and partially rebuilt from 1789 onwards, and was found to contain mosaic pavements of the very highest quality, many of which have been conserved. It may well have been built by one of the town's magistrates (*quattrovir*) Gnaeus Satrius Rufus at the beginning of the first century AD, since an inscription noting other building projects which he funded was found in the theatre. The architectural style and method of the lower arcade, the most substantial survival of the original structure, is sophisticated, employing rusticated blocks of local stone clothed with a high-quality, expensive stone veneer. The upper arcade has been restored in brick, so it is easy to distinguish it from what remains of the original, as is the case with both the *cavea* (seating area) and the stage, the latter decorated with a series of niches alternately curved or rectangular. Every summer a festival of classical plays revives the glories of the early Roman Empire, and the characters of the tragedies of Seneca or the comedies of Plautus himself and his successor Terentius once again command the attention of enthusiastic crowds.

The most substantial remains of another similar theatre to have been excavated in Umbria are those of Spoleto which, from its position within the city's walls and because of damage from an earthquake in antiquity, was subject to extensive adaptation in the Dark Ages and after. The former Church of St. Agata was built over part of the *scena,* and the noble family of the Ancaiani quarried the site for materials to use in the construction of their nearby town palace during the sixteenth century. It was only in 1870 that a substantial effort was made to conserve what was left of the first-century structure. Most interestingly, the architectural remains for

Roman theatre, Spoleto

maneuvering stage machinery (post holes and track) have survived. The theatre is visited as part of the adjoining archaeological museum.

A trip to ancient Carsulae, an Augustan *municipium* straddling the western bifurcation of the Via Flaminia and abandoned after the classical period, sadly reveals even less of the original theatrical splendour of the auditorium. Excavated only in the 1950s and not even then in its entirety, the theatre's scale, however, matches the claims made by Strabo in the first century BC that the city was a centre of Umbrian affluence. This is backed up by its interesting position immediately next to the remains of an amphitheatre, both set in a natural declivity and creating an entire "entertainment quarter" for what can only ever have been a medium-sized town.

Roman remains other than theatrical structures in the region have long been the subject of interest by foreign commentators, especially those with a theatrical flourish of their own. And there is no Roman monument better-known than the so called Bridge of Augustus at Narni. This was undoubtedly a major engineering work of the Augustan age, coinciding with the modernizing of the Flaminian Way; 525 feet long and 100 feet above the River Nera, it originally boasted four huge travertine arches of which only the one nearest town now survives intact. Henry James in his *Italian Hours* finds himself with time on his hands changing trains at Narni Scalo and marvels at the bridge's grandeur:

> One day in midwinter, some years since, during a journey from Rome to Florence perforce too rapid to allow much wayside sacrifice to curiosity, I waited for the train at Narni. There was time to stroll far enough from the station to have a look at the famous old bridge of Augustus, broken short off in mid-Tiber. While I stood admiring the measure of impression was made to overflow by the gratuitous grace of a white-cowled monk who came trudging up the road that wound to the gate of the town. Narni stood, in its own presented felicity, on a hill a good space away, boxed in behind its perfect grey wall, and the monk, to oblige me, crept slowly along and disappeared within the aperture. Everything was distinct in the clear air, and the view exactly as like the bit of background by an Umbrian master as it ideally should have been.

To whatever degree the Master catches the mood and "makes theatre", it does not stop him from this time mistaking the Nera for the Tiber: even

Corot's *The Bridge at Narni*

Homer nods... There is hope for us lesser authors, then. Among artists who have memorialized their view of the bridge is Jean-Baptiste-Camille Corot, who within a few months of his arrival in 1826 to take up the Prix de Rome with study at the French Academy in the Villa Medici had travelled to Narni to paint the ruin *en plein air*. The painting is now in the Louvre's collection.

The stabilization of Roman power, accompanied by a spread of definitively Roman culture within our region, followed on the Battle of Sentinum in 295 BC, which saw a triumph for the Republican legions of the metropolis over the assembled troops of the Etruscan league. Ian Campbell-Ross, however, neatly expresses the dilemma about the precise direction and dynamic of the resulting flow of influence: "It was the degree to which Rome was itself Etruscanized... that enables us to understand certain aspects of the relationship between the city and such centres of Etruscan power as Perugia, so important in the development of Umbria."

The intricate nature of the "cross-over" can be discerned in such important sculptural pieces as that of *The Orator*, an early first-century BC votive offering featuring the Etruscan nobleman Aule Mettele with an accompanying inscription in the Etruscan language—yet the style and dress are entirely Roman of the late Republic. As we saw in the last chapter's account of Etruscan burial practices, what was once distinct and unique gradually acquired Roman elements. Trade in the area endured, politics favoured first one side then the other, and almost imperceptibly a single culture of central Italy emerged which we now term classically "Roman". Symbolic of this change is another statue found near Amelia in 1963, a massive and hugely costly bronze of the wildly popular member of the Imperial family, Germanicus. The statue, made about a hundred years after that of Aule Mettele, establishes Umbria as a mainstream part of the Roman "homeland". The presumptive heir of his uncle Tiberius, the second emperor, Germanicus died while acting as governor of Syria, and sustained mourning for him across the Roman world caused an unprecedented breakdown of industrial output and mercantile life. The statue is probably a memorial bronze which was erected in Roman-Etruscan Amelia emphasizing the inhabitants' loyalty to the reigning Imperial house—quite a development in the history of assimilation.

It was undoubtedly this context that produced the greatest writer to emerge from Umbria in the Roman era. Little is known about the early life of Sextus Propertius (even his name is incomplete lacking the patronymic, and sparsely attested), but Assisi has long claimed to be the place of his birth in about 45 BC. His poems after the Greek model of Callimachus in elegiac couplets (thus *Elegies*) recount the bitter-sweet affair he conducted with the older woman he calls "Cynthia", and have the conventional landscape of "Arcadia" as its setting. An occasional topical reference confirms his knowledge of Umbrian geography. Allusions in the poems to the contemporary political scene, charting particularly the rise to unassailable power of Octavius Caesar as the first emperor, Augustus, occasionally break through the amorous cloud-cover. For example, we learn that his father, an Umbrian landowner, had estates confiscated probably in 41 BC, when the increasingly powerful Octavian granted land to his veteran troops. For the rest, Propertius' rather tortuous, recondite and heavily allusive verse focuses on life in the capital, his house on the Esquiline and trips to the hill resort of Tibur (modern Tivoli). But in what has become perhaps his most famous poem Elegies IV, 7 (praised by such modern poets as the Russian Nobel laureate, Joseph Brodsky) an innate theatrical skill is incontrovertibly evidenced. Here in a masterpiece, written it seems not long before his own death around 15 BC, the poet recounts his final encounter, *post mortem*, with his beautiful but cruel mistress, Cynthia:

> There are ghosts after all, then; death is not the ending:
> the soul, like smoke, escapes from the funeral flame.
> Beside my bed I saw the wraith of Cynthia.
> From that new grave by the noisy road she came
> to me who, shaken, still, by the rites, lay restless
> in the bed that was once our kingdom and was no more.
> Her eyes, her hair, were the same as I had known them;
> fire had charred one side of the robe she wore
> and had eaten away the beryl ring on her finger;
> her lips were withered from water drunk underground.
> Her spirit, her voice, were living, but as she stood there
> her brittle finger bones made a rattling sound.
> "You forget so soon?" she said. "No woman ever
> had a truer lover, yet sleep can erase the sight
> of the little room we shared in the noisy Subura,

my window worn by ruses of the night,
the rope tossed over the sill where I'd hang for a moment
and hand over hand climb down into your embrace.
Under our cloaks the earth has been warmed by our bodies
as we lay by the crossroads in some shadowy place.
Our pledge was wordless, but our lies, our cheating,
the deaf south-western wind has brushed away.
When I came to death, no man's voice called my name out,
though yours would have kept me alive another day;
for me no watchman troubled to sound his cleft reed;
a broken tile props up my fallen head.
Who has seen you stand by my grave grief-stricken?
Who has seen your robe grow wet with the tears you shed?

༂

You will have dreams, and you must learn to trust them;
through holy dreams the truth may be revealed.
At night we dead can wander—even Cerberus,
his chain cast off, will stray through forest and field,
until with dawn hell's law returns us to Lethe
where Charon the ferry-man counts over his own.
Take your new love. I shall share you with no other
when you come to me here, and bone shall grind on bone."
And suddenly, her sad complaining ended,
she was gone, and I stood with my empty arms extended.
(Translated by Constance Carrier)

It may not be the work of Homer or the Greek tragedians, or even of his most celebrated Roman contemporary, Publius Vergilius Maro, "Virgil", but it has power and I would challenge anyone to deny its theatricality.

GOLDEN AGE

After the confusion of the Civil Wars, and then the long years of Augustus' increasingly stable *Principate*, the full-blown Imperial period must have been something of a golden age for Umbria. In easy reach of the greatest city the world had ever seen, fertile and an essential corridor of communication and the passage of goods, it was also the magnet for luxury settlement, with Roman aristocrats buying up farms and constructing villas from where they might simply holiday or more probably hunt. These "incomers" joined the Romanized Etruscan aristocracy to secure the vibrancy of a balanced countryside/town culture whose theatres are among the most abiding features. The most celebrated of these new Umbri was Gaius Plinius Caecilius Secundus, Pliny the Younger, whose villa by the side of the Tiber was excavated in the 1980s. Long known as Colle Plinio, a tumulus near the village of Selci-Lama at the very northern-most tip of our region revealed the foundations of the country house which has long been known in considerable detail from a couple of the letters to his friends published by Pliny towards the end of his distinguished political career (consul 100 AD, proconsul of Bithynia in modern-day Turkey 110-113). A native of Como in what was technically not even Italy for the Romans (the province of Gallia Cisalpina), Pliny is either captivated by the area or at least wants to appear to be. The most bookish of bores, he describes in a short letter addressed to the historian Tacitus (Epistles Book 1, 6) a hunting expedition to which he brought his secretaries and writing tablets to avoid wasting time or indeed, no doubt, one of his many *bons mots,* which would have to be immediately noted down:

> CERTAINLY YOU will laugh (and laugh you may) when I tell you that your old acquaintance is turned sportsman, and has taken three noble boars. "What?" you say, "Pliny?" Even he. However, I indulged at the same time my beloved inactivity, and whilst I sat at my nets, you would have found me, not with spear and dart, but pen and tablets by my side. I mused and wrote, being resolved if I returned with my hands empty, at least to come home with my pocket-book full.

Even if the unsportsmanlike writer is not terribly funny, he is honest in his response to the natural beauty of Umbria's surroundings. He continues:

> Believe me, this manner of studying is not to be despised; you cannot conceive how greatly exercise contributes to enliven the imagination. Besides the sylvan solitude with which one is surrounded, and the very silence which is observed on these occasions, strongly incline the mind to meditation. For the future therefore let me advise you, whenever you

hunt, to take along with you your tablets, as well as your basket and bottle: for be assured you will find Minerva as fond of roaming the hills as Diana. Farewell.

(Translated by Betty Racice)

Pliny is also good at describing the landscape around his villa, which forms a natural amphitheatre, a huge bowl half Tuscan and half Umbrian, with the Tiber watering fertile fields on either bank. This effect can today be best experienced with a visit to the small town of Citerna. There, half way up its main street, is a "balcony" open to this natural amphitheatre, which perfectly gives the impression of being the best box in the house. Far away across the valley can just be discerned the location of Pliny's villa, to the north the gloomy shadow of St. Francis' Monte Verna looms, to the south the winding of the Tiber around Città di Castello, headed for Perugia and the widening of the valley. As well as housing some superb art works the other principal feature of this town is the covered passages which circle the majority of its ancient fortifications, reminiscent of what we find on a grander scale in the Portico di San Filippo and other arcaded features of Nocera Umbra's townscape.

Another natural amphitheatre is formed by the hills which half circle on its eastern side the great Umbrian lake, Trasimeno. The largest of the non-alpine Italian lakes (49 square miles) it has the remarkable feature of being no deeper than twenty feet at any point, and only fourteen on average. Henry James, travelling between Perugia and Cortona, noted it and gives it yet another spelling:

> Between Perugia and Cortona lies the large weedy water of Lake Thrasymene, turned into a witching word for ever by Hannibal's recorded victory over Rome. Dim as such records have become to us and remote such realities, he is yet a passionless pilgrim who doesn't, as he passes, of a heavy summer's day, feel the air and the light and the very faintness of the breeze all charged and haunted with them, all interfused as with the wasted ache of experience and with the vague historic gaze.

It was by the side of this enormous puddle, on 24 June 217 BC, that probably the most famous event in Umbrian history occurred. After he had crossed the Alps with his notable elephants, Hannibal Barca, generalissimo of Carthage, the North African trade-rival of Rome, lay in wait for the enemy legions. Hidden by mists and reed banks, he surprised the commanding consul of the Roman forces, Gaius Flaminius (he of the eponymous road), and inflicted the gravest defeat on the Republic's armed forces that they had ever known or would know again. Titus Livius (Livy) tells the story with a historical flourish which works up the set piece into the equivalent of a Greek tragedy.

> In order still further to exasperate his enemy and make him eager to avenge the injuries inflicted on the allies of Rome, Hannibal laid waste with all the horrors of war the land between Cortona and Lake Trasumennus. He had now reached a position eminently adapted for surprise tactics, where the lake comes up close under the hills of Cortona. There is only a very narrow road here between the hills and the lake, as though a space had been purposely left far it. Further on there is a small expanse of level ground flanked by hills, and it was here that Hannibal pitched camp, which was only occupied by his Africans and Spaniards, he himself being in command. The Balearics and the rest of the light infantry he sent behind the hills; the cavalry, conveniently screened by some low hills, he stationed at the mouth of the defile, so that when the Romans had entered it they would be completely shut in by the cavalry, the lake, and the hills. Flaminius had reached the lake at sunset. The next morning, in a still uncertain light, he passed through the defile, without sending any scouts on to feel the way, and when the column began to deploy in the wider extent of level ground the only enemy they saw was the one in front, the rest were concealed in their rear and above their heads. When the Carthaginian saw his object achieved and had his enemy shut in between the lake and the hills with his forces surrounding them, he gave the signal for all to make a simultaneous attack, and they charged straight down upon the point nearest to them. The affair was all the more sudden and unexpected to the Romans because a fog which had risen from the lake was denser on the plain than on the heights; the bodies of the enemy on the various hills could see each other well enough, and it was all the easier for them to charge all at the same time. The shout of battle rose round the Romans before they could see clearly from whence it came, or became aware that they were surrounded. Fighting began in front and flank before they could form line or get their weapons ready or draw their swords. (Livy 22.4)

For almost three hours the fighting went on; everywhere a desperate struggle was kept up, but it raged with greater fierceness round the consul. He was followed by the pick of his army, and wherever he saw his men hard pressed and in difficulties he at once went to their help. Distinguished by his armour he was the object of the enemy's fiercest attacks, which his comrades did their utmost to repel, until an Insubrian horseman who knew the consul by sight—his name was Ducarius—cried out to his countrymen, "Here is the man who slew our legions and laid waste our city and our lands! I will offer him in sacrifice to the shades of my foully murdered countrymen." Digging spurs into his horse he charged into the dense masses of the enemy, and slew an armour-bearer who threw himself in the way as he galloped up lance in rest, and then plunged his lance into the consul; but the triarii protected the body with their shields and prevented him from despoiling it. Then began a general flight, neither lake nor mountain stopped the panic-stricken fugitives, they rushed like blind men over cliff and defile, men and arms tumbled pell-mell on one another. A large number, finding no avenue of escape, went into the water up to their shoulders; some in their wild terror even attempted to escape by swimming, an endless and hopeless task in that lake. Either their spirits gave way and they were drowned, or else finding their efforts fruitless, they regained with great difficulty the shallow water at the edge of the lake and were butchered in all directions by the enemy's cavalry who had ridden into the water. About 6000 men who had formed the head of the line of march cut their way through the enemy and cleared the defile, quite unconscious of all that had been going on behind them. They halted on some rising ground, and listened to the shouting below and the clash of arms, but were unable, owing to the fog, to see or find out what the fortunes of the fight were. At last, when the battle was over and the sun's heat had dispelled the fog, mountain and plain revealed in the clear light the disastrous overthrow of the Roman army and showed only too plainly that all was lost. (Livy 22.6, translated by Aubrey de Selincourt)

The event was certainly indelibly printed on the local mind. Two hamlets still recall the carnage in their names: Ossaia (Bone-field) and Sanguineto (Place of Blood). It is also from these events that Barry Unsworth named his deliciously pessimistic novel, *After Hannibal,* cited in the previous chapter, to typify Perugia's gloom. And the effect of fog on the plain and visibility higher up the slope is certainly an abiding meteorological feature of the entire region.

The next major bust-up in Umbria's history was her involvement in Rome's Civil Wars (80-27 BC). Ringing in the death-knell of the five centuries' old Republican constitution these clashes between politicians-cum-generals culminated in the emergence of a new Roman state first ruled by groups of magnates together (the First and Second Triumvirates), soon reducing itself to power concentrated in the hands of a single leader, designated at first *princeps* and later *imperator,* hence the Empire. The *Bellum Perusinum* (Perugian Campaign) of 40 BC, which saw a brief coalition between the future Caesar Augustus and Marcus Antonius, is memorably recalled in Shakespeare's *Antony and Cleopatra,* when Octavius envies Antony's iron digestive system:

> It is reported thou didst eat strange flesh,/Which some did die to look on:…

Punished for its support of the losing side (Shakespeare's consuls Hirtius and Pansa), Perugia was technically abolished only to be re-founded as Perusia Augusta, glorying in the style of the Civil Wars' ultimate victor, Augustus, and celebrated in the inscription above the city's Etruscan Arch leading to the university quarter. A neighbouring town which had backed the winning side, Spello, did even better out of the naming game, becoming *Hispellum Splendidissima Colonia Julia.*

Other towns of the region to gain from the spread of definitive Roman development are Narni (Roman Narnia), which replaced the Umbrian settlement of Nequinum in 299 BC, and Spoleto (Spoletum, 241 BC). Each of these was a Roman *colonia,* a colony, whose inhabitants were automatically Roman citizens. Remains of this flourishing are to be found in the impressive series of Roman cisterns underneath the Church of Santa Maria in Narni, a rocky bastion whose provision of water might well be as tricky as that of Orvieto, considered in the last chapter. Orvieto itself, of all the towns of Umbria, fared the least well in the high Roman period; identified with the Etruscan *Volsinii Veteres,* Old Volsinii, it was destroyed by a Roman army in 264 BC, and then the settlement was moved to what is now Bolsena (*Volsinii Nuovi*), which is not even in our region.

Terni (*Interamnia Nahars*), though apparently an important Roman centre (producing no fewer than three second-century Roman emperors), has little evidence of its Roman greatness, the imposing remains of an amphitheatre apart. Now once again used for summer theatrical performances (though employing modern raked seating set in the middle of the *arena* rather than any of the scant original tiers of the *cavea*), part of the medieval cathedral complex is built into its walls. I once got a splendid view of the whole while using the bathroom in the private apartments of Terni's bishop. Having revealed this biographical detail I can further back up an aesthetic claim that smaller Roman centres such as Bevagna, Amelia and even Giove speak much more eloquently than Terni of the affluence and sophistication of this period in the life of Umbria.

MODERN THEATRICS

Although the Roman period set the standard for the theatrical tradition in Umbria, something of a "come back" has been staged more recently. One of the most extraordinary aspects of this renaissance is to be found within the *Città ideale* project of Milan-based architect, Tomasso Buzzi. At the convent of Scarzuola, founded as a hermitage by St. Francis of Assisi in 1218, a mile and a half from Montegiove, the Milanese professor worked to create an idealized fantasy space from 1958 to 1982. At its centre is the Teatro all'Antico, a Greco-Roman-style auditorium surrounded by other classical, alchemical and esoteric follies. Excavated from the hill as it falls away from the Franciscan convent, the ensemble of pavilions, fountains and formal garden recall both the whimsy of the Parco dei Mostri at Bomarzo across the border in Lazio, and the exuberance and classiness of Villa d'Este at Tivoli. Too remote to act successfully as a venue for theatre, the project was worked at by Buzzi to be what has been described as a tapestry of Penelope: never completed, perpetually tinkered with. To visit it one must make a special booking with Buzzi's heir, Marco Solari, who receives groups of no fewer than eight persons.

If La Scarzuola seems surreal in the sublime setting of Umbria's rolling hills, olive groves and vineyards, then surely Terni, so recently disparaged by me, might seem even more out of place as a setting for a flourishing film industry. Three miles from the centre of the city and based in the industrial plant which previously supported a hydro-electrical unit, Papigno now houses studios set up by Rome's Hollywood, Cinecittà. Chosen as

A view of the *Città ideale*

the studios in which the sets for two enormously successful films of Roberto Benigni, *La Vita è Bella* and *Pinocchio,* were constructed, both productions also utilized nearby outdoor Umbrian locations. And the Oscar-winning Tuscan clown and popularizer of Dante's *Comedia Divina* has not been alone in recognizing the cinematic potential of Umbria: Arrone and Ferentillo, two ancient *borghi* close to Terni, were used as locations for Mario Monicelli's 1966 historic epic, *L'Armata Brancaleone,* while Fellini set part of his *Intervista* (1987) at the Cascata delle Marmore.

It seems that the big screen has by no means exhausted the celluloid possibilities of Umbria's natural theatricality or picturesque settings. Two long-running Italian TV shows have found their locations (and much of their character and colour) in Umbrian towns; Città della Pieve has for five seasons of *Carabinieri* hosted the comings and goings of the eponymous law enforcers impersonated by a cast of popular artists, while Gubbio is the setting for the crime solving of *Don Matteo,* a parish priest much given to Father Brown-like snooping. Don Matteo is played by Terence Hill (an entirely Italian actor, baptized Mario Girotti) who functions for his home nation as an equivalent to the USA's Richard Chamberlain. Enormously popular when young (unforgettable alongside Alain Delon in Visconti's *Il Gattopardo, The Leopard*) he became a national institution by playing in a series of Westerns together with another Italian who bears an Anglo-Saxon name, Bud Spencer. Hill, now well into his late middle age, still keeps his blonde good looks, and his priestly sleuth weighs in as one of the nation's most popular television characters.

None of these film personalities is, of course, Umbrian. But Monica Bellucci is. Undoubtedly one of Italy's most celebrated modern actresses, and a considerable "sex symbol" or even for some "the most beautiful woman in the world", she is an ex-model who has moved between the small and large screens of both domestic and foreign productions with apparent ease. Born in Città di Castello (either in 1964 or 1968, depending on which biography is consulted), a town with a tradition (self-assessed) of producing beauties, the young Monica's middle-class family (mother an artist, father a business owner) sent her to study law at Perugia University. But it was part-time modeling that launched her film career, later to make her internationally known for her Persephone in *The Matrix Reloaded* (2003) and Mary Magdalene in *The Passion of the Christ* (2004). Her connection with this last project did not, it seems, imply the same revivalist Roman Catholic agenda so often imputed to the film's director, Mel Gibson, since "La Bellucci" outraged Italian bourgeois opinion and the Vatican in 2003 by posing nude for a photo-shoot while pregnant as part of a campaign to broaden Italy's highly restrictive donor sperm programmes. (Unless, of course, this was the sin for which she was atoning as the Magdalene.) Umbrians are proud of this international recognition of their theatrical potential, if not exactly its realization. It still seems that really to "make it" one has to get out: but if you can take the girl out of Umbria, the question remains whether you can take Umbria out of the girl. I with many others would like to think not.

Chapter Four

TEMPLE TO CHURCH

A PERIOD OF INVASIONS

I have lived some part of every year in Umbria for over ten years, and I have never stopped being aware of the degree to which I remain an intruder, in spite of that longed for "becoming Umbrian" that has been my declared dream. The way I feel this the most keenly is in my relationship with the most basic of the region's "inhabitants", its plant and animal life. A friend once suggested that it is the Umbrian passion for hunting, with its toll of birds large and small, that leads there to be a concurrently higher density of insects. It cannot be proved, *ma se non è vero, e ben trovato*, if not true, it makes sense. The country hums, buzzes, chirps and chirrups. *Tarli,* woodworm, infest the beams of every traditionally built dwelling, requiring an annual poison spray in likely spots. *Tafani,* horse flies, dive bomb pool- and sun-bathers, and are extraordinarily persistent, even when doused with water. *Callabrone,* giant hornets, have more than once found a home in my chimneys, warranting the services of the local sweep, and each May a queen-bee somehow squeezes between the closed outer-door of the kitchen to build her colony all too visibly against the glass partition inside. Then, of course, there are the scorpions. It is at this point that virtually every visitor from Britain screams and retires to the nearest stool, taking refuge well above floor level. Let me hasten to add that these decidedly ugly little arthropods are not deadly like their much larger red cousins, found in Africa and Asia. If the tail should strike, then it would be like a bee sting, only really dangerous to those with particular allergies. I can attest to it, since I have been stung and have lived to tell the tale.

No, if Umbria is to offer deadly, then let it do so in reptilian form. *Vipere,* adders, are native to the region, and in fact about ten years ago they were the object of a national project for re-stocking the countryside with endangered species; young snakes were literally parachuted in from helicopters. It is also suggested that wolves were let free in the mountains. Un-imaginable but true! Today the reinvigorated brood of vipers accounts

Not a brood, but viper enough

for a considerable annual death toll. Not however of humans, rather their pets. I have known of a friend's cat which was too inquisitive about what was down in the old outhouse, and another's very large and healthy dog which only just made it through with immediate veterinarian intervention and a month's convalescence. I have even had to kill a viper in my own larder, when it went for a sleepy guest looking for a bottle of water to take to bed. Our weapons—a broom and a mop, but it took the two of us and was not easy. A serum against viper venom used to be on sale at chemists but so much more damage was done to humans who were administered this antidote in the mistaken belief that they had been bitten that it was withdrawn from sale. Oddly it remains available in the Vatican City's pharmacy. "Vatican Gardens Infested with Vipers" would surely make a sensational headline.

And if this wildlife was not challenging enough for one sojourning in summer Umbria, then the constant fight with the undergrowth would surely provide the rest. Suspiciously quiet during the winter months, and then with spring arriving comparatively late in this majority upland landscape of hills, so violent can be the growth of every invasive plant that your daffodils might well still be in bloom, with cherry blossom on the bough at the same time as the thistles, briars, and nettles launch their annual surprise attack. Of course, one does just have to accept that things grow fast here—nothing faster than the vines, and the cash crops of tobacco and sunflowers in the valley bottoms display a similar haste later in the season. And it would be churlish not to mention that the presence of so many poppies growing as "weeds" adds a new meaning to the word; wild flowers around here are something special. The memory of cyclamen and wild orchids growing along a limestone path near Assisi often returns to delight me. But woe-betide a sluggish gardener or an occasional visitor to their lonely country place. Without constant attention the most attractive of gardens can be transformed into a jungle.

So yes, I am decidedly a stranger! Why is it so obvious? Not because I do not get on with the locals, nor because I have failed to make Italian friends round about. No, simply because all the real Umbrians have long since sold their houses on the hills and moved down to new properties in the valleys where they need no longer worry about the swarms of insects, the lurking snakes or indeed the inconveniences of water being supplied by a well liable to run dry. They leave that to the latest horde of incomers

Umbria was no stranger to the movement of peoples either in prehistory or throughout the classical period, and one might add that the ethnic mix of central Italy has been almost constantly provisional and evolving. The establishment of a fixed Roman/Etruscan population, the main subject of the last chapter, would always have been leavened by the presence of slaves from elsewhere in the empire, and there is little reason to doubt that the lowest strata of local society also picked up inherited traits from this rich genetic pool. People will simply keep on having sex. However, the fairly rapid decline of the Western Roman Empire in the period 380-470 AD led to decisive, large-scale waves of different groups of settlers to peninsular Italy. And this was to be a continuous feature for the next two or three hundred years. Visigoths, Ostrogoths, Huns, Lombards, they all came and some of each of them stayed. Later other foreigners would arrive with passing armies: Germans with the Holy Roman Empire's Hohenstaufen dynasty, and even raiding parties of Turks or other Muslim groups from North Africa (lumped together by the more or less abusive catch-all term, "Saracen", like those against whom St. Clare protected Assisi). Trade also led to diversity; stories tell that St. Francis' mother was from Provence and even his own sobriquet Francesco ("the little French guy"—his baptismal name was Giovanni, John) underlines links between southern France and central Italy, opened up no doubt by his father's cloth trade. But the invasions go on, especially in a globalized economy and with the natural tendency of Umbria to de-populate; there are simply not enough job opportunities to entice the young to stay. But the present day invaders fall very much into two different categories: the rich and the poor.

A springtime market day in any one of the pretty smaller towns of mid-Umbria will coax out even the shyest of the regions most recent invaders. A stroll round the food stalls, maybe splashing out on some really good pecorino or mozzarella brought up from Campania, picking up the staple broad beans and artichokes of April, and perhaps treating themselves to a piece of fish brought into the interior from Adriatic ports: all this the invaders might well do, but they will not go home to their tastefully renovated *casale* without spending some time in the bar of the piazza to drink a beer, Campari or whatever, and gossip with other Anglophone exiles. As many as 1.5 million British citizens emigrate annually, at least half ending up in Europe. Now parts of Italy are nowhere near to matching the swamping of localities which has happened in coastal Spain, where British expats regularly win local mayoral elections, but it would be idle to deny that the influx of new Umbrians has had no effect on the place and its longer established residents. I know a former British army vet who as well as renovating old houses for a living undertakes the duties of a mayoral deputy for a tiny community of twenty families up in the mountains between Umbria and Tuscany. He, I would hazard, is among the most integrated of the British invaders I've come across, so much so that he is known locally and unaffectedly as Claudio, a fairly regular name in Italy, rather than his baptismal Claude, not so common in today's UK. He shows every sign of having found his place.

Then there are also those who have invaded perhaps primarily because it is easier to sit and drink the day away here in company and in good weather than it would be elsewhere. Generally a bit cheaper still than northern Europe, but less cheap than it used to be, Umbria has become one of the sought after destinations for settlement of Britons (and some other nationalities) determined to create the expat dream, or should that be nightmare. I well-remember coming across a raddled group of hard drinkers on the gin and tonics when I was having my breakfast in a local village bar: "Back in India of course…" "Aren't there any bitters?" "Don't you know Phoebe?" These were conversations from which I was happy to beat a swift retreat. Apparently loath to learn Italian or at least communicate in it at a level higher than ordering a drink, they recall an attitude expressed by Maggie Smith's character in Zefferelli's film *Tea with Mussolini*—we British, having the whole world to choose from, have bestowed a great honour in choosing Italy in which to live.

Of course, Tuscany was first in the recent phase of this game, developing its "Chiantishire" as long as forty years ago, and then Umbria was discovered as the cheaper option offering much the same (or better, depending on taste). And that explains why not all these invaders were or are super affluent. Though the aforementioned *casale* or *casa colonica* is the "type" to which most incomers aspire, plenty have bought small sections of bigger buildings or even an apartment in an unattractive strip village with no views, hillsides or even space to build a swimming pool. Nonetheless, they all can be classified as "rich" in the face of the poor immigration from North and West Africa.

These economic migrants, too, have touched the fabric of the place. *Halal* meat is not difficult to find in any town in Umbria and women wearing the *hijab* push children in buggies along pavements the length and breadth of the region. Originally dependent on finding employment only in factories and canning plants, or doing seasonal back-breaking work harvesting cash crops, the African immigrants to Umbria have gradually won a foothold that seems to be lasting. Buying up small businesses, diversifying and servicing the tourist trade's need for cheap manual labour has born fruit, and many families, having "won" recognition and legal status, are beginning to add a welcome diversity to the region's largely homogeneous culture, especially in its school system. In this their presence is far more significant than the developed world's immigrants who are typically in at least later middle age if not already retired, and rarely accompanied by children. If statistics are looked for, however, the numbers of these new Umbrians still remain very small indeed. Only 3.5 per cent of the Italian population is Muslim, even if this reality does not prevent the "talking up" of such extraordinary events as the 2007 uncovering of an Al-Qaeda cell attached to a *madrassa* in Ponte San Giovanni, a hamlet just outside Perugia. One of the issues foremost in the public debates during the 2008 general and regional elections was that of immigration and multiculturalism. Despite the posturing of the triumphant Right, it was just a few weeks into his premiership that Silvio Berlusconi declared that being a clandestine immigrant in Italy should not be considered a crime as much as an abuse. He was more than thoroughly aware of the contribution that this kind of immigration adds to the economy without costing what properly recognized workers with holiday rights, pensions and healthcare demand.

EARLY CHRISTIANITY

Leaving current issues and taking up once again our timeline trail through the development of the region, we have arrived at what can be best described as Late Antiquity or the Early Middle Ages. It was the Age of Invasions *par excellence* for Umbria. Yet the invading cultural force which preceded the settlement of actual foreign bodies was one that marks the era as not only a clash of arms but also of ideas. To what extent Christianity was an invader into the peninsular heartlands of the Late Roman Empire rather than a faith which took root there naturally is a question difficult to resolve. Legends of local martyr saints who clash with paganism and are executed for it are as common here as elsewhere in the Roman world. The first to be documented in 169 AD are the martyrdoms of Victor and Medicus at Ottrìcoli. Archaeological evidence comes to the aid of tradition and hagiographical writings when we note the catacombs at San Faustino near Massa Martana, which abound in Christian symbols dating from the middle of the second century.

Perhaps the most typical saintly type represented in Umbria is that of San Crescentino or Crescenzio, who in the third century AD is believed to have been a Roman soldier (stereotypically a centurion therefore middle-ranking) who, ridding the Morra Valley of possession by a dragon (or serpent, back to the vipers), was tried for his faith and executed at Tifernum Tiberinum, modern Città di Castello. Venerated as a martyr and the first public witness to the Christian faith in the area, Crescentino won the hearts and minds of the locals. A battle with a dragon is a neat figure for the more philosophical struggle that Christianity faced in addressing the classical culture of state paganism. (Most typically of all, the same metaphor is, of course, elaborated in the legend of St. George, who would eventually develop into the Crusaders' patron of choice and the English national saint.)

Yet there is a second strand of early Christian Umbrian sanctity, that represented by its early bishops. It is believed that Felicianus, first Bishop of Foligno, died in the mid-third-century persecutions of the Emperor Decius. The same fate is recounted for a whole string of Perugian bishops (St. Constant and Saints Ercolano I and II). There is no martyr-bishop more celebrated, however, than the first Bishop of Terni, St. Valentine. Almost certainly a historical figure of the late third century, he is of course now feted in the western world on his feast 14 February as the patron of lovers. The legend has it that Valentine exposed his own life to danger and ultimate martyrdom under the Emperor Diocletian by taking the place of a young Christian condemned to death, whom he wished to see reunited with his betrothed. The fact that according to the story the lovers both later suffered a similar fate only goes further to prove that Valentine was a romantic at heart, certainly ready for the big gesture. Terni's recent attempts to cash in on the St. Valentine trade by directing visitors to the saint's tomb and basilica by a complicated system of road signs also might best be thought of as a touch of whimsy. Visitors to this town are rarely tourists, certainly not of the sort looking for romance—industrial Terni will never replace Sorrento, Capri, Venice or Rome as principal resorts for lovers or a particularly favoured location for a dream wedding.

Following these tribulations and triumphs for Christianity in the second and third centuries, by the end of the fourth century it was paganism that was now officially censured and Christianity promoted by the Roman authorities. But the question remains about the effectiveness of such official positions in preventing more basic and local superstitions. Eventually the legends of such heroes as Crescentino and cults based upon places associated with their lives melded with the fertility rites and the sanctity of springs, caves and groves to make a religion if not entirely orthodox then at least truly local.

There can have been few natural sites with more sacred associations in Umbria than the springs of the River Clitunno (classical Clitumnus). Set in the heart of the Vale of Umbria south of Trevi and north of Spoleto, an abundant spring of water rises direct from the ground and gives rise to thick groves of willows and beeches. From thence it flows into the Topino, itself a tributary of the Tiber. It was concerning these pools sacred to Jove that Virgil in his *Georgics* (II, 146ff) describes the miraculous effect of washing sacrificial animals in their waters—they would come out perfectly white, making them now spotless offerings, all the more acceptable to the gods.

> ... here are your snowy flocks, Clitumnus, and, the noblest sacrifice,
> your bulls, that, drenched in your sacred stream,
> have often led Roman triumphs to the gods' temples.
>
> (Translated by A. S. Kline)

Pliny the Younger, too, describes the area in another of his Umbrian letters (VIII, 8), showing that in antiquity the extent of the pools and the breadth of the river which emerged from them was much greater than it is now.

> There is a small hill which is heavily clothed in a wood of venerable cypress trees; at its foot the spring emerges and bursts out into a number of different channels, great and small, which once the force has slowed unite in a large pool of mirror-like stillness. It's easy to count the coins which have been tossed into the pool and the pebbles which line its bottom. The banks are wooded with ash and poplar, the reflections of which twin their originals as so many more of those trees. The water feels and looks like sparkling snow.
>
> (Betty Radice)

What we can see today is in fact an entirely nineteenth-century recreation of the natural feature planned and executed by a local landowner and engineer, Paolo Campello della Spina. The lake was excavated and the water course was channeled in 1852 in order to power the mills which were then established by the side of the stream. Thus Byron's apostrophe of its natural beauties in Canto IV, 66-8 of *Childe Harold's Pilgrimage* was prior to the industrialization:

> ... the purest god of gentle waters!
> And most serene of aspect, and most clear;
> Surely that stream was unprofaned by slaughters—
> A mirror and a bath for Beauty's youngest daughters.

Whereas Giosuè Carducci's even more celebrated poem, "Alle Fonti del Clitunno" from the collection *Odi barbere,* written while he was acting as school inspector for the district, reflect the changed, modern situation. Even so, Carducci is largely nostalgic in his purpose and tone, especially in the poem's most famous lines

Hail, green Umbria, and you Clitunno
Spirit of the pure spring!
I feel our ancient home within my heart and
The Gods of Italy resting on my brow inspired.

For a "new" Italian (post-Unification, 1860) to discover his roots in this place, when we note that it was itself an elaborate recent recreation of a rustic idyll, captures precisely the shifting nature of belief, identity and significance that typifies Late Antiquity. It comes to me as no surprise that we find so close to the Fonti del Clitunno what may well be the oldest church to have survived in the region, the so called Tempietto. Set below the Via Flaminia and above the *forma nuova*, the artificial channel carrying the waters of the springs past another of the locality's mills, the Tempietto is a small chapel which appears to be dedicated to the apostles Peter and Paul, from their apse mosaic images which may be as early as fourth-century AD. Byron describes it thus:

And on thy happy shore a temple still,
Of small and delicate proportion, keeps,
Upon a mild declivity of hill,
Its memory of thee; beneath it sweeps
Thy current's calmness; oft from out it leaps
The finny darter with the glittering scales,
Who dwells and revels in thy glassy deeps;
While, chance, some scattered water-lily sails
Down where the shallower wave still tells its bubbling tales.

A big question remains as to whether the structure is an adaptation of a pre-existing pagan sanctuary or a freshly built Christian place of worship which used elements of older buildings. With its crypt supporting an arcaded porch leading to the cruciform brick chapel the building is certainly hybrid in form, to such an extent that some have even suggested that it is a pastiche of a much later period. Its real charm, however, is im-

The Tempietto

material to quibbles about dating. It is also virtually unique in Italy, let alone Umbria.

So what was going on historically in Umbria as Christianity was established and the power of Rome declined? Gothic armies moved repeatedly through the region during the fifth century both before and after their symbolic double sacks of Rome (410 and 437 AD), the Via Flaminia being the most important link between the ancient capital and the new seat of Imperial power, Ravenna. It is also the period when Bruno Toscano's definition of the region as the "Byzantine corridor" becomes intelligible: the Flaminia is simply ideologically transformed into the Via Ravennina, a symbolic cultural spinal cord of the old civilization. The almost continuous warfare which raged along this conduit, however, meant that the region's economy and agriculture suffered accordingly.

The first barbarian with sufficient authority to spend energies on revitalizing the region was Theodoric, Gothic "King of Italy", following the abdication of the last Roman emperor, Romulus Augustulus, in 470 AD.

During the 490s, from his base in the new capital on the Adriatic, he re-established garrisons along the Flaminia/Ravennina, thus guaranteeing links with Rome, and he further remitted taxes in the region to stimulate prosperity, especially a return to regular farming. Unfortunately this was but a brief respite in a procession of warfare and the subsequent degradation of a well established infrastructure. Umbria became one of the principal theatres of war in the struggles between Theodoric's successor Witges, and the Eastern Roman general, Belisarius, attempting to re-establish the imperial hegemony of Constantinople on the central provinces of Italy.

Another saintly bishop emerged in this period, Florus or Florido of Città di Castello, earning his status as the city's patron by his extremely practical action of restoring the town's walls. And if this contest was resolved in favour of the Byzantines in 540 AD it was almost immediately re-challenged with the campaigning of Totila, the new Gothic leader from 542 AD. Umbria saw the final defeat of this new challenger in the Battle of Tagina, a hamlet just north of Gualdo Tadino, in 552 AD at the hands of another imperial general (and a eunuch to boot), Narses.

It was most probably during this turbulent period that one of the most startling archaeological treasures to have been discovered in Umbria was hidden away for safe keeping. The so-called *Tesoro di Canoscio,* the Canoscio Hoard or Treasure, consists of a collection of silver plate with most of the items almost certainly used for the liturgical celebration of holy communion; six great dishes (two engraved with elegant symbols of Christian ritual), two smaller ones, nine spoons, three chalices and a ciborium with a lid. This unique and extremely precious collection of fifth- or sixth-century silverware was uncovered by chance during the ploughing of a field near the village of Canoscio near Trestina in 1935. The shock and delight at the find was such that it has become proverbial among Umbrians to refer to a re-found object of value as "another Canoscio".

The finds are now to be seen as the principal exhibit of the Diocesan Museum in Città di Castello (frustratingly, though somewhat typically, without any explanatory labelling). The pieces, found carefully stowed under a large plate for protection (itself broken by the plough when re-discovered) as they were being buried in a shallow pit, are not all in forms that can be directly related to the liturgy, though the Christian context is attested by the inscriptions and inscribed iconography. Names of Aelianus and Felicitas, probably donors, appear on one of the patens.

The largest of the unbroken plates was clearly designed for liturgical use: in the centre is a raised surface like those in pagan *paterae* which kept the thumb free of libations when making an offering. On a number of the items unmistakably Christian symbols have been engraved; a Byzantine Cross with alpha and omega; the four rivers of the Book Genesis; the hand of God and the dove of the Holy Spirit; two lambs facing each other. These are beautiful objects which display a dignity transcending their religious design and purpose, and they attest the persistence of what was at least a spasmodic culture of luxury goods well into what we might call the Dark Ages.

If it seemed that the (Eastern) Empire had struck back in a definitive way, with Narses' triumph and the beheading of Totila, and that central Italy had finally been delivered from Gothic influence, then these barbarian-free dreams were short lived. A fresh wave of invasion by a new Germanic tribe, the Langobards (literally Longbeards), quickly established a duchy around Spoleto (571 AD), under Faroald I, the founder of a noble house whose power would last centuries. A strip of western Umbrian territory as far as Perugia and then branching east via Gubbio to Ravenna was maintained for nearly two centuries by the Byzantine exarchate in the face of the *de facto* dominance of the Langobard duchy. This toehold for those who claimed descent from the legitimate imperial past, and who had so enriched Ravenna with art works of the Christian east, would itself finally be lost when the Langobard Duke Aistulf conquered the city in 751.

To whatever extent Langobard culture was revolutionary in political terms, it was not above using the remains of the classical past, and it was determinedly Christian from the outset. The city of Spoleto and the surrounding countryside are liberally sprinkled with examples of buildings dating back to the early Middle Ages which substantially reflect previous Roman architectural projects. The Tempietto del Clitunno itself is typical of the trend: a structure either adapted from, or built out of the remains of, a classical age building. On a grander scale but following the same principles is the Basilica of San Salvatore just outside Spoleto's walls on the road to Foligno. Dating from the late fourth or early fifth century, the church was reconstructed in the high Middle Ages after a major fire, and has suffered in a string of earthquakes since. It can nonetheless still be claimed as "the most substantial antique monument in Spoleto" (Giuseppe

San Salvatore

Sordini). It employs an entire series of Doric and four massive Corinthian columns, which appear to have belonged to the same classical pagan temple. As in the Tempietto, experts detect a local architectural style which melds traditions of the classical past with orientalizing features, such as the squared presbytery and apses.

Of course, it can hardly be said to be an especially Langobard trait to build new buildings from the *spoglia*, remains, of Roman buildings. Rome itself is full of them. It is the distinctiveness of the churches associated with the Langobard duchy that makes the difference. Elsewhere in Umbria we find plenty of other examples of the general waste-not-want-not approach to church building, but without any special architectural quirks. Santa Maria in Pantano, in the Martani hills south of Todi, for example, is an early building (perhaps sixth-century) which utilizes as much of an antique temple and villa as was possible. At Carsulae a bit further south along the original Via Flaminia we see a church abandoned in the Dark Ages after it had been built into the remains of much older secular buildings in the city's forum. Most obvious of all is the use of a major classical temple façade on the forum of Assisi to house a church dedicated to St. Donato at least as early as the eleventh century. Only later would this construction acquire the name of the Temple of Minerva, when it stopped being even a church and was used partly (lower level) as the town gaol and (upper level) as the council chamber of the city's government. Reverting to sacred use in the fourteenth century, the building became known as Santa Maria sopra Minerva, and survived to be the highlight of Goethe's visit to the town in the mid-eighteenth century.

സ

Umbria virtually disappears as a political or even geographical idea as this historical period unfolds. In the compromises which the papacy made with the local Langobard overlords or later in its alliance with Charlemagne's Franks, it might still claim to have a legal right to the lordship of most of the region, but with no army of its own could not exert real power. This does not mean though that the Church did badly out of Umbria in the period. By the early tenth century as much as one-third of the land was owned by religious institutions, primarily Benedictine abbeys like that of San Pietro in Valle, in the Val di Nera north of Terni, which enjoyed special patronage from the Langobard ducal family. Founded around 720 AD by Duke Faobard II, this church enjoyed substantial local and international patronage, and its rebuilding by the German Holy Roman Emperors Otto III and Henry IV in the tenth century marks it as special as we approach the full-blown Romanesque. Its extraordinary cycle of frescoes, recounting Old Testament stories from the late twelfth century, are unique in Italy.

With the high Middle Ages Umbria reasserted itself and to some extent emerged from a period in which invaders had manipulated and profited from the region. It would have to wait another four or five hundred years until substantial emigration from the region in the late nineteenth and early twentieth centuries, especially from its increasingly barren uplands, seriously disturbed the balance of a stable population once again. This trend is excellently described in the small but well illustrated museum in the Rocca del Flea at Gualdo Tadino. And if invasion remains a feature of an area which to some extent will always be a natural thoroughfare, then we have at least to be satisfied that subsequent invasions have largely been friendly and have not provoked any further trend in the displacement of peoples. Which brings me, oddly, back to my garden, the starting point of this chapter.

In June 2002 I was subject to perhaps the happiest kind of invasion imaginable. The producer of an exceptionally successful TV show, *Ground Force*, is also an Umbrian foreigner and wanted to make an episode while hosting the show's "stars" at her own place. The programme's format was quite simple: a team of gardeners and DIY adepts gains access to someone's garden without their knowledge, and transforms it from wilderness to demi-paradise, or at least as near as three days' endeavours can so effect. After making discreet local enquiries my own particular wilderness was selected as that with the most transformative potential. Despite three day's unseasonal early summer rain and the difficulties of access to my hilltop hide-away, the magic was done. Alan Titchmarsh, Charlie Dimmock and Tommy Walsh, household names to British TV viewers, laboured to transform my gardening life forever at the same time as making a watchable show. I was subsequently "surprised" (joining the ranks of such previous recipients of their invasion as Nelson Mandela and Bette Midler) and filmed being so (a process which I am sad to admit took five takes). In the subsequent eight years I have tried my best to maintain the transformation and even believe that in some ways I have improved upon what the professionals left behind. This is fortunate because the show still gets occasional airings on satellite or cable channels in the middle of the night. I will have to battle against nature annually for just a little longer to keep up appearances.

Medieval tower, near Foligno

Chapter Five

THE CASTLE

MIDDLE AGES I

I closed the last chapter in my garden, and I'm going to open this next in the same place, but for entirely different reasons and with a definite shift of time and theme. Driving along any Umbrian valley and looking up to the hills, you will see a tower, some crenellated ruins or an entire fortress on just about every spur of the surrounding hills and at the very least every two or three miles. Some form part of a fortified *borgo* or small town, others represent the maxim that an Umbrian's original dream home was his castle.

The house I own in Umbria is by no means such a knightly dwelling—in fact it is quite specifically a reconstructed version of the *canonica* or vicarage of a small hillside hamlet which was occupied by a succession of parish priests for probably about six centuries. Yet exactly where and how it has been constructed is significant for our tale of chivalrous doings, especially where its garden is concerned. You can only get into the garden through the house since otherwise it is walled and perched on what seems to be an artificial mound, held in place on the hillside by huge bastion walls of ancient masonry. Below my house is a large, rambling noble pile, not a fortress (*rocca*) but a late medieval country gentleman's seat (*castello*). What my garden represents, then, is the trace of a much earlier fortification, a defensive tower, which could be given over to being the vicarage orchard in an age when comparative peace encouraged the knightly class to build for (slightly) more comfort rather than (slightly) less security.

The next three chapters in this book are going to consider different elements of medieval Umbrian society: 1) nobility, knights and castles; 2) the middle class, town councils and town halls; 3) the Church, churches and popes. I choose to start with the "upper crust" and their warlike pursuits since they are in some ways prior to the others, but so interdependent are the three that I might have started literally anywhere. Neither are the themes which each emphasis raises limited only to a consideration of the Middle Ages—there are strong after-currents in and around Umbria today which originate here. And in each chapter I will include the description of a characteristically flavoured (military, civic and religious) *corteo storico*, historic pageant, which has been recreated in modern Umbria specifically to celebrate this formative period.

FEUDAL UMBRIA

Our last chapter talked of the frequent Dark Age passage of armies through Umbria, and it is from this painful reality that the need for the locals to defend themselves sprang. Retreat to a nearby stronghold, with as many of your goods and animals as are transportable, is of course the only sensible option in the face of a marauding horde. Then you sit it out and wait for the horde to move further down or up the Via Flaminia, or the Tiber Valley, depending on the phase of its invasion. Roman towns were only systematically re-fortified in the latter part of the empire, and then not always; San Florido's late sixth-century walls (see Chapter Four) around Città di Castello are a kind of exception that proves a rule. But strongholds can take many forms, not only within the urban context, even if most kinds try to benefit from natural geological advantages; so that hills, rocky outcrops, un-scalable cliffs all come in useful. And the utility of finding a strong place is mirrored by that of finding a strong lord, who even if unable to provide protection from a full-scale marauding army of invasion, ought to offer some help when it comes to that army's skirmishers and scouts—or indeed when it comes to another local lord.

Much has been written about the emergence of the feudal system in early medieval Europe, and though much of it is highly debatable (even whether feudalism as such really ever existed, or is in fact simply a theory constructed by later commentators) what actually happened clearly has something to do with the collapse of Roman economic systems such as a stable coinage, slavery, a huge "common market" and the well developed manufacturing industry which supported an affluent middle class. For the early Middle Ages were undoubtedly the age of all that was local: crops, goods, art, vision and authority. It was the age in which the local strong man, however barbaric, brutish and long-bearded, translated himself into the image of a chivalrous Christian nobleman. It is in this period that heraldry slowly emerges, and also the titles which stretch down the centuries to the present—knights and barons, *conti* and *marchesi*.

Those who still advocate an understanding of medieval society in Italy and elsewhere in Western Europe based on feudalism (from Latin: *foedum,* an agreement or pact) demonstrate that all land was held, farmed and lived upon by individuals and their families in lieu of service to their lord. And everyone had a lord. At the base of a huge societal pyramid were the peasants, whose lord was their local boss in the local castle, be he named knight or baron. The local boss returned service to a regional boss, be he count or duke. The counts and dukes offered service to the highest level boss, king or emperor. And what was especially important in the case of our particular region was the proliferation of ecclesiastical lords, as noted in the previous chapter. Clergy also fitted into the above outline system, resulting in the fact that the pope himself claimed to be the highest level boss for the whole of central Italy, and at various times the highest level boss of all for everyone everywhere. Theologically this was further explained and justified by demonstrating that the pope's lord was Jesus, King of the Universe. The outworking of this particular logic of the theory, however, was highly contested by succeeding dynasties of Holy Roman Emperors, almost constantly at war or preparing to be at war with the pope.

The peasants served their lord by providing him with food and by serving as foot soldiers in his armies; middle-ranking lords provided the peasants of other lesser lords, and also the cavalry provided by the lords (knights) themselves. The claim to property was step by step established as the centuries of the Middle Ages passed so that in the end "rents" were paid in lieu of actual physical service (perhaps as early as the ninth century, more likely a century or two later). At this point money became more important to the higher-level lords as soldiers came to be paid, and armies raised on a professional basis. One feature remained unchanged in this developing economy of man power and capital: the castle or fortress (*rocca*) was still necessary, whether the army was feudal or mercenary.

The classical examples of nobility to be found in urban centres such as Perugia at the end of the medieval period all held "fiefs" (the feudal landholding) around the city and especially the fertile land of its lake, Trasimeno: the Montemelini, the Bourbon-Sorbello, the Oddi, the Baglioni, the della Corgna and the Florenzi. And it is their castles that still dominate the landscape, as their town palaces dominated the city. Neither are they architecturally all that different. A single tower of great height rising from a cluster of buildings (an *isola* or island) set around a series of open or closed courts. The urban landscape so proliferated with these *torre* that there was even the possibility of aerial bridges linking allied towers. Perugia was likely to have had over fifty of these structures, but today only one remains, that of the Torre degli Sciri rising over 150 feet above Via dei Priori's street level.

Often said to have given medieval Umbrian towns the skyline of an ancient Manhattan, these towers are still also regularly discernible on the hills along any of the major valley road routes of the region. For example, if we take just one stretch of the upper Tiber Valley, that between Città di Castello and Umbertide, a distance of no more than seven miles, we find town castles associated with town walls at both extremities, and each sitting beside the Tiber. But there are no fewer than six easily observable medieval fortifications on the slopes above both sides of the river as it passes between the two towns: from south to north at Canoscio, at Castellucio above Trestina, on the height above Montone, at Verna, at Montecastelli, and then the dreamily beautiful Castello Montalto above Niccone, followed by a similar but less elegant tower attached to a big farmhouse a step nearer to Umbertide. And then only two miles to both the west and the east of Umbertide we find the massive Civitella Ranieri and the ruins of the Castello di Monestevole. If we were to add small-scale fortifications and some other walled villages or fortified churches/monasteries, we would arrive at a figure of nearly thirty substantial medieval defensive structures in an area of about thirteen square miles.

If this phenomenon is easily observable in the broad Tiber Valley, it is brought even more to our attention in a corridor-like valley such as that of the Nera. High up on the crags at every one of the river's turns, a tower strikes up into the patches of visible sky. The defensible towns of Cerreto di Spoleto and Ponte, with their accompanying fortifications perched on eminences above the Nera, were fought over for centuries by Norcia, Terni and Spoleto itself. Their fine churches and sixteenth-century *palazzi*, surprising in such small, isolated towns, indicate the investment that the eventual winner of the violent game (Spoleto) would be willing to lavish on these strategic powerhouses.

From its southern extremities, to the eastern and western marches, and as I have noted in detail throughout the far north, Umbria teems with

PERUGIA - Torre degli Sciri (XIII sec.)

Norcia's *castellina*

these signs of its chivalric past—the Paglia Valley has heights so crowned, the winding roads of the Martani hills are so guarded, the great *conca* across which modern Terni sprawls has its watchtowers all around. Along the whole length of the Valle d'Umbria from Spoleto to Assisi, and up past Nocera along the course of the Topino to Gualdo Tadino, look to a geographical eminence and you will find it crowned with human expressions of power, security and strength, medieval-style. At Gualdo the town's medieval fortress, Castello Flea, elegant in its simplicity and reduced scale, has lent its name to a locally produced but nationally marketed (and really quite pricey) mineral water, Rocchetta, "Little Castle". So it is true, these buildings can be iconic, can even become a brand; a fact not diminished by the activities of Cristina Chiabotto, a recent Miss Italia winner, as the principal element in Roccchetta's TV marketing campaign—*Sana dentro, bella fuori,* "Healthy on the inside, beautiful on the outside."

But of all small castles surely the most perfectly formed, reflecting its late date and Renaissance sensibility, must be the *castellina* of Norcia built for Pope Paul III by the architect Vignola between 1554 and 1564. Set on the east side of Piazza San Benedetto, the city's main square, this miniature fortification is immaculately symmetrical with angled towers at the four corners. Not sufficiently imposing to claim the distinction of dominating this civic space, unlike its elder cousin the Rocca Paolina of Perugia, it merely hints at the papal policy to keep their dominions under close guard. Here then for once the ecclesiastical scarlet velvet glove is far more evident than the iron papal fist.

Not all of Umbria's castles are small or "local" in the feudal sense. The most dominant are simply enormous, and they are there as a result of a political struggle which, as we have already noted, lasted through the latter part of the Middle Ages—that between pope and emperor to claim, among other even broader interests, supreme lordship over central Italy. Supporters of the former are termed Guelph and those of the latter Ghibelline. Having got their names established, so determined were they to get the distinction between support for the Church or the emperor clear that a different pattern of crenellation was used by the two sides on their castles. So in the Niccone Valley we find rival castles on either side of the river (and now straddling the modern division between Umbria and Tuscany) sporting their appropriate distinctive battlement decorations: that of Castello di Reschio, Guelph, that of Sant' Andrea di Sorbello, Ghibelline. Throughout the centuries-long struggle cities changed their allegiance even more frequently than individual families, depending upon the relative strength of pope or emperor at a particular time—not apparently necessitating continual refurbishment of the crenellation of town walls. After all, relative strength might change rapidly and none of the town councils (*communes*) wanted to over-commit themselves.

The most decidedly Guelph city in the twelfth and thirteenth centuries, however, was Perugia. In the high Middle Ages a whole series of popes made the city their principal residence, starting with Alexander II in 1068. But even this partisanship did not guarantee the safety of the resident pontiffs; no fewer than four of them met untimely ends in the city within a hundred years: Innocent III (1216), Urban IV (1264), Martin IV (1295) and Benedict XI (1304). This led to a correspondingly large number of medieval conclaves for the election of successors to the suddenly deceased popes. Poison was often posited as the explanation, while the Perugians blamed the water. Be warned.

The hotspot within the papal-imperial struggle might well be identified in the years between 1180 and 1250, a period book-ended by the extraordinary reigns of the Hohenstaufen emperors, Frederick I, Barbarossa, "Red-beard", and his grandson Frederick II, Stupor Mundi or "World Wonder". Both these princes campaigned extensively against papal interests throughout the region. One of the actions considered by his contemporaries to be a miracle performed by Gubbio's patron saint, Bishop Ubaldo, was his successful negotiations with Barbarossa to leave the city unsacked. Towns did, however, fall, and on a sickeningly regular basis. Frederick II might have been expected to have a bit more respect for the area since he had been brought up as an infant in Foligno and Spoleto, and was baptized in the cathedral at Assisi. As a brilliant general and probably the most cultured monarch of his time, he made Foligno the centre of his adult campaigns to recapture cities for the Ghibelline cause. His successes included Nocera, Spoleto, Gubbio (by now St. Ubaldo-less), Terni and Montefalco. After Frederick's death in 1250 Umbria lost its central place as theatre of the papal-imperial war.

The majority of the monster castles and forts in Umbria that we see today owe their origins to a struggle which, though connected with this last one, developed a hundred years later. In 1353 Pope Innocent VI, who, like his immediate predecessors, was a Frenchman and continued the establishment of the papacy in the so-called Babylonian captivity at Avignon in Provence, sent the Spanish Cardinal Gil Alvarez Calvillo de Albornoz (born 1310) to subdue papal territories in central Italy. This prelate's fourteen years of highly successful campaigning would ultimately make it possible for the popes to return to Rome—both a growing theological and political imperative. Italian saints, foremost of whom a Dominican nun from Siena, Caterin Benincasa, were calling for the restoration of the papacy in Rome, and many wanted to force a division between the papacy and the French monarchy.

Cardinal Albornoz arrived in Umbria at exactly the period which we have anticipated, that in which feudal relationships gave way to mercenary arrangements in the waging of war. Immense mercenary bands ranged over much of Europe offering swords for hire, and the most notable to enter our story is the White Company, that commanded by Giovanni Acuto, or more properly Sir John Hawkwood. A knight from East Anglia, he fought in the opening moves of the Hundred Years War, only independently to threaten papal Avignon in an attempt to feed and pay his soldiers left high and dry after the Battle of Poitiers. Bribed to cross the

Alps to annoy the anti-papal rulers of Milan, Hawkwood finally led his troops south and entered a new phase of the Guelph/Ghibelline struggle playing out under the command of Cardinal Albornoz. Frances Stonor Saunders, in a masterful study of the diabolical Hawkwood, who fought on both sides in the war, changing more than once, has much to say in praise of one his chief paymasters, the military prelate Albornoz:

> He was a consummate soldier and a wily politician who skilfully exploited the common factor in all the Italian states: the fear that one of their number might become pre-eminent. Known as "the Tamer of Tyrants", his method was simple, but effective: divide your enemies, overcome each one separately, then lure them on to your side with promise of reward, and use them to proceed against your remaining enemies.

He was also a prodigious builder of castles. To this day Narni, Spoleto, and Assisi are all dominated by the huge military bases which Albornoz constructed to consolidate his gains in the deadly game of chess played out on the "board" of Umbria. Orvieto had one too, but it was dismantled and replaced by a public park at the Unification of Italy. Grim and forbidding, these forts were used as prisons and garrison quarters right until the fall of the Papal States in 1860. The cardinal's political solution, named the Egidian Constitutions in his honour (Egidio is the Italian version of the name Giles/Gil), were equally well-founded; they were maintained from the date of their promulgation at Fano on 13 April 1367 until 1815 in the reorganizations following the Napoleonic period. If gains were made by the papacy (the keys of every town in Umbria save one were brought to Pope Urban V in 1370 as he made his ultimately futile attempt to bring back the papacy to Italy) there were also losses— in 1367 Perugia (the single missing city) revolted against the pope and cardinal. Notwithstanding this disaster the cardinal's military legacy is not to be underestimated.

GOOD FRIDAY PROCESSIONS

It is this abiding chivalric heritage, sketched out and then firmly inked in between the eleventh and fourteenth centuries, which still colours the broadly historical mood that can be identified in today's Umbria. Festivals and competitions recalling the high Middle Ages and early Renaissance are the stock in trade of the Umbrian sensitivity to the past. And in order to describe what I mean by this I must here present the first of my promised three set-pieces—a description of the mysterious mix of church, heraldry and history, but above all else, fun, which one encounters at every celebratory turn in the region.

You could go to see a Good Friday procession in any one of forty or so Umbrian towns, the most famous being in the Valle dell'Umbria at Assisi, Bevagna, or Trevi, but my own exposure to the form comes exclusively from Città di Castello in the upper Tiber Valley. The first thing to note is the way in which the processions are publicized; a considerable amount of their annual budget is used on posting notices throughout the territory of the commune, listing the events, their location, timing and principal participants. This is a genuinely "popular" occasion, and advertisements also appear in the local papers. The name of the bishop will figure somewhere, probably in letters considerably bigger than those of *cristo morto* or the *madre dolorata*, the statues which form the centre of the things processed, and he will undoubtedly be billed as going to deliver *brevi parole*—a few words, which everyone hopes, usually hopelessly, to be the case. He may also be going to bless people with something at the end of it all, best of all a Relic of the True Cross, but one of the Thorns from Jesus' Crown (see *La donazione della Santa Spina* below) would do just as well.

All guidebooks to Umbria talk about the tradition of the Holy Week processions which persist so extensively in the region, citing flaming torches, barefoot penitents and beating drums as the chief attractions. The armchair tourist who never actually makes it to one of these exhibitions could easily be tempted, therefore, to think that their purpose was principally connected with religion, albeit with a particularly medieval twang, something far from the truth. Like virtually all Umbrian (and, one might add, Italian) public festivals the guiding spirit of the celebration is a statement of, and an attempt to reinforce, community. Local ties and solidarity are at the heart of what goes on here. One could, of course, make a strong case for these being, in the broadest sense, "religious" values, and the majority Roman Catholic Church of Italy (83 per cent of the population baptized, more than forty per cent claiming to be practising Christians) is keen still to foster them. But the events themselves owe relatively little to

Christian theology or indeed liturgy—in fact, the splendid Italian adjective *folcloristico*, deriving from the English term folklore, captures the mood precisely. They even somehow capture something of the truth lying behind feudal system theory. It is thus without apology that *Venerdì Santo* is making its appearance here in the Castle medieval chapter rather in the later Church themed section.

On arrival at the commune of your choice you will almost certainly have to park outside the almost certainly remaining medieval town walls, unless of course you have arrived much earlier in time for an unseasonal meal—Good Friday is an obligatory fast-day for Catholics. The attempts made by puzzled when foreign, and mischievous, if local, motorists to get out of the *centro storico* moments before the procession passes can only be described as heroic. So might the efforts of pedestrians trying to reach the published assembly point (in the case of Città di Castello, Piazza Santa Maria Maggiore, at the southernmost of the city's gates) through streets in which electric lights have been switched off for the night. Before my first time here, I never had really appreciated how easy the medieval assassin's job must have been, unhampered by modern street lighting. Not only was it difficult to see people's faces, it was difficult to see people, as we passed through the winding allies overhung by so many *quattrocento* palaces. The menacing mood was coloured further by distant drum rolls. Emerging from these architectural gorges, we found ourselves in the piazza lit only by candles held by the thronging faithful, or perched on the window ledges of the cliff-like surrounding buildings. Here finally a little electric light also seeped from the open west door of the church. It is from here that we are to join in the procession.

Anyone who has been to Bruges/Brugge for the Ascension Day procession (boringly but sensibly held by daylight, and with admittance to reserved seats only by ticket) or Seville in Holy Week (hysterical in every Almadovarian sense) will have identified the national flavour behind each of these celebrations. England's very own Nazareth, Walsingham, boasts a National Pilgrimage on the late Spring Bank Holiday which might best be described as "tongue-in-cheek", manifesting a substantial degree of what foreigners like to call English humour. Let us say it could be described as *Carry on Processing.*

Umbrian processions are no different, entirely characteristic of place and local temperament. They are gossipy, disorderly, all-age events, in

Ecce Homo, a Passiontide statue

which *bella figura* (yes, it matters that you are seen to be there) meets comic-carnival-cum-historical-pageant. People are having just a whale of a time: kids on parents' shoulders, old ladies pushing to the front, all brandishing their lighted candles, helpfully shielded by plastic holders (the fire-brigade is also on hand should things turn nasty). And those who have a uniform to wear are taking full advantage of the fact. The *carabinieri* are in the so-called *divisa dell'epoca,* tail-coats and cockades, whilst the *vigili urbani* exercise their privilege of being under the mayor's entirely local command to monopolize the *gonfalon,* the City Flag, and then there are the Dames of the Red Cross (rather posh nurses), straight out of a 1950s American film, white gloves, white tights and white shoes to accessorize their dinky navy blue capes and veils. And this is only the crowd.

The procession proper is headed by a mast-like cluster of flaming branches held aloft by two stout yeomen dressed as if they were members of Sir John Hawkwood's White Company. Other swashbuckling extras follow, with crossbows, broad swords and battle-axes, if not exactly at the ready then much in evidence. Then come the members of the religious confraternities, the major surviving link between the present celebration of this event and its origins in the liturgy proper of the Church. Originating as self-selecting charitable organizations, dedicated to the burial of paupers or the provision of medical care in medieval towns, they still function as clubs loosely connected with religious observance. Some still maintain the tradition of their members wearing towering pointed hoods, Ku Klux Klan-style, in order that no distinction can be made between the rich and poor in their ranks. Their officers wield great ceremonial maces, and they stride in time to the solemn drum strokes, drawn up around their distinctive banners and the statues being processed. At Città di Castello the two confraternities represented are those of La Madonna del Buon Consiglio (Our Lady of Good Council) and Gesù Legato alla Colonna (Jesus Bound to the Column—a non-biblical traditional reference to his scourging before crucifixion). Many more confraternities from outlying villages join a second annual procession around San Florido's Day in November, the so-called *donazione del cero* (Candle Giving), but for now pride of place is given to those city corporations most associated with the holy images recalling the passion of Christ.

The most important statue of Christ represents his lifeless corpse, and this is in effect his funeral procession. His mother Mary follows after—the most revenced of the city's Madonnas is chosen for this distinction. In some towns these statues date from the Renaissance and there is some evidence of an extremely long tradition for these rites. At Gubbio's Santa Croce della Foce, for example, it is claimed that a sort of passion play has been held every Good Friday since the Middle Ages. Here the use of the wooden instruments called *battistrangoli* (elaborate football rattles) is accompanied by singing, whereas they are normally used in other processions to draw attention to the passage of the most important items, since bells, more usual for this purpose, would strike too joyous a note. More often, however, the religious images employed are nineteenth-century objects of devotion, indicating the way in which the processions reflect the antiquarian project of reviving medieval traditions and local rituals in the wake of the Unification of Italy. And with a trend for even more towns and villages to discover their "traditions" there are modern examples of religious images still being created. In fact, even some of those used at Città di Castello today are modern, designed and carved by the atelier of Giovanni Mattiacci located at the village of San Giustino, just to the north of the town on the border with Tuscany.

The aim of the procession, then, is to carry these images to a recreation of Christ's sepulchre in one of the town's churches (in Città di Castello's case, the cathedral) and there to inter *cristo morto,* to wait for the empty tomb of Easter morning. We finally get our chance to join in the procession behind the town brass band (yes, there still is one here despite the content of Chapter Fourteen), which now starts up a Verdian medley of suitably doleful operatic extracts, though quite what the prelude to *La traviata* has to do with the observance of Good Friday I just do not know. The mood is still on the whole more boisterous than sorrowing, with individuals and groups noisily chatting and wishing each other well for the holiday weekend (*Auguri! Buona Pasqua!* etc). This continues unabated even during the ceremonial climax of being blessed with the Relic of the True Cross. The bishop at the time I attended this event, Monsignor Pelegrino Tomaso Ronchi, a good-natured looking Cappuchin Franciscan friar, takes it all in his stride, however. We will find him (and his successor as bishop) again at the Church-themed *corteo storico,* the Commemoration of the Donation of the Holy Thorn at nearby Montone, which will be the subject of my "set-piece" in Chapter Six. I bet you can hardly wait, or indeed keep yourselves from attending a Good Friday Procession just as soon as possible.

Chapter Six

THE TOWN HALL

MIDDLE AGES II

I wanted a new cheque book, so I went to the bank. Simple. Not so simple. After waiting twenty minutes patiently in the queue for the one teller operating in my Umbrian small-town branch of a well-known Florentine Cassa di Risparmio I was informed, after some frantic computer tapping on teller's part, that my *codice fiscale* (fiscal identity code) was incorrect and that I would have to verify it before I would be able to get another block of cheques. Still not overly perturbed, I explained that it had been the bank which had first given me my fiscal code in the period some five years before when I was negotiating a mortgage with them. Further flurried tapping on keyboard. Since a really serious queue was now building up behind me, the teller asked if I would like to speak to the manager. I said that I would be delighted. When I had been granted the mortgage, the director of the bank had been a smartly dressed, leggy brunette, Dottoressa Rossi, before whom all such problems as the failure of my money to arrive on the day of the exchange of contracts melted like a May-time Umbrian snowfall. It was now a red-faced, middle-aged man in a crumpled suit, with a pronounced hang-dog look, Dottor Bruni. My confidence began to wane. Bruni sat me down, while on the other side of the desk he began the now familiar computer concerto. After two or three minutes of tapping he pronounced that I would have to go to the local tax office to retrieve my tax code, and accompanying documentation. I explained that I had already been told this, but that if the code which I had resolutely continued to quote was incorrect then this was not my fault but his, since it had been supplied me by the bank.

Still wishing to be polite, I asked "How quickly will I receive a reply from the tax office?"

"Oh, in no more than a month."

With a hint of impatience now: "But all I want is a cheque book—can't you issue me one in the meantime?"

"Under no circumstances. We must act in accordance with the designated procedures set out in our protocols."

With my voice now louder and indicating more than impatience, "But you know who I am. My wages are paid into this branch each month and I've been paying my mortgage repayments for five years. I am your client."

With aggression in his voice, "Yes Signor Boardman, we know who you are but rules are rules."

Nearing hysteria (I had made the two-and-a-half-hour journey to my bank principally to perform this task which occurs via post automatically in the United Kingdom), "I'll sort out the problem, I promise. But I need a cheque book to make some necessary payments in the next few days."

Bruni glanced at the computer screen, and with something that I could only describe as a snarl and with a voice raised so that it would have been easily audible to the queue still waiting for the teller, "With what are you going to make the payments, your account only has fifty euros?"

Shouting now, "That is none of your business—how do you know I'm not about to deposit a million? But if I were to have so intended, I do so no longer. And tomorrow I will close my account here. Good day."

I do not think I had ever previously stormed out of an office, but that is exactly what I did next. Of course, I had no idea what to do then. I could not afford to liquidate my mortgage, which still had fifteen years to run, and so I had no real hope of closing my account. All that was left was to calm down and think about how to make the payments I needed to without the facility of cheques. I drove home and mixed a stiff drink.

It was about three hours later that there was a knock on my door. I was not expecting anyone, and we do not get casual callers at my house, which is two miles from the main road, at the end of an unmetalled, unsignposted and precipitous track. For a stranger to find me may well have taken a couple of hours asking around the locality. It was Dottor Bruni, still in the crumpled suit, and looking even more red-faced, and decidedly out-of-breath. "Our mistake, Signor Boardman, please accept my apologies. I wanted to rectify the mistake as quickly as possible. And so here I am and"—with something of a theatrical flourish—"here is your cheque book."

I thanked him and signed for the consignment in a state of wonder. It was only when he had gone that I began to ask myself whether I really wanted to be part of a bank (for which I paid charges) which could engage in such questionable management.

Umbria, like elsewhere in Italy, is like this. Everything is much too much trouble until nothing is too much trouble. Perhaps they had checked their records, and I would not have been at all surprised if they then found I was the biggest regular depositor, from the *bonifico* of my relatively modest stipend. Lots of people round here do not trust the bank, mainly because they would then have to pay tax, and a good deal of business is still done *in nero,* illegally. But of course you have to take the rough with the smooth. My opening business with the bank had centred on my mortgage as previously stated, and I was horrified at the time at the apparent casual attitude to the paying of the balance to the vendor enabling the contract to be signed. But then when I enquired about the method of repayments which I would have to set up from the UK in the couple of months which remained till my definitive move to Italy, I was told that I need not bother making any repayments until I started getting paid in Italy. I shall say it again: everything is too much trouble until nothing is.

The Urban Ideal

Italians, of course, invented modern banking back in the Middle Ages, but it sometimes feels like it has not moved on much since then. It is still impossible to make a deposit, even in cash, without being at your bank in person. It makes the idea of internet banking (which is apparently available) somewhat redundant. Yet it cannot be denied that growth in population, relative political stability and outbreaks of peace between papacy and empire meant that for central Italy the period 1100-1345 was truly as extraordinary as the Industrial Revolution would be for Britain in the mid-eighteenth and nineteenth centuries, and this was facilitated by one thing and one thing alone: the new attitudes towards, and methods of dealing with, money. It was a boom in trade, manufacture, political development and artistic confidence, and it made Umbria what it still is today—a landscape of prosperous bourgeois towns. It is the period which is termed the "Rise of the Communes", not a reference to later Marxist theory, but the establishment of local political identity in the urban context, in other words the emergence of what are virtually small city states. These towns, fortified and beautified by the merchant class, which increasingly pulled as much weight as local lords, temporal and spiritual, would gradually also acquire direct control over the rural districts surrounding them, forming their hinterland, the so called *contrada*. This was partly the reason for the decline in the feudal system which had arguably (see Chapter Five) dominated the economic and political scene in previous centuries. The only thing it seemed that could stop economic growth was a disaster as major as that of the epidemic outbreak of plague, which has long been termed The Black Death (1348). But much needs to be told of what was achieved in the two and a half centuries of glory before we reach that grim episode.

What is an Italian *piazza*? It is, of course, a space which is to be filled with people, or for some reasons (weather, the hour, war) remains empty of them. It is the location of prestige, civic architecture. It is a place of assembly, especially when something like democracy begins to develop as an aspect of government. And it is a theatre for display, religious, dramatic or judicial. But what this amounts to is that the piazza is quite simply the continuity of the life of a community. The markets are held here; special sporting activities take place in this arena; originally bankers themselves would simply have set up their tables of exchange here. Life, death, fun and money are the piazza's life blood. And in these days when tourism is so important to the Umbrian economy it will not and should not come as a surprise that events as varied as film festivals, jazz concerts, speciality food markets, opera performances and civic barbecues take place in these eminently multi-purpose spaces.

In Umbria the principal piazza of a town with any claim to a distinguished past is more often than not the place where the *forum* was located in Roman times. Todi, Perugia, Spoleto, Città di Castello, Bevagna, Foligno, Spello all follow this pattern. It is true that some towns moved from their original Roman sites in this medieval, golden-age of growth, such as Gualdo Tadino and Gubbio, but this was largely from a desire to take up a more defensible position, and their citizens' ability to make such choices are exceptions which prove the rule of continuity amidst change.

Making the choice about which Umbrian *piazze* to visit "virtually" is quite difficult. Why? Because while they are in a sense a *genre*, at the same time, like the people whose lives have been lived out therein, they remain strongly individual. So we can range through our region and make distinctive nominations. Piazza Grande in Gubbio, or Santa Chiara in Assisi both would be strong contenders for their locational eminence—the views to be had from these monumentally significant spaces are simply without parallel. We will in fact visit Gubbio's main square later in this chapter, but that town is too peripheral to the main thrust of our narrative to take this prime place, whereas Assisi claims such a priority elsewhere that for once we can give it a miss. Piazza del Duomo in Spoleto will be visited much later in this book when we consider it as a place of performance within the region's traditions of modern music festivals. Piazza Caprera in Nocera Umbra might be chosen for its ordinariness in being that extraordinary thing found commonly in Umbria, a civic space where a mixture of styles from high Middle Ages to the present day compete for notice and prestige. But Nocera is a town which other than for its beautiful position above the old Via Flaminia and its fine waters and many fountains is not in the first rank of our region's settlements, and it is also marginal geographically. Suffering the same fate, Città di Castello will still get more than its fair share of coverage for the reasons I explained in the introduction so we can forget Piazze Mateotti and Gabriotti close as they are to my heart. One of Foligno's squares might make a strong claim when we recall the town's aspiration to national centrality, a feature mirrored by its own central Piazza della Republica. But it would be flying in the face of nature to choose as uniquely representative the main square of a city of the plain in this landscape of hill towns. So where have we arrived?

Palazzo dei Priori, Todi

Climbing the steep, still-medieval streets of Todi, Umbro-Roman Tuder, you will eventually emerge in a surprisingly large open space, the Piazza del Popolo, People's Place, bounded on three sides by perhaps the most perfect combination of civic and religious buildings that the high Middle Ages have left Umbria, if not Italy. The square is in fact smaller than its ancient Roman equivalent, which originally stretched further north beyond the *duomo.* The space still owes its extraordinarily flat surface to the success of the Roman engineers who constructed a series of cisterns here which were then roofed by travertine paving, the original finish of which can be seen through a glass viewing panel. And it was in and around this space that the story of Umbrian politics was played out in the era of the communes.

The first phase of the political development of the independent city state around the start of the twelfth century was to be governed by a ruling class of *boni homines,* the Good Guys, self-assessed, of course, and largely dependent upon aristocratic lineage and local landownership. Gradually this system evolved into the choice of a much smaller number (anything between two and twenty) variously named *Priori* (First Men) or *Consuli* (consuls, borrowed from ancient Roman use). At this stage the nobility still managed to hold the majority of these offices though often a small number of places were reserved for those termed plebeians. Divisions in the *commune's* fabric, however, were common, whether arising from the external pressure of Ghibelline-Guelph hostilities or simple family rivalry or polarizing class distinctions. A solution was found to these threats to the unity of the commune by the appointment of a *podestà.* A guarantor of the city's agreed laws rather than a ruler, this official always came from outside and was often restricted in the social contacts he was permitted to develop with the citizens. Usually the podestà, in office for a specified term (a year or six months) was elected in some way—from a vote of the consuls, or the whole council of Good Guys, but the election was often restricted in particulars. The pope or the emperor might have the right to nominate candidates, or even another city might be the nominator (as Perugia acted for Spello), or the candidates themselves might only be drawn from either Ghibelline or Guelph lists. Phenomenal economic growth in the later thirteenth century added a further refinement to the political tensions apparent in the communes. The guilds of merchants—collectively described as *il popolo*—increased their influence on government by establishing the role of People's Captain (*Capitano del Popolo*). Always an outsider, just like the podestà, these two officials came to split responsibility for all things necessary for the everyday running of society: food and water supply, sanitation, education, policing, public building, relations with the Church. If the tendency to develop structures which seem to overlap, or even be in rivalry, seems puzzling, then just recall the continuing Italian practice of multiple forces of law and order: *Carabinieri, Polizie, Vigile Urbani* and *Guardie di Finanze*.

But back to Todi's Piazza del Popolo. Here we find no fewer than three civic buildings dating from the mid to late thirteenth century and a cathedral from the same period. Originally the architectural homogeneity was underlined by the fact that entrance to the square was through one of four gates at each corner of the slightly tapered rectangle, each leading from one of the town's quarters (only three remain). Earliest is the Palazzo del Popolo or del Podestà, which was built and then modified to permit sessions of the full council between 1213 and 1267. Next to it and showing more Gothic features, with its lancet windows and pointed gable, than its firmly Romanesque neighbour, is Palazzo del Capitano. Once completed around 1300 it was linked to the Palazzo del Popolo with the addition of a broad staircase rising from the piazza to unite the entrance to each building, illustrating that the town's medieval architects also conceived the piazza as an architectural unity. Today the twin palaces house both the local municipal administration and the civic museum, whose collection contains such diffuse exhibits as fifth-century Etruscan bronzes, paintings by Lo Spagno and the saddle used by Anita Garribaldi in the retreat from Rome with her husband's troops (1849). On the short south side of the square rises the Palazzo dei Priori (begun in the 1230s but only completed in the 1380s), considerably more severe than its predecessors, emphasized by battlements at roof level and a tower. It was here that the podestà actually lived, later to be succeeded by papal rectors, vicars and governors, as variously designated. Now it is the seat of the *prefetura*, the controlling body of local law and order. High on its façade is placed the massive bronze eagle, the town's symbol, crafted by Giovanni di Gigliaccio in 1339.

If we travel some twenty miles north, to Perugia, we find similar bronze symbols on the façade of Perugia's Palazzo dei Priori, of all Umbria's town halls by far the grandest. What are actually in place today on the building's exterior are copies of the original civic bronzes, the *grifo perugino*

Perugia;s Fontana Maggiore

(Perugia's Griffin) and *leone guelfo* (the Lion of the Guelphs), the works which set the trend of municipal monumental statuary copied later in Todi and elsewhere. The originals are inside the building which today houses the Galleria Nazionale di Umbria, the most important of the region's art museums, and they certainly date from the 1280s and are probably the first examples of bronze casting *a tondo* in medieval Italy. Some scholars have even suggested that they may have been made by Arnolfo di Cambio, the famous Tuscan sculptor, when in the city for the construction of a second town fountain, now lost. But one fountain from our period remains in Perugia, and of all the civic works to have survived in Umbria from the thirteenth century it must stand out as the most extraordinary, in some senses typifying the urban ideal of engineering, art, politics and public utility to which the communes aspired.

Fontana Maggiore (or della Piazza) delivered the town's water carried from Monte Pacciano in an aqueduct constructed laboriously between 1254 and 1278 under the direction of Boninsegna Veneziano. The monument consists of two concentric polygonal marble basins, the lower of

28 the upper of 11 sides, both placed upon a stepped podium and surmounted by a bronze bowl, born aloft by a bronze figure group of three
nymphs. The decoration of both the lower and upper basins in *bas relievo*
by the father and son team of Niccolà and Giovanni Pisano attempts to
unite the ordering of the cosmos (months of the year, signs of the zodiac),
ancient history (biblical and pagan, Adam and Eve and Romulus and
Remus) and contemporary science represented by the seven liberal arts,
with the mythic history of Perugia itself. The reliefs are supplemented on
the upper level with statues in the round mainly representing the religious
figures who had played a part in the creation and defence of Perugia
through the centuries. This extraordinary monument, startling in the bold-
ness of the techniques used to complete it as well as in its cultural politics,
was completed with the casting of the bronze basin in 1277 by the local
metal worker Rosso Pedellaio, and it remains the undoubted star of Piazza
IV Novembre, despite strong competition in the form of the Archbishop's
Palace, the duomo and the Palazzo dei Priori which frame it.

In Umbria the only fountain which might be said to rival Perugia's at
least in popular affection is that to be found just a step down the hill from
Gubbio's splendid Piazza Grande dominated by its own mid-fourteenth-
century Palazzo dei Priori. La Fontana dei Matti, the Madmen's Fountain,
is in the charming Largo del Bargello, named for the beautifully propor-
tioned palazzo (1302) which turns the corner down the hill at this point.
The legend has it that it is only necessary to run wider-shins round the
fountain's basin splashing yourself with water to go mad. Documented
proof of this can then be obtained in a local trinket shop where a certifi-
cate is obtainable to confirm your madness and, incidentally, confer honorary citizenship of Gubbio—a bargain, surely.

THE DAY OF THE MAD
Gubbio and its inhabitants might well be considered at the very least eccentric when you consider their claim to have the largest Christmas tree
in the world. Before you start getting excited about the prospect of visiting fir trees of giant redwood proportions, let me explain. This is a Christmas tree in shape only, laid out in lights and stretching all the way up the
thickly wooded Monte Ingino behind the city, which itself viewed from a
distance appears to be the bucket in which the tree is sitting. Why bother?
Why, indeed. But this is to question the genius of being Gubbian, some-

thing that since I have performed the necessary ritual of the anticlockwise fountain running, I can surely claim. And it is with just such adoptive authority that I begin the second of my set-pieces: La Festa di Sant'Ubaldo di Gubbio, St. Ubaldo of Gubbio's Day, which I cite in my series as one most able to express the civic and corporate character of Umbria's abiding medievalism.

Sometimes also known as La Festa dei Matti, The Day of the Mad, it is witness to some seriously insane annual feats, especially those of the Corsa dei Ceri, The Candle Race, which focus like the Christmas tree on the heights of Monte Ingino. *Eugubini*, Gubbians, from all over the world return home every year specifically to participate in this event. It is actually held on the eve of the feast of the town's patron Ubaldo, 15 May, and so reasonable weather can at least usually be expected. It consists in forming up in three distinctively dressed teams representing the towns districts, *terzi*, the thirds, each carrying a hugely heavy wooden totem (*cero*, literally a candle) crowned by a representation of a Christian saint through the streets for the entire day. The community weight-lifting begins in Piazza Grande at noon when the three *ceri* are baptized by the bishop and the mayor. At the end of the day the three teams join in the *corsa* itself, a race through the narrow winding streets which goes on up and up the mountain behind and above town to reach St. Ubaldo's sanctuary on the summit (2,713 feet).

It is clearly a mad kind of race, suited to the claims of instability by the locals, as tradition dictates that the *cero* with Ubaldo on top always has to win. It is also obviously a pagan spring festival in origin, with its phallic *ceri* proving to be considerably more "challenging" than most English Maypoles. And I have to admit to having been incredibly moved following one team as it visited the district from where it came. The real effort involved become only too clear as team members almost collapsed out of the running, immediately to be replaced by the next reserve. The complexity of turning a narrow corner with an overhanging building ahead evoked laughter as well as the straining of muscles. As they passed geranium-heavy balconies, ancient inhabitants now house-bound emerged and the team strained yet further to lift the *cero* to receive the devoted attention of these virtual ancestors, which consisted in nothing more than flapping a handkerchief in the direction of the crowning figure of the saint. Engaged in something apparently so meaningless, magnificently trivial,

Raising the *ceri* at Gubbio

you could feel the city coming together, recreating itself, re-establishing the idea of communal effort and reveling in a guileless camaraderie.

Team building exercises of the sort that can be discerned even today in such *feste* as that of Gubbio were an essential element in the life of a medieval commune, so manifold were the tendencies to fragmentation. We have already noted the ubiquity of Ghibelline and Guelph strife in these towns, and further polarization between noble and plebeian, rich and poor, as well as that between factions gathered around leading families. But a further uniting force working against these centrifugal forces was the inter-city rivalry which gathered opposing groups in a single city together beneath the *campanile* of their town-hall, ready to engage in petty wars with their neighbours. Perugia against Assisi, Spello against Trevi, Narni against Terni—it was on this level that the concept known as *campanilismo*, an extreme local patriotism, emerged. And some would say it has stayed that way. But can Umbria's civic identity still be said to have been formed definitively in this period?

It was to answer this kind of question that I decided to talk with a couple of native Umbrian politicians, who from their different levels in local government might cast some light into the murky area which is the abiding myth of campanilismo. Where does the power lie in today's Umbria? Are the political groupings significantly different from those that direct national affairs? Do people put party or place first? Andrea Lignani Marchesani comes from an old Città di Castello family, and has served two terms as a regional councillor for the right-wing Alleanza Nazionale party. The council meets in Perugia and commands considerable resources throughout Umbria to direct transport, health, education, and economic development and to oversee law and order. To be *consigliere regionale* is to cut a considerable figure, and Andrea, thick-set with a square face topped with bushy brown hair, is only in his early forties. His penchant for wearing an English Barbour jacket and brown brogues might lead you to think he was a typically British country-gentleman. But he is far from it. His promotion prospects lie in being made *assesore*, director, for a particular department in the regional government or even eventually gathering so much local support and national approval that he might be his party's candidate to be regional president. Of course, an alternative route might be to leave the local and try for the national level, but to understand the different dynamics which would then be involved is exactly what we are trying to find out.

Andrea works hard at being seen locally; from a get-together to celebrate the local chestnut festival, to visiting all the stalls at the annual flower and produce fair, going to home fixtures of the most successful local football teams, and the really important church festivals. He keeps his local image very well worked. The only time he ever told me about going to the political centre was his attendance at a big rally in Rome organized by all the right-of-centre parties, and he seemed particularly put out at having to go. Talking over breakfast after he had put me up in what his family calls the cardinal's bedroom, a room about twice as large and three times as high as my own living room and decorated with ancient portraits of dignified ecclesiastics, his cell phone rings repeatedly. Has he seen this morning's *Corriere della Sera*? What does he think about Gianfranco Fini's intervention in the debate about assisted dying? Has he made contact with possible sponsors to help keep afloat an ailing local trade fair? It is not that he seems like a small time politician in terms that I have thought of them before, more that small time politics seems bigger here. He is a likeable man, and a generous and attentive host, and I feel that I get to something like the "real" him when he suddenly says as I am drinking my second cup of coffee: "Today is not a busy day, but I have to do a lot of the things I do not like doing: making phone calls to push local causes with those who have national resources."

Andrea is able and is required to play the role of a party politician more than his friend Cesare Sassolini, who is for the moment simply a town councillor at Città di Castello, and who can talk about putting aside party principles to achieve a project which is agreed upon by all his colleagues, irrespective of their right- or left-wing labels. As one of only six centre-right deputies in a city council which has been dominated and run by centre-left coalitions since the end of the Second World War, he knows the value of "common cause politics". His cheery greetings and amiable conversations with the Democratic Party's *sindaco,* mayor, witnessed by me whenever I have attended civic gatherings, are more than just an exhibition of his obvious charm and good nature. This is the way things get done, if they are to get done. However, reflecting on Cesare's decision to run for sindaco in the spring of 2011, I finally saw that his ambitions are serious. Talking through his chances with another mutual friend we noted that Cesare had no political skeletons in his closet and that he is liked by members of all parties—a recipe that might have spelled success, perhaps. In fact, not; he polled a creditable 27% of the votes and came second.

Both these men, then, would have to be driven by a considerable force (overriding ambition or outside patronage), neither of which they seem to exhibit, to arrive at the point of escape velocity from their local context. Life is just too good here. And I am sure that they would never have to threaten the bank manager to get what they wanted. And I have a feeling that now, since I know them, neither will I.

Spoleto, the cathedral

Chapter Seven
THE CHURCH
MIDDLE AGES III

It is the very quintessence of the Gothic style. Crowned by shining pin-
nacles, loaded with sculpture, three elegant pointed gables soar upwards,
the central one slightly taller than those at its flanks. It tells a story and it
opens to reveal the faith of medieval Christendom. It looks like the façade
of a church building, and what is more it even seems to be designed to look
like the church in which it is to be found, but it is in fact a precious reliquary crafted to contain Orvieto's most venerated relic: the Holy Corporal of Bolsena.

While travelling on pilgrimage to Rome in 1262 an otherwise pious
Czech priest, Peter, was assailed by doubts about the doctrine of transubstantiation in the Eucharist, that is the belief that the bread and the wine
used in the rite become the actual body and blood of Jesus Christ. During
a celebration of the mass at the lakeside town of Bolsena Peter found the

Pope Urban IV venerates the Holy Corporal on its approach to Orvieto

bread he was blessing to be bleeding; he wrapped it in the small linen cloth, the corporal, which is always laid over the ordinary linen altar cloth during mass. This corporal was duly stained with the miraculous blood. The pope, Urban IV, residing at nearby Orvieto quickly heard the story, and so sent Bishop Giacomo to verify it. The bishop was quickly convinced and so made a suitably solemn return to the pope bearing the holy relic (the corporal) with great reverence. The pope came out of the city when word was brought to him of the procession's approach, and he personally carried the bloodstained cloth inside the walls.

Peter was now convinced that the elements of bread and wine used in the mass truly became the body and blood of Jesus, that transubstantiation is true. In honour of the miracle the pope decreed (with a Bull issued on 11 August 1264) a new feast to be kept by the whole church, that of Corpus Domini or Corpus Christi, the Body of Christ, the special prayers for which explaining the mystery of transubstantiation were then commissioned from Thomas Aquinas, the super-theologian of the time. The feast is celebrated on the Thursday after the Feast of the Holy Trinity, which is itself dependent for its date on Easter—so usually in early June. In addition the pope ordered the *commune* of Orvieto to build a church as their cathedral which would be worthy of receiving this relic. To this day Orvieto keeps this feast, in some particular way its very own, in splendid style. Carpets of flowers are laid along the streets costing hundreds of hours of work—simply to be walked over by the procession carrying the Eucharistic host and the relic of the corporal. Elsewhere in the region Spello rivals this devotion with its flower-carpeted streets, but no one really can steal the show from Orvieto, the originator of the tradition.

This account of the miracle is at least the *legenda* of what happened in and around Orvieto in 1262. That is not quite to say that it is a fiction, a legend, in our ordinary sense of the word, but it does mean that it is the "official version" of the events. Sufficiently official, in fact, to be transformed into pictorial form in the fourteenth-century frescoes decorating the corporal's chapel inside the cathedral and in precisely the same iconographic terms with enamels which enrich the silver-gilt reliquary itself. The stages of the story are laid out in sequence, from the miraculous moment at the Bolsena altar, right through to the promulgation of the feast. It is often claimed that medieval wall paintings were the bible and theological primer of the illiterate poor; yet it should be noted that the scenes chosen to narrate the key moments of this *legenda* are far from being self-explanatory. What they are, though, are political, stressing those points in the story which the Church counted as significant: the pope's role in deciding to send an emissary to verify the story, the pope's piety in leaving the city to greet the relic, the pope's authority in making the proclamation. Such fixing of an approved version of events in artistic programmes was commonplace in Umbria during the high Middle Ages, though that is not perhaps to say a great deal, since artistic programmes everywhere and always have generally recorded the official version since it is the person(s) who decide(s) the official version who generally pay(s). In this place and at this time the principal sponsor was the pope. The Guelph-Ghibelline struggles at last seemed to be being resolved, the House of Hauenstaufen disintegrating in claim and counterclaim, and the papal candidate to the Kingdom of Sicily was safely installed. Theological claims to authority and the rebuttal of heresy, even conveniently local and well-timed miracles, were political as well as religious coin.

Umbria saw a great deal of the popes in the thirteenth century as generally Rome itself was too dangerous a place in which to reside, or at least a place too difficult to control. So the preferred seats of the Holy See at this time were the smaller towns of Viterbo and Montefiascone in Lazio and Orvieto and Perugia in Umbria. We have already noted how many popes died in Perugia in this period, and she was not the only city to be so dignified. Popes are generally a little older than most other rulers when selected and so concurrently there are more of them than most other holders of office as a fact of human life. With the regular papal sojourns at Orvieto and its accompanying patronage, then, the town might be said to have thoroughly emerged from its difficult period following utter destruction and re-founding at Bolsena under the Roman Republic. The name itself points to the fact: Orvieto = *Urbs Vetus*, Old Town. The supremely advantageous position atop a volcanic plug of tufa, 1,066 feet above sea level, commanding the valley of the River Paglia not far from where it meets the Tiber, rendered the location irresistible to Dark Age fortification of the type talked about in Chapter Four. And given the conditions during the growth of the communes, Orvieto showed itself among the most successful in both developing its urban environment and dominating the local countryside. In a remarkable census of 1292 we learn that the city state divided its territory into 34 *privieri* or districts each with its castle, and its

territory stretched west as far as the Tyrrhenian Sea, far beyond the boundaries of today's Umbria. The economic life of this unit explains how the
population of 20,000 city dwellers, a very high figure for this period, could
be sustained.

Today Orvieto is perhaps the most obvious of Umbria's *città dell'arte*,
Art Towns. Why? Because it has retained little civil importance, and its
considerable significance in the past has been distilled to leave the very
essence of sophisticated medieval charm. Its superlative Gothic cathedral,
the house for Bolsena's relic, is alone enough to qualify this town as artis-
tically extraordinary. Substantially completed within the hundred years
which followed the miracle, the church is in the Sienese style. A lofty hall
church supported by massive black and white chequer-board marble pillars
with apsidal niches along the nave walls, it originally closed in a shortened
transept and octagonal raised sanctuary. Added to this were two lateral
chapels, one for the housing of the holy corporal on the left side of the
transept, the other on the right willed in honour of the Virgin Mary (but
known as San Brizio) by a rich Orvietan Tommaso di Micheluccio, and
frescoed magnificently by Fra Angelico and Luca Signorelli (see Chapter
Eight). But it is the church's façade that most impresses, recalling the

Orvieto's cathedral

glories of its model—the corporal's reliquary. Using a wonderful combination of grey, white and pink marbles set out in layers, four enormous piers divide the lower space into three. The piers are then used in themselves as the vehicle of the cathedral's most ambitious decorative scheme—bas reliefs depicting the life of Christ, his genealogy and the Last Judgment, a theme which Signorelli was also to exploit to sublime effect inside the church. Then four massive bronzes of the symbols of the evangelists, winged ox, lion, man and eagle, break up the space higher up, before we reach the perfect central rose window, surrounded by sculpted decorative motifs and figures of saints and royals. Personally I do not even mind the nineteenth-century mosaics in the gables, which have little to add to the general scheme, but are at least representative of a local pride in and ownership of this building which abided through the centuries. At the very least their colours are sympathetic.

Because of its singular history as part of the Catholic Church State, Umbria has developed a singular relationship with the Church and its clergy. Antic-clerical is too strong a word for the irritated resignation that the people of the region show to the functionaries of their religion. That religion is important in their history and remains so is part of a pragmatism which recognizes and celebrates the value of such monuments as Orvieto's *duomo* and the real distinction they bring to the region. Umbrian Perugia was in effect the capital city of central Italy for half a century in the1200s due to the presence of the papal curia, Rome never being the most sensible of locations to exercise rule over territories that stretched (largely over mountainous terrain) 250 miles to the north and east. And a city never forgets that she has been sovereign, be the period of that sovereignty ever so brief.

But to return to the Church and the clergy; it is important to make a distinction between the saintliness of notable Umbrians, Francis and Claire of Assisi most obviously, and the lives of those called to serve the Church in its myriad interventions in daily Umbrian living. We will in fact consider "Umbria Santa" in our next chapter. For the clergy were not just "holy men" if indeed they were that; they were in a special privileged sense civil servants, tax collectors, judges, policemen, spies, diplomats, politicians, medics and entertainers. In such multi-purpose activity it is hardly surprising that they aroused a variety of responses from those around them, ranging from fear and respect to contempt and genuine devotion. And to a degree that is perhaps surprising these clerics of old have bequeathed much to contemporary attitudes of clergy to laity and vice versa.

One of the most extraordinary exchanges between clergy and laity in Umbria took place as a result of the banning in the thirteenth century of monks of the Abbey of Sant'Eutizio near Norcia from their traditional employment as expert surgeons. In some manner (a renegade monk?) their skills were transmitted to the males of about forty families in the nearby town of Preci, who then continued to pass on their knowledge, father to son, down the centuries. Particularly noted for eye surgery, in 1588 one of the most noted practitioners of his age, Cesare Scacchi, was summoned to the court of Elizabeth I to treat her (successfully) for cataracts. And the Queen of England was not their only royal patient, other European monarchs patronizing Precian surgeons right down to the end of the eighteenth century. The singular success of this very widespread practice led to the tiny and remote town developing some particularly handsome architecture both domestic and civic, both secular and religious. Tangentially, another small town falling under the dominance of Norcia for most of its existence, Cerreto, but this time in the Nera Valley rather than that of Castoriana, also had inhabitants—cerretani—who roamed over the whole of Europe in the Middle Ages. Famed as spice dealers, and sometimes not so honest in their dealings, a corruption of their name to ciarlatani gives us the English word, charlatan.

Visiting a small church just north of Perugia I was fascinated to read a typed notice pinned to the door, designed to set fear even into the heart of a charlatan. Here the "mortal dangers" of not making one's confession and refusal to receive holy communion were recounted with what can only be described as ghoulish, medieval glee—such a vivid belief in hellfire obviously a substitute for what in the past would have been real clerical power to punish the "heresy" of staying away from church and refusing to participate in the sacraments. A priest on Palm Sunday castigated the faithful in my hearing for our being so few; preaching to the converted in the real sense. Another priest, the uncle of a friend, closed his church and posted a notice outside that it would remain closed until the people of the village repented of their wicked ways and returned to mass in such numbers as represented their clear penitence. Once in conversation with an elderly parish priest I was waxing lyrical about the special character of Umbria, the way it seems to inspire an unselfconscious spirituality, the way the landscape itself seems to be a lesson in holiness, how the spirit of Francis and Claire lived on etc., etc. He looked at me with stony resolution and snarled a response, "The people round here are animals". (Shades of Smollett's *bestia,* the English Heretick.) It was in this priest's parish that Lisa St. Aubin de Terán lived while writing her book *A Valley in Italy* in which she is observant of the way in which religious rhythms still form people's lives, but also notes the way in which the young, furnished with fast cars and scooters, can travel long distances to taste the modern delights of nightclubs, music, liberated sex and a drug culture.

> The Beauties [her term for the two young Irish au pairs who lived with her family] knew all the places to go and they did not have to go alone, since their considerable charms were more than fully appreciated by the local male talent. Leaving after an early dinner in a noisy posse of cars the care-free twenty somethings thought nothing of driving to Livorno or Rimini to dance, creeping back just as dawn broke.

But of course if most of the priests are locals, they are also Umbrians before they are priests. Don Giuseppe, a sprightly seventy-odd-year-old, confesses to me, half ashamed, half elated, that his main passion in life is hunting. And indeed I have the proof of this explained to me by a friend when he recounts his family's horror at not being able to find the old rogue when his grandmother is on her death bed—a Thursday in November he was over the hills and far away with his faithful dogs at his heels and his rifle braced over his arm.

If the thirteenth century, that of the Bolsena miracle, was the pinnacle of papal residence in Umbria, it did not really mark the emergence of a political unit which we might describe as the Church State. Individual popes had to deal with, influence or force, local governments, the communes, to do more or less their will as overlord. But it is noteworthy that the popes made similar claims to be overlords of the Kingdom of Sicily to the south, and indeed intervention in that sphere dictated much of their attitude to the rest of their territories (as sources of fundraising and the recruiting of armies) in the politically volatile period of rivals to the throne of the Sicilian *regno,* Charles of Anjou and successive Kings of Aragon. The credibility and indeed the reality of the Papal State was further stretched by the withdrawal from the peninsula of the pope and curia in the fourteenth century, and as we have already recounted it took over twenty years of bitter, bloody and costly war waged by Cardinal Albornoz finally to make anything like the unified state emerge.

Many historians credit Albornoz with the creation of the state rather than its restoration. But even this state was dependent upon the goodwill of the ruled, or at least the richest and most powerful of the locals. It was in this phase of political evolution, moreover, that we gradually see the communal form of government shift to that of rule by a dominant family, the *signori*. The first town to adopt this form of government, or have it thrust upon them, was Orvieto when the Monaldeschi family seized power in 1334. It was this noble house that brought the building of the cathedral to its triumphant conclusion. And it would be other great houses within and beyond Umbria's borders, the D'Este of Ferrara, the Montefeltro of Urbino and Gubbio, the Malatesta of Rimini, whose cooperation was needed to float effectively the idea of the pope's temporal power. It was these signori who presided over the Umbrian Renaissance, and we will consider them in more detail in Chapter Ten.

If the rise of the communes had marked an end to the mobility of Umbrian populations, providing a golden age of settled prosperous city dwelling in the thirteenth and fourteenth centuries, the ending of the politically volatile yet creative years of warfare across the region led to stagnation and a different kind of instability. As Ian Campbell Ross puts it: "with no capital investment, agricultural improvements were limited or non-existent, and while the region evidenced no growth in manufacturing it simultaneously declined as a centre of trade and commerce."

Agricultural decline resulting from the sudden, steep fall in population and changes in trade routes made central Italy much poorer after the great plague ("Black Death") of 1347-49 than it had been before. Poverty itself led to a vast increase in lawlessness; there were an estimated 27,000 people living by banditry in the Papal State at the end of the sixteenth century. Then in the seventeenth and eighteenth centuries the formerly active, competitive and more-or-less competent signori gradually became a complacent, absentee nobility, returning from Rome to their ancient city palaces and country villas only for brief summer holidays. The cities further declined in population and the system of *mezzadria* developed in the countryside, share-cropping by peasants with the vast part of profit leaving the immediate economy to go straight into the pockets of absentee noble landlords.

Church-within-a-church, la Porziuncola inside Santa Maria degli Angeli

Yet even in this atmosphere of decline churches continued to be built, but for external rather than local reasons. The fifth largest church in the world was raised from 1569 to 1679 by the Order of Friars Minor and with the patronage of Pope Pius V to mark the end of the Council of Trent, at Santa Maria degli Angeli near Assisi. It was built over the tiny chapel and its "little portion", la Porziuncola, which had been the place of St. Francis' death. The architect was Galeazzo Alessi, who somehow managed to dwarf the Umbrian landscape with this grandest of mannerist churches, an urban visitor to the most rural of locations. Its building was also an exercise in religious rivalry between this branch of Franciscanism and the other most venerable branch, the Franciscan Conventuals, who held the custody of the great medieval basilica up in the town and the location of the saint's tomb.

More interesting and more to Umbrian scale and tradition, recalling the miracle of Bolsena, was the bumper crop of late Renaissance shrines dedicated to the Virgin Mary on sites where her apparitions had been reported. These came in the wake of the extensive preaching tours of the immensely popular, even beloved, fifteenth-century Franciscan, San

Bernadino di Siena, with his attractive biblical teaching and colourful devotion to Mary, Jesus' mother. Pope Sixtus IV (another Franciscan and the builder of the Vatican's eponymous 'Sistine' chapel) confirmed the authenticity of these Marian "sightings" with a Bull, and as a result a string of exquisite churches arose at Castel Rigone (do not miss the humorous bas-reliefs in the side chapel), Trevi (with a superlative Adoration of the Magi by Perugino), Passignano and most perfectly at Todi. Some have seen the hand of the young Michelangelo Buonarroti in Santa Maria della Consolazione, a sober centrally planned near octagon (in fact a Greek Cross whose arms on three sides are polygonal and on the fourth apsidal) crowned with a stately cupola and found just outside Todi's Perugia gate. However, the continuous oral tradition since the end of the sixteenth century has attributed this masterwork to the design of Bramante, while more realistically the documents themselves attest the involvement, over almost a century of construction (1508-1607), of Caprarola, Peruzzi, Vignola and Ippolito Scalza. Not an inconsiderable list in themselves.

Church building in Umbria has not ceased to this day; large, generally ugly, parish churches in growing towns such as Terni in the south and Trestina and Umbertide in the north supplement the profusion of smaller, more ancient structures which are sadly neglected because now of little practical use—difficult to heat, too small for modern liturgical styles and in need of repair. Churches built more recently on a truly monumental scale are, of course, fewer though no less important if we assess their negative impact on their rural or urban environment.

One simply cannot ignore among the former the Sanctuary of Merciful Love (Santuario dell'Amore Misericordioso), only some four miles south of Todi with its beautiful Santa Maria della Consolazione, at the hamlet of Collevalenza. This modern structure (1965) by the Madrid architect Julio Lafuente is quite a different beast. Information prepared by Todi's tourist office comes up with some extraordinary ways of describing it considering that it is supposed to be a recommendation: "severe and shocking" upon its "mastodontic platform". Its "heaviness" is apparently, according to the civic architectural apologist, a way of urging the pilgrim to lay aside the weight of sin which she or he carries. At the same time, puzzlingly, the structure is described as tall and airy—surely it cannot be all of this? Dear reader, it isn't. It is just about the most depressing agglomeration of reinforced concrete lumps ever to have been assembled

Mastodontic? The Sanctuary of the Merciful Love

upon an attractive hillside. A good deal of mercy needs to be shown it to make any case for its horrific impact. This is no doubt supplied by the community of Merciful Love founded here in 1951 by Mother Speranza Alhama di Gesù, and she is buried inside. She died in 1983 just a few months after Pope John Paul II bestowed the rank of basilica on the church. I think we may safely say that good taste was never one of his concerns.

Returning to modern town churches, mention should also certainly be made of the Basilica di Santa Rita at Cascia, which in the words of the definitive Italian guide, that of the Italian Touring Club, "inserts itself into the urban context destroying every rule of scale and style." Built from 1937-47 over the former Augustinian convent in which the saint died (fourteenth century) the structure employs what might be described as a Byzantine gigantism which is far from appealing, however rich the marbles of the interior. St. Rita is known as "the Saint of the Impossible" through her own dogged tenacity in prayer against all the odds, and she is turned to by modern believers for assistance typically when there are metaphorical mountains to be climbed. Well, it really would be a miracle for any serious commentator to make a case for this ecclesiastical monstrosity. Together with the Sanctuary of Merciful Love it might be said to stand at the extreme opposite end of a continuum of beauty and appropriateness to place from that held by Orvieto's duomo from where we started and to which I for one am very happy to return again and again.

HOLY UMBRIA

So what of the famed "Umbria Santa", that Holy Umbria of nineteenth-century sentimentalists? Is the Church at best an aesthetic component for good or ill in the life of the region, and is local theological thinking reduced to the levels of anticlericalism that may or may not be aroused by its peculiar experience of priestly rule? We will, as I have already indicated, encounter the individuals whose personal charismatic sanctity has impacted upon the area in a later chapter—but what of an ideology of sanctity? Some ecclesiastical historians have seen the communes of Umbria and the support they gave to the emergence of Franciscanism combined with the residence of the popes in the region through much of the thirteenth century as locating here a theological laboratory which would ultimately trigger elements essential to fifteenth-century Christian humanism. This movement itself played its hugely important role in making the intellectual bullets for the Reformers of the sixteenth century to fire. The imagining of Umbria as a *terra del Riforma,* Land of Church Reform, might seem perhaps far-fetched when we reflect back on the "official version" of the Bolsena miracle which opened the chapter. But certainly the radical impact of St. Francis, the *Corpus Christi* revolution in theology provided by St. Thomas Aquinas, and the election of the former penniless hermit Pietro Angelerio da Morrone as Celestine V in Perugia at the very end of the thirteenth century are signs of a cutting-edge role for Christian theology in our region in this period.

What was happening in thirteenth-century Umbria brought to an end the theological elaboration of the ideal of crusade begun two centuries before, a movement which for all its political, kingdom building elements was originally to secure the possibility of pilgrimage for the Christian faithful to their Holy Land. The 1216 proclamation of the so-called *Perdono d'Assisi,* the declaration of a general indulgence for the forgiveness of sins, at the request of St. Francis, materially suggests that the need to make a pilgrimage to Jerusalem (to earn grace, i.e. forgiveness) has been replaced by a more local and internalized form of repentance and penance. Francis' own encounter with Islam in a mission that took him to the court of

Egypt's most famous sultan, Saladin, was one marked by peaceful dialogue rather than bloody confrontation. Even if the high idealism of such developments were later dashed by the martial pride of Celestine's successor and probable murderer Boniface VIII, it never departed entirely from the region, surfacing again in the preaching of San Bernadino and destined to flower even in the humanistic projects of Federico Cesi, friend and patron of Galileo Galilei (see Chapter Ten).

But to step back now to the main period of these three chapters and to end my medieval triptych of set-pieces, I want to stray once again northwards from Orvieto's heights, where we started, to a similarly elevated but far less grand (if no less proud) commune; that of Montone. This time the event communicates something I believe of the abidingly ambivalent attitude of Umbrians to their church and her clergy, suggesting perhaps that it will always be a Land of Reform.

Montone is a charming and exceptionally well-kept hill town positioned on a low Apennine spur overlooking the confluence of the Carpina and Tiber rivers. Dating from the ninth century it was briefly an independent commune but was always the subject of struggles between Gubbio, Città di Castello and Perugia because of its strategic position. It has twin "peaks" crowned severally by ruins of a small castle, the defences of which once included the *collegiata* (collegiate church) dedicated to St. Gregory the Great and the Assumption of the Blessed Virgin Mary, and the Franciscan church and adjacent convent now transformed into a small museum, with some really excellent early Renaissance detached frescoes and canvases. In between the two eminences, from which marvellous views of the upper Tiber Valley and the mountains of the Marches are to be had, wind the charming streets which at times transform themselves in to flights of stairs.

What distinguishes Montone from many such towns in Umbria, however, is the fact that it was the birthplace of one of John Hawkwood's successors as most important Italian *condottiere*, mercenary generals, Andrea (known as Braccio) Fortebraccio. A figure who rather fancifully has been attributed with an early desire for Italian unity, he was to play a key part in central Italian politics and war for the first quarter of the fifteenth century, commanding armies of the Kingdom of Naples, King Ladislaus of Poland and the Papal States, and finally achieving the Lordship of Perugia between 1416 and 1424. Montone remained his lifelong family base and it continued so after his death. His son Carlo took up the family business as "General-for-Hire" and it was while commanding Venetian troops against Turkish incursions in 1473 that he was presented by a grateful local cleric with a relic from Christ's passion, a spine from the Crown of Thorns (Santa Spina). This he subsequently offered to the Franciscan convent of Montone, and legend has it that the bells of the town broke into a spontaneous peal of joy at the approach of the count and his troops.

Since 1635, when the thorn was housed in a richly tooled silver shrine, the tradition has been to venerate the relic on Easter Monday (known in Italy as *pasquetta*, "little Easter", or *lunedì del'angelo*, "angel Monday") with a subsidiary event on the penultimate Sunday of August. (Interestingly, a festival celebrating an identical relic is held at Preggio on the other side of the Tiber Valley and in the hills overlooking Lake Trasimeno about six miles from Montone on Easter Tuesday. In this tiny hamlet of seventy persons the celebration has maintained its principally religious character, rather than a pseudo-historical taste as at Montone, and probably for this reason is less well-known.) So it was after a leisurely seasonal breakfast of boiled eggs, *torta di formaggio* ("cheese bread") and *coppa* ham, typically Umbrian Easter fare, that I set off for the court of the Fortebracci.

Montone means "ram", and it is rather a rampant ram that forms the heraldic device on all of the town's public buildings, notices, flags and even shop fronts. Easter Monday can occur on dates almost a month apart (24 March to 20 April), and yet astrologically the event always occurs under the patronage of the Zodiac's sign of the Ram—perhaps a further reason for the original choice of the recurrence. Near the main heraldic ram and likewise affixed to the façade of the commune are inscribed tablets commemorating the town's other illustrious sons: Sant'Albertino , "Little St. Albert", who founded Camaldolese monasteries in the vicinity, and Domenico Lupatelli, one of the heroic thousand led by Garibaldi whose invasion of Sicily in 1860 led to the Unification of Italy. So it was literally in the shadow of these courageous examples of spiritual and patriotic virtue that the crowd assembled in the Piazza Fortebraccio was addressed as *Arieti* ("rams" in Latin) a little after the advertised hour of 10.30 a.m. by the *Gran Gonfalone*, a kind of town crier-cum-mayor's mace bearer.

A good deal of messing around checking the apparently temperamental microphones had kept the gathering on-lookers amused for the half hour before this, and so it is with a sense of relief that his summons and greeting boom out across the little square. Dressed in an elaborate recreation of fifteenth-century civilian chic, the Gonfalone proceeds to recount the story of the original arrival of the relic and to announce groups representing the three *rioni* of Montone, each named after one of the town's gates, del Monte, del Borgo Vecchio and del Verziere. This forms the heart of what is generically termed *un corteo storico* (historical pageant), and the pride taken in the preparation of the costumes and the competition to represent your district is still surprisingly strong, even among the most modern of Montonesi, from the eldest to the youngest. Here are venerable grandfathers and noble-looking matrons, women and men in the full pride of middle age and in the first flush of youth, and there are babes in arms and toddlers too.

The last "character" to enter the piazza before the relic's arrival is the married woman nominated that year to represent Count Carlo's wife, left in charge of the family castle. This really has more to do with a beauty contest, or the choice of the Queen of the May in Anglo-Saxon culture, than anything to do with the Holy Thorn, once again underlining the community values at the heart of these festivities. In fact, the arrival of the Santa Spina *in piazza* had already taken place about twenty minutes before these theatricals, slung quite casually over the parish priest's arm, albeit veiled in a red liturgical cloth. There he had greeted the bishop, affably chatting with acquaintances in the growing crowd, and together they had retreated into the *palazzo del commune* to vest and to join the only other participants not in medieval drag, members of the Confraternity of the Blessed Sacrament who would carry the canopy above the relic in the later procession to the collegiate church. These church functionaries were also the only participants absolved from the necessity of maintaining the Renaissance illusion—among them spectacles or sunglasses in fact seemed *de rigueur*. The town has invested in a set of impressive silver trumpets which together with a drum corps punctuate the proceedings, further providing opportunities for the town's youth to participate with something nearing unembarrassed enthusiasm.

At last the Gonfalone's narration of the *proclama* draws to a close, a horse bearing this year's Conte Carlo Fortebraccio enters the piazza from the Borgo Vecchio Gate, and the relic is delivered to the bishop who, together with *Castelana* Samantha, has shuffled to a set of more or less grand-looking chairs set at the square's opposite end. With a theatrical flourish in keeping with the occasion he then unveils the reliquary and briefly raises it to be greeted/adored/applauded by the crowd. Very few of its members cross themselves, more take photos. A procession of relic, clerics, actors and the rest then proceeds to the collegiate church on castle hill to cele-brate mass. A trumpeter, costumed in slashed velvet doublet and party-coloured hose leaning against a pillar inside the church, could well be a model for a Piero della Francesco fresco; even his modern hairstyle, an unkempt pony-tail, not at all out of early-Renaissance keeping.

The bells ring out, and it feels good to be alive on this Umbrian spring morning. This is an antidote to any medieval gloom cast by the thought of Cardinal Albornoz's castles. This is the Middle Ages alive and well and having fun. Attending the event a couple of years later after a change of bishop to Mgr. Domenico Cancian, a rather serious modern religious, some of the fun seemed to be being challenged—or at least that was the import of his sermon. I do not think that he is going to get very far, though—or at least I hope not. The fun to be had with the Middle Ages in Umbria is just too strong to be stifled.

Chapter Eight

THE CONVENT

UMBRIAN SANCTITY

St. Francis of Assisi is undoubtedly the most famous Umbrian. The sense of his belonging to the region is emphasized by the fact that he was not only born but died here, notwithstanding his extensive journeys in Italy and beyond. His rootedness in the place might best be described with a consideration of his final resting place. Unlike many people identified as holy during their life time his corpse was not exhumed, dismembered, rendered down or divided so that relics might pass among his followers and the faithful (the graphic account of an autopsy on the body of St. Clare of nearby Montefalco by one of the sisters of her order—revealing the image of the crucifixion tattooed on her heart—is enough to illustrate the gory possibilities and the flesh hungry piety of clerics and laity). Rather Francis was buried, whole, beneath the massive church begun at the northern edge of his home town quickly after his death (1226) and unprecedentedly rapid official canonization (1228). Was this a true sense of discreet piety, a following of his own wishes, or just an attempt by his fellow citizens to protect his relics from being stolen? We cannot be sure. It was only at the start of the nineteenth century that excavations under the lower basilica's high altar revealed the plain stone coffin embedded within the massive foundations twenty feet down, now visible but still unreachable from a modern crypt chapel.

Jonathan Keates in his charming *Philip's Travel Guide* stresses Assisi's Umbrian pre-eminence,

> There can be no question as to which is Umbria's most famous city. Perugia and Spoleto are ancient and illustrious, Orvieto has its respectful following among lovers of renaissance art, and Terni, "the Manchester of Umbria", is, well, big. The wider world however has chosen to celebrate a much more modest place, a small grey town crowning one of those hilltops running south-eastwards above the old road to Rome

Temple-piled-upon-temple, the Basilica of St. Francis of Assisi

and already historic when, in 1181 or 1182, a boy called Giovanni was born to the wife of a merchant newly returned from France, who added Francesco to the child's baptismal names in honour of his journey.

As stated, the town was historic before Francis' time, and there are many features of its architecture and life which underline its longevity. As we have seen in Chapter Two, the Augustan-age poet Sextus Propertius was almost certainly born here. And then the Temple of Minerva, the façade of which is still so dominant in the town's main square and considered of much greater interest by Goethe than St. Francis' basilica, and the remains of an amphitheatre, cisterns and first-century houses, all attest to its classical status. It has a fine Romanesque cathedral (begun 1140 AD) dedicated to San Rufino which legend says was founded by Bishop Basileus as early as 412 AD. But it is the Basilica di San Francesco, which, limb-like, extends the view of the town from the valley and truly transforms the dynamic and significance of this charming hillside city. Consideration of this extraordinary building, surely the most interesting and important in the region if not in the whole of Italy, follows naturally on from our last chapter, though the emphasis here will leave the Church, her churches and their clergy behind as we consider more rarefied topics: sanctity, sense of place and genius, religious and otherwise.

The Basilica of St. Francis is not only an architectural marvel, but itself a spiritual tool, resourced by a collection of artistic works that have no western Christian equal in richness and quality with the possible exception of the Sistine Chapel in Rome two and a half centuries later. A happy fact is that although we do not have so-called primary relics of the saint (i.e. body parts) we do have a wealth of secondary ones—things he owned, wore, touched and, most tellingly, wrote and drew. His autographs are few but very significant, and there even exists an image, a coloured Hebrew letter "Tau", on the wall of a tiny chapel at Fonte Columba in the Rieti Valley just over the Umbrian border in northern Lazio, which has long been believed to be from his hand. It is in fact very similar to the same symbol on the letter to Brother Elias which is incontestably his autograph. To have manuscripts from this period, the late twelfth and early thirteenth centuries, is rare enough, but to have them from such a significant historic and religious figure is most unusual.

Francis' use of the Tau and its continued use by his followers through the ages (the tau cross can be bought in every gift shop in Assisi and probably throughout Umbria as a whole) relates to a passage in the Hebrew scriptures, the book of Ezekiel, in which those to be saved are marked on the forehead with this letter (the last in the classical Hebrew alphabet). As often Francis startles with the uncompromising use of this apocalyptic sign, shattering any sentimental image ("animal lover", "peace warrior") that a superficial knowledge of him might have established. Francis remains a figure who can continue to scare as much as attract in the directness of his living the simplest life inspired by the words of Jesus Christ recorded in the Christian gospels—the simplicity could often be harsh. But the power of its impact was undeniable.

As Henry James put it, any visit to Assisi must start with the basilica, and this is how that visit left its mark upon him:

> This two-fold temple of St. Francis is one of the very sacred places of Italy, and it would be hard to breathe anywhere an air more heavy with holiness. Such seems especially the case if you happen thus to have come from Rome, where everything ecclesiastical is, in aspect, so very much

of this world—so florid, so elegant, so full of accommodations and ex-crescences. The mere site here makes for authority, and they were brave builders who laid the foundation-stones. The thing rises straight from a steep mountain-side and plunges forward on its great substructure of arches even as a crowned headland may frown over the main. Before it stretches a long, grassy piazza, at the end of which you look up a small grey street, to see it first climb a little way the rest of the hill and then pause and leave a broad green slope, crested, high in the air, with a ruined castle. When I say before it I mean before the upper church; for by way of doing something supremely handsome and impressive the sturdy architects of the thirteenth century piled temple upon temple and bequeathed a double version of their idea. One may imagine them to have intended perhaps an architectural image of the relation between heart and head. Entering the lower church at the bottom of the great flight of steps which leads from the upper door, you seem to push at least into the very heart of Catholicism.

It must be a commonplace for visitors, pilgrims or tourists, to reflect that this mighty structure seems distant from the charisma of Francis the *poverello*, the poor little man whose preaching of the Christian gospel took Christ's directions to his disciples to have little and give away what they had with the utmost seriousness. However, such personal humility which was evident in the life of the saint by no means excluded a concern for the physical condition of the buildings in which God was worshipped. Indeed, part of his conversion lies in the mission he is said to have received med-itating before the crucifix of the ruined church, San Damiano—a direction to restore this house of prayer, something he took quite literally, labour-ing with his own hands and encouraging others to do so. (This church is still to be found a little down the slope from the south end of the town. Following Francis' death it became the home of St. Clare's enclosed com-munity of sisters and it was here that she died in 1253. Meanwhile the "speaking" crucifix is now in the principal side chapel of the Basilica di Santa Chiara, built in the second half of the thirteenth century to receive the tomb of Francis' sister saint.)

This concern with brick, stones and mortar is reflected also in the iconography which soon developed around episodes from his life (visible in the Francis Cycles of both upper and lower basilicas) in which the pope,

Innocent III, dreams that Francis is holding up the collapsing Lateran Basilica in Rome with his bare hands. (It has to be noted that the Dominican Order, the most significant rival to the Franciscan movement in the thirteenth century, also adopted the image as an icon of their founder, Dominic de Guzmán, with the obvious difference that it is their saint who is doing the architectural weight-lifting.) One of the simplest but most basic devotions which Francis taught his followers was the prayer that God should be blessed in "all the churches of the world", a specific reference to his concern and respect for the buildings themselves. With these considerations in mind, then, we can easily make the case for this church of churches, not least because it is based upon a particular model which Francis knew and loved, having made more than one pilgrimage to it: the Sacro Speco at Subiaco, the site of St. Benedict's solitary meditative life as he lived in a cave at the beginning of his ministry (c.500 AD). Attentive readers will recall the link between the two saints made by the legend of the thorn-less roses, recounted at the start of Chapter Two. And so again, curiously, to understand thoroughly St. Francis and the basilica dedicated to conserving his tomb and legacy, we have to start with that other much earlier holy man.

At least for the integrity of this book's subject, Benedict was fortuitously also a native Umbrian. Born in Norcia about 480 AD, he did not, however, spend his life in the region. After an education in the decadent atmosphere of early Gothic Rome, he travelled south and east to found his monasteries, most famously at Monte Cassino but also seminally at Subiaco. He is commemorated at Norcia (Roman Nursia) itself with an externally beautiful late Romanesque church (the sadly bland interior, the result of seventeenth-century remodelling, does nevertheless contain a couple of really rather good paintings). The church is built over a late Roman aristocratic house, which, as tradition would have it, was the birthplace of the saint and his equally saintly sister Scholastica (Umbrian saints seem to come in neat male/female pairs). You can visit the excavations, and the resident Benedictine community sings vespers to Gregorian chant most days there at 5 p.m. In some way Francis, although his own eventual rule for the friars would be very different from that Benedict wrote for his monks, was inspired and directed by the example of his venerable predecessor and fellow Umbrian. The spirit of reform and renewal was clearly what lay at the heart of this self-association. What Benedict had done for

Subiaco's portrait of St. Francis

Christianity at the beginning of the Dark Ages, Francis felt called to do in the high Middle Ages.

We know that Francis visited Subiaco because of a couple of extraordinary frescoes in the decoration of its chapel of Pope St. Gregory the Great. In portraits believed to be from life, Francis is pictured taking part in the ceremony of dedication of this tiny sanctuary scooped out of the rock-face above the cave venerated as that inhabited by St. Benedict. He stands, gaunt, bearded with head covered by a tall hood, alongside his patron Cardinal Ugolino, who as Pope Gregory IX would canonize Francis, and here the celebrant at this mass of consecration. These images of Francis are unique in being taken apparently from life and showing him without the canonical stigmata ("holy wounds") with which he is conventionally depicted. They make the link between Francis and Benedict, this church and the great basilica at Assisi, explicit. Subiaco also explains much of the motivation for the plan to which the church in Assisi was constructed, "temple piled upon temple" as James describes it. For the church at Subiaco is also built as a lower and upper sanctuary—but it is done so perforce because of its position on a narrow ledge running alongside a steep cliff of fifty feet, and because of its intention to monumentalize a natural feature, the cave which had been inhabited by the saint. A visit to the architectural complex is designed as an ascent, or rather a series of ascents—though sadly today this is obscured since access is gained from the modern path which leads to the highest level, and thus ruptures the original spiritual intention of its planners.

At the original entrance to the complex a further natural feature binds the two saints even closer together. Here grow roses which rather obliquely commemorate the legend that Benedict rolled in thorns to relieve himself of the mental torments of unchaste imagining. This was a practice imitated by Francis (as we noted in Chapter Two) who was rewarded by a species of rose miraculously developing without thorns—which one might think rather defeats the object of the exercise. The lower church, with its multiple chapels either embedded in the rock or projecting out from it, finally establishes itself securely on the plain of an entrance to the Holy Cave itself (*sacro speco*). A central stair then leads to the upper church, which is as conventional as it might be in its precarious position.

THE BASILICA DI SAN FRANCESCO

The Basilica of St. Francis at Assisi follows its Benedictine model precisely, though there is no absolute topographical necessity to do so. Here, too, a visit is designed as a two-part ascent. You are supposed to enter from the lower piazza immediately next to the entrance to the convent. A huge Gothic portal divided in two by a slender twisted column forces the visitor to enter by the narrow gate, according to Christ's injunction in St. John's gospel. And here, as already noted by Henry James, you instantly feel as though you have plunged into a space which is in some ways hidden, interior, mysterious and communicative of instinct rather than rationality— "the very heart of Catholicism". Once you get used to the comparative gloom, though, the richness of the space's decoration becomes gloriously apparent. A series of late thirteenth-century frescoes by an artist simply known as the Master of St. Francis run along the walls of the lower church. Rough and ready but with undoubted power, they are the earliest examples of images canonized as elements necessary to any "Life" of the saint: the renunciation of his father's wealth, his holding up the church, his preaching to the birds. At intervals, however, this cycle is brutally interrupted where arches were punched through the massive walls to give access to later side chapels, themselves beautifully decorated with lives of other saints (St. Martin by Simone Martini, St. Mary Magdalene by Giotto). James believed that the great painted vault above the lower church's High Altar, with a depiction of Francis in glory and the three evangelical virtues (poverty, chastity and obedience), was by Giotto, but stylistically this cannot be so. The artist is now simply known as the master of the Triumph of St. Francis. One transept, that on the left, contains a superb Life of Christ by Pietro Lorenzetti, the Siena-born painter, who worked here probably contemporaneously in the 1320s with his fellow Sienese Simone Martini. In the other transept is found an enthroned Madonna and Child flanked by St. Francis by Cimabue, and scenes with the saint and his early followers more probably by Giotto.

All this rich decoration, made even more mysteriously sumptuous by the filtering of the limited light through the panes of jewel-like medieval stained glass, can blind you to the spiritual meaning of this lower church. This part of the building represents mortal life with its challenges, problems and pain, albeit enlightened by belonging to the Church and the actions of that Church's heroes, the saints, and observance of the rule which St. Francis in particular might teach you. No quantity of bright decoration can really lift the sense of weight generated by the architecture, a feature further reinforced by yet another descent to the crypt tomb-chamber, as already described, a modern creation. The entire lower church, then, is purposefully oppressive, acting as a distinct contrast to the impression caused by climbing the stairs from either of the transepts and entering the upper church, what James describes as "the head". Here we find ourselves in what is imagined as a true foretaste of heaven; a lofty hall with myriad shafts of light striking down from the high slender lancets. And we find here decorating the walls what is substantially the same artistic programme as that beneath in the lower church starting with a Life of Francis with the famously disputed Giotto/School of Giotto authorship, dating from the 1290s. These are the most celebrated of the images of the saint, and notable both for their size and clarity—his preaching to the birds near Bevagna, the story of the wolf of Gubbio and the ridding Arezzo of its resident demons.

Ian Campbell Ross catches something of the scale of their impact:

However often seen and however familiar from reproduction, the cycle never fails to impress… In part it depends on the magnificent setting of the paintings in the four bays into which each wall is divided on each side of the nave, reinforced by the dazzling fusion of actual architectural features with illusionistic pillars and cornices painted to contain the different scenes. More important, though, are the dramatic qualities of individual scenes and the cycle's overall narrative cogency, taking Francis from his first calling through the principal events of his mission to his death and posthumous miracles.

The cycle is remarkably varied in mood and tone, including as it does images which have never failed to inspire popular religious devotion, or which act as records of institutional reform, or simply act as examples of divine revelation or sympathetic grief. The cycle passes from the right hand of the altar (nearest the entrance you will have come in) all around the nave crossing the west end until we arrive at the left hand of the altar. Here the life of the saint gives way to the life of Christ, which runs around the transepts and apse. The painter here is Cimabue, among the first masters to have worked on the basilica's decoration in the 1260s and 1270s, but

Lorenzetti's angels

whose fresco technique has suffered a strange chemical reaction, creating a black/dark green image on white, as in a negative photograph. They continue to exercise considerable power, however, and it is easy to imagine how the Crucifixion with its sky crowded with sorrowing angels must have inspired the same subject in Lorenzetti during the following generation. And then we are back at the altar having made a full circuit of this glorious church. This is to have made no comment on or to have noted only in the most fleeting of manner the frescoes higher up the nave walls by a series of Roman artists including Rusuti, Torriti and the Isaac Master. Some of these if not all were also Franciscan friars responding to the first Franciscan pope Nicholas IV's appeal to further adorn the church in the 1290s.

What is stressed theologically in all of this is what was important for Francis. It implies a strong sense of belonging to the community of the Church with its recognized hierarchy; participating in its liturgy, being fed by its sacraments, being modelled to the Likeness of Christ. The natural egress is now through the west end door of the upper church. This was the traditional place in medieval churches to place a representation of the Last Judgment—a warning before the worshipper returned to normal life that, in spite of belonging to the community of the saved, there were still temptations and there would be retribution. Such a theology is entirely absent here. Yet a glance up at the ceiling vaults reveals a series of massive depictions by Cimabue and others of the four evangelists, interrupted notably by a bald patch of plaster where St. Matthew should be. This is the last remaining record inside the building of the disaster of 26 September 1997, when an after tremor following a major earthquake brought down the ceiling on top of two friars and some art experts assessing the damage caused by the first shock. The two friars were killed. Eight people died in the region as a result of the quake which was centred on Foligno, and reached 5.3 on the Richter scale. A sobering thought in this most life-filled of spaces.

Thankfully though, the last artistic works one notices before leaving the basilica return us to the intended mood of the building. These are stained-glass panels high up on the right with representations of Christ carried in his mother's arms and Francis carried in Christ's arms, a touching and evocative equivalence. Then it is out into the fresh air and the spectacular view in summer or winter of the Vale of Umbria, as if this itself is a comment on the lesson/sermon which has been delivered—here in this very place that I, Francis, lived and died and found heaven, you can and should go and do the same.

In his lifetime Francis often came dangerously close to being classed as a heretic and imprisoned, punished or even executed for straying from orthodoxy. But his straying was always within bounds, pushing at the edges but not leaving the centre.

FRANCISCANS AND DOMINICANS

And it is perhaps at this point that we ought not to forget the (limited) influence made in Umbria by the Dominican Order, the substantial rival religious movement of the thirteenth century to that of St. Francis. Had Francis actually transgressed the bounds of what was acceptable to orthodoxy it would have been to Dominicans that he would have finally been delivered as the principal agents of the Church's Inquisition. But it is not, fortunately, as inquisitors that we meet this other order here. We have already seen how a Dominican friar, Thomas Aquinas, was called in to Orvieto to prepare the theological back-up to the miracle of Bolsena, and a few other towns would become dominated by their convents. Most notably, the massive thirteenth-century Church of San Domenico in Perugia was Umbria's largest until the construction of Santa Maria degli Angeli in the sixteenth century (its extensive monastic buildings now house the National Archaeological Museum). The church itself is now among the least attractive of such large constructions, having undergone a particularly brutal but at the same time ineffective Baroque makeover. But Umbria inevitably belongs to the Franciscan heritage and although the two orders rank *pari passu* elsewhere in the Catholic world, here it is clear that the followers of Francis triumph. We need only remember how often, outside Assisi, Franciscan buildings dominate Umbria's townscapes—it is only necessary to cite the imposing presence of the gargantuan but elegant preaching hall of San Fortunato at Todi, towering over the town, to make the point.

This centrality to the local tradition is something that cannot be taken from Francis, then. It is something that his basilica splendidly captures, allowing the full mystery of a life of faith lived within the Catholic tradition to emerge, presenting something new but also something deeply rooted in a living tradition. But I cannot deny that this is hardly what is universally appealing about the man. People who come to Umbria simply looking for Francis and what inspired him are more likely to be impressed by the many so-called "beds" of St. Francis, which are in fact little more than ledges in caves or under the slight overhang of a cliff beside an ancient path. His wandering of the medieval tracks which wound around the hillsides and through the woods can, of course, be recreated and much trekking and rambling will be little disturbed by other human contact, unless your journey is at the peak hunting seasons. He did really get about for one who used only his own feet, and traces of his sojourning in every corner of modern Umbria let alone Lazio, Marche, Abruzzo, Tuscany and even as far south as Molisse and Puglia, witness to his spiritual restlessness.

Flying in the face of this refusal to settle down was another religious tradition that Francis helped establish, in which the women inspired by his example should remain in closed houses, strictly cloistered. Much has been written of the spiritual closeness which existed between Francis and the young noble woman Clara Offreduccio (St. Clare). She is variously imagined as his muse, like Beatrice for Dante, or a type of spiritual sister, filling in for the lack of a real one so that he could be even more like his model Benedict who was balanced by his sibling nun, Scholastica. She was certainly received by him into religious vows on 20 March 1212, apparently fleeing her parental home for fear of an arranged marriage. It took time for her to found her group, the Order of Poor Ladies, spending as she did some time as a member of a variety of already existing religious houses for women. She was eventually successful, however, settling with her "sisters" at the church which Francis had restored just down the hill from the walls of Assisi, San Damiano. She would live a strictly enclosed life until her death in August 1253.

Much has also been written about the degree to which this adhering to stereotype of the wandering male (the "friar") and the stable woman (the "enclosed Poor Clare") was itself a watering down of Francis' original revolutionary message in order to be more acceptable to both social norms and the expectations of the Church. That Clare herself seems more than to have acquiesced in this turn of events is proof that it was by no means a compromise to the mood of its founding, but fitted the charisma of the Franciscan movement from the start—the key feature being the permission to live the simplest form of life "in poverty", whether enclosed or free to wander. It is true that even this principle was called into ques-

St. Clare of Assisi

tion following the saint's death as a worldly Church found ways of "permitting" the Franciscan movement to own property, invest money and gradually become indistinguishable from the other rich religious orders, as recipients of hefty legacies in the wills of lay devotees. Clare, too, had to battle repeatedly in founding her Poor Ladies to avoid the imposition of a rule based on that used by contemporary Benedictine nuns by successive popes, preferring a stricter version more in keeping with Francis' example. Despite being a "difficult" character for the Church authorities, she was still swiftly canonized by order of Pope Innocent IV in 1256, who also changed the name of her order to that of the Poor Clares. Perhaps a little comically, she was named patron of television by Pius XII in the 1950s since there were many accounts of her being able to watch mass being celebrated in a miraculous projection on to the wall of her cell when confined there by illness. Well, I suppose we might note that TV has undoubtedly been a godsend for the housebound, but perhaps not really as a religious tool.

"Umbria Santa", predictably, has many other examples of saintliness to offer. Already mentioned at the start of this chapter we have encountered St. Clare of Montefalco, a town across the Vale of Umbria from Assisi, but clearly in view of it. Here another Renaissance master has left us his rather "chocolate box" version of the life of Francis: Benozzo Gozzoli, the best-known of Fra Angelico's assistants, working here in the mid-fifteenth century. But back in the 1290s little Clare, aged six, followed her elder sister Giovanna into a hermitage for Third Order Franciscans. But her devotedness to the memory of Francis and Clare of Assisi was questioned by the then Bishop of Spoleto who preferred that the house founded by the sisters follow the rule of St. Augustine. When she was finally considered for canonization in the middle of the fourteenth century, after a noted life as a mystical abbess, an unholy wrangle broke out between the Franciscans and Augustinians to claim her sanctity for themselves. So fierce was the battle that the campaign stooped to dirty tricks with claims being made that the posthumous finding of the marks of the passion on her heart was a stunt mounted by the rivals. (It did not always in fact pay to be too unusual.) Confusion caused by the contradictory evidence slowed down the Montefalco Clare's cause to such an extent that she was only beatified 1737 and canonized in 1881. Exceptionally slow in contrast to her models.

Political events, as ever with a religious flavour, prevented another significant Umbrian example of early Franciscanism from ever making it to official sainthood. This was Jacopone de' Benedetti, more commonly known as Jacopo da Todi, one of the most influential medieval Italian poets. Not only is he the likely author of the Latin hymn *Stabat Mater*, but he was also a leading example among writers of the so called *laudi*, "praises", in an early literary form of Italian. Married and following a secular legal career, Jacapone was converted in 1268 to a strict form of Franciscanism following the tragic death of his wife in an accident during a dance (the floor of the room collapsed). The convent he then most probably entered was that at Pantanelli near Terni, which belonged to the "Spiritual" movement (the *Spirituali* or *fraticelli*) within Franciscanism, very much at odds with the majority group, the "Conventuals" (*Conventuali*), who favoured a moderate interpretation of St. Francis' rule. Passing some time at Rome around the election of the hermit Pope Celestine V, he addressed one of his laudi to the rigorist pontiff, who subsequently recognized the Spirituals as a new order: *Pauperes heremitae domini Celestini*. Jacapone and his brethren were not to triumph for long, however. Persuaded by his powerful legal advisor, Cardinal Caetani, to abdicate, Celestine's attempts to reform the Church were countermanded when Caetani himself was elected as Boniface VIII. Allying himself with the powerful Colonna cardinals, Jacopo and Pietro, bitter rivals of Boniface, Jacapone was among the signatories of the so-called Lunghezza Manifesto of May 1297, a demand to the pope to submit to the rulings of a general council. Jacapone and his collaborators were then excommunicated, taken prisoner after a siege of their headquarters at Palestrina and publicly dishonoured and condemned to life imprisonment. This Jacapone served in the Convent of San Fortunato (doubling as a prison) at Todi. He was released only in 1303 following the death of Boniface, and spent his remaining few years with likeminded spirituals at nearby Collazone. His verse is strenuous and key in the development of Italian as a literary language.

La Bontate se lamenta
Che l'Affetto non l'à amata;
La Iustizia à appellata
Ché i ne deia rason fare.

Goodness complains
That Affection doesn't love her;
Justice gets called in
To say who is in the right.

RELICS

Our consideration of all this classical Umbrian religiosity began by noting that we do not have any primary relics of St. Francis. Medieval piety placed enormous emphasis on the ownership of and reverence due to these physical reminders of human holiness. But it was a true theological revolutionary, once again inspired by the example of Francis himself, who challenged this cult of relics in the first half of the fifteenth century: Bernardino Albizzeschi, born in 1380 and rapidly canonized as San Bernardino da Siena by Pope Nicholas V after his death in 1444. If he was Tuscan, why include him in our consideration of things Umbrian? For two reasons: he made a number of his "special preaching appearances" in

Perugia, and his most celebrated secondary relic, the monogram of Christ, IHS, a sort of visual aid in his preaching, is now in the town museum of Montefalco, where we can also see the Gozzoli frescoes of the life of St. Francis. Bernardino would frequently claim to have the most precious relic of Jesus Christ in his possession, working up the interest of his relic hungry audience, only to surprise them by holding up a manuscript copy of the gospels. Then he would preach (sometimes for as long as seven consecutive days) expounding a theology which contained startlingly "modern" ideas such as the dignity of labour, the common good of a free market and the responsibility of the ruler to the ruled. He was particularly beloved in Perugia where Fortebraccio invited him to resolve the fighting of factions attached to the various noble families. He is celebrated there with a beautiful jewel-like oratorio next to the ruined Church of St. Francis. Its façade, rich in coloured marbles and decorated with bas reliefs by Agostino di Duccio, was constructed between 1457 and 1466. Bernardino continued this role as "civic peacemaker" right up to his death at L'Aquila in Abruzzo, for which he was adopted as the city's patron. An Umbrian master composed the most complete account of his life in iconographical form when in 1486 Pinturicchio frescoed a chapel dedicated to him in Rome's Church of Santa Maria in Aracoeli.

There may be no physical relics of St. Francis, but as we have seen the region and regions far beyond it teem with the traditions which he inspired; countless women and men have been moved to change their lives in the most radical ways. Regional art and the region's countryside witness to the uniqueness of this strange little saint with his enormous power of will. It is impossible to value Umbria without developing some response to her most famous child. I hope this chapter has given you some tools with which to work.

Chapter Nine

THE FRESCO

UMBRIAN ART

For many English-speaking visitors to central Italy its artistic heritage is one of the principal reasons for their choice of holiday destination. A half-remembered documentary, a reading of John Mortimer's *A Summer's Lease* or Frances Mayo's *Under the Tuscan Sun,* the slightly tipsy enthusiasm of a fellow dinner guest in London, Boston or Sydney: each could be the contributory factor in firing up an appetite for art previously unsatisfied. Many are the hire-cars which have followed the Piero, Perugino, Pinturicchio trails. Forty years on from Kenneth Clark's classic BBC TV series *Civilisation,* an iconic appreciation of decidedly western traditions with a disproportionate consideration of the Italian Renaissance, scholars and art historians are still insistent that this place merits attention—and clearly my own advocacy of its special character and quality is a wholehearted affirmation of the same.

There are masterpieces to be found here on a scale which simply astounds. But this is not to say that only the best art is worth looking at. The culture of a life-with-art persists in Umbria: the Church and aristocracy may not fund it with such enthusiasm as they traditionally did; the *commune* may not be as big a patron as it was in the nineteenth century, riding high on the wave of Italian Unification—but the habit of simply being exposed to good art enables the inhabitants of the region to develop a sophisticated taste which both defends its heritage and promotes the expectation that common space should be beautified by artists. This attitude itself could perhaps be what defines "Umbrian art" for, as we will see in the account which follows, there are few clearly unifying factors, other than perhaps good fortune.

And so it has often been argued that there is no such thing as Umbrian art. Umbrian artists yes, of two kinds, those born in the region and those who lived and produced masterworks within her boundaries. Undoubtedly the landscape and even the region's history influenced the style of the painters and the subject of much of their painting, but to claim some special status for Umbria as a natural nursery for artistic talent is far-fetched. Ian Campbell Ross expresses it well:

> Attempts to locate certain essential features in "Umbrian" art throughout a long chronological span tend to simplistic reduction of art in the region to a restricted number of (frequently mystical) features, often arbitrarily attributed to artists of quite different characteristics. In the process, such attempts inevitably deny—or at least obscure—the variety and diversity of cultural influence in Umbrian painting.

Umbria is to be found in a particularly fertile spot for Renaissance art much as it was as a theatre of Dark Age hostilities—it was on the road between important places, and with just enough patronage, prestige and money to afford to keep a slice for itself. Painting dating from the fifth century at the Tempietto di Clitunno and from a little later at San Salvatore at Spoleto reinforces this lesson. Other rules and motives apply, of course, to a spectacular local project such as the Dukes of Spoleto's interest in the tenth-century decoration of San Pietro in Valle, or an international project such as the decoration of the Basilica of St. Francis, both of which are purposefully in Umbria—they could, as previous chapters argued, have been nowhere else. But much of the oeuvre of Perugino, Pinturicchio, Signorelli and others might have been (and indeed often is) somewhere else.

IL PERUGINO

Perugia is neither Florence nor Rome, and even if Pietro di Cristoforo Vannucci exhibited a certain loyalty to the metropolis of his adoption, he was not a native (Città della Pieve where he actually was born is nearly an hour's drive away across the hills, and a hearty day's walk). He was awarded honorary citizenship of the metropolis in 1485 following his triumphant collaboration with such Tuscan masters as Botticelli and Ghirlandaio on the decoration of the walls of the Sistine Chapel. *Il Perugino*, even with its contemporary chocolate associations, is a better soubriquet than *Il Castrino* could ever be. He continued to sign himself, however, as "Petrus of Castrum plebis", the Latin name of his birthplace. Loyalty, then, really does begin at home.

So yes, perhaps we can say that there is a school and a kind of family likeness between the best of the painters, most readily associated with the works of the aforementioned Perugino. But where did his inspiration come from? And was it really Umbrian? Well again, neither Piero della Francesca nor Andrea del Verrocchio, Pietro's main influences, can accurately be described as Umbrian, but examples of their work could be studied by the apprentice painter, and elements of both their particular styles incorporated to create a new distinctive one for Il Perugino himself.

Born in about 1450, Perugino found himself growing up not far from Arezzo where Piero della Francesca, throughout his impressionable years (1455-66), was at work on his masterwork, the frescoes for the Franciscan church illustrating the Legend of the Finding of the True Cross. Outside Umbria, Arezzo and indeed Borgo San Sepolchro, where Piero had been born around the turn of the fifteenth century and where he had often worked, were both in the orbit of an aspirant artist. Vasari, the artist-cum-art historian of the Renaissance, claims that Perugino came from an impoverished family, but more recent scholarship reveals that his father was a householder and his mother an owner of considerable property—well, Vasari also believed that he was born in Perugia, a mistake that was continued right down to the nineteenth century. The young (and apparently affluent) Vannucci then could easily have visited these expressions of the radical modern art before heading off to Florence to study under Verrocchio by 1472, and his response to the light-filled monumentality of Piero was softened by his new master's subtlety of handling form and shape. He eradicated what can be eccentric and even nervous in Verrocchio and went on to coin the most saleable and sweet series of "Madonnas and Child" that any wealthy patron could have imagined or coveted. They were, however, for centuries misattributed to his teacher. Today they are in museums as widespread as New York's Metropolitan, Paris' Louvre, and St. Petersburg's Hermitage.

Early works can be found in Perugia (National Gallery) and Deruta (Palazzo Comunale), but it was his call to Rome by Pope Sixtus IV from 1478, culminating in his frescoes for the Sistine Chapel, where he first worked on the frescoed altar piece (*la finta pala*) with the Assumption of Mary surrounded by the births of (left side) Moses and (right side) Jesus, that made his name. These paintings (eventually destroyed when Paul III commissioned The Last Judgement from Michelangelo) together with the

The *illustri* of Perugia's Collegio del Cambio

others that survive show signs of close collaboration with his best-known student of the early years, Bernadino di Betti, who himself earned the soubriquet *Il Pinturicchio*. As we have heard of him before, so we will hear more of him later.

Celebrity brought orders for the maturing Vannucci. During the second half of the 1480s he opened two studios, one in Perugia the other in the artistic capital and school for the Renaissance in general, Florence. Italians of the period, including Giovanni Santi, a minor painter who would father one of the greats, *Il Rafaelo*, wrote of Vannucci that he was foremost together with Leonardo da Vinci among Florentine painters. For this public-relations exercise Umbria did not even get a mention. It was Santi who also coined another soubriquet for Pietro, *il divin pittore,* the Divine Painter, while writing a poetic account of contemporary artistic talent for his patron Federico da Montefeltro, Duke of Urbino. Santi's praise was real as he was soon to practise what he preached by placing his son, the young Raphael, as apprentice to Perugino.

The 1490s saw Perugino working more concentratedly in his adoptive city, with considerable patronage originating with the Baglioni *signori*. It is from this period that perhaps his masterwork dates, the decoration for the Collegio del Cambio, with a scheme of biblical and classical themes elaborated within a complex humanistic philosophical programme illustrating the compatibility of pagan and Christian wisdom. Completed in 1500, the frescoes display typically Peruginian figures of a cool refinement within airy land- and townscapes. Though the Master's hand is discernible in the work (the superb self-portrait, for example), there is also plenty of evidence of a large team working with him, among whom could well have been the young Raphael Santi himself. Summoned to Rome once more by a new pope, Julius II, Perugino frescoed the vault of the Stanza dell'Incendio in the new private apartments. But this marked a turn in his fortunes. Pope Julius found the effect old fashioned and summoned new blood in the form of the Master's promising pupil. Raphael never looked back as he poured out masterpieces of the level of "The School of Athens" for his new Roman patrons, while Pietro Vannucci began what has been described as a long, slow decline in which he repeated versions of his best works (for example, a 1520s virtual copy at Trevi of the 1490s Adoration of the Magi from Città della Pieve). But an artist of Perugino's stature and commitment never really disappoints.

Look, for instance, at the extraordinary (and innovative) work he completed during 1505 for the tiny dependency of Perugia, Panicale, perched on a hill on the south side of Lake Trasimene. Here he created two masterpieces, now contained in the Church of San Sebastiano just outside the town walls: a coronation of the Virgin brought from its original home in the Church of Sant Agostino, and a haunting account of the martyrdom of the church's patron, Sebastian, tied to a pillar with four archers about to take aim. The landscape beyond an arched arcade is that of an idealized Umbria, and somehow more spiritual than the rather conventional figures, reminiscent of the statuesque kings and *illustri* of the Collegio del Cambio.

Perugino was a noted sceptic where religion was concerned, but this had never stopped him from creating works of considerable power for the Church. In fact, the atmosphere of detachment which seems to be his particular gift was consonant with the spiritual expectations of the time. Giving room for the meditative appreciation of the subject was at the heart of the humanistic religious project—that and a refined taste inspired by the rediscovery of Greek and Roman antiquities, which were prized for their intense, abstract perfection rather than any emotions which they might stir. And even if he had been rejected by a pope with modern taste, casting some sort of blight over his middle career, Perugino could always boast that he had created one of the mòst iconic representations of the papal claims to dominion over the whole of Christendom and the Church: the Confession of St. Peter in the Sistine Chapel. Here Christ delivers the keys of the kingdom to his leading apostle who has just acknowledged him as Messiah. (Legend has it that it was lucky as a cardinal to be seated beneath this fresco during papal elections, as repeatedly the holders of this position were subsequently elected pope, ironically including Cardinal della Rovere himself, who took the name Julius II on election.) But even here the architectural townscape which forms the background seems to grab the attention more than the main subject matter. In some ways Perugino's interest in the setting for his rather generic formalized figures matches his contemporary, Leonardo da Vinci's dream-like landscapes which back his most famous portraits or frame his religious figure groups. Giovanni Santi's grouping of the two together displays perhaps more discernment than might at first sight appear.

Works by Perugino are scattered around the whole district surrounding his eponymous city. His birthplace, Città della Pieve, is perhaps unsurprisingly particularly rich in them, with three religious paintings and a self-portrait in its cathedral and the incomparable Adoration of the Magi in the Confraternity chapel of Santa Maria dei Bianchi, already mentioned, and a recently discovered Deposition in the hospital chapel of San Giacomo Villa. But you can also find extraordinary works in the smallest places: a late Coronation of the Virgin in the *collegiata* of Corciano, and another, very early frescoed altar piece of St. Sebastian at the hamlet of Cerqueto. Other works are to be found in Bettona, Spello (in Santa Maria Maggiore, close to the masterwork of his former pupil Pinturicchio, see Introduction), Foligno, Montefalco and even perhaps (it is a contentious attribution) on the reverse side of the Porziuncola chapel at Santa Maria degli Angeli of Assisi. This peppering of the countryside with works of great artistic merit has enabled more than one special exhibition to be mounted in the region which has not only centred upon a single museum and a temporary "show" dedicated to the Master but also a suggested itinerary and excellent notes to accompany visits to these isolated gems. The last of these was a great success in 2004.

Great he may have remained even to the end of his career but no one can deny the poignancy of his completion of a large fresco at the Church of San Severo in Perugia in 1521, fifteen years after it had been left unfinished by Raphael. The Figures of the Trinity (God the Father now lost) in the upper part of the composition point to the crescendo of genius which was just beginning as the pupil headed off to Rome, whereas the collection of Benedictine saints in the lower part of the painting represent Perugino's continuity of style and artistic values even after the untimely death of his renowned apprentice. An expression of Schadenfreude on the part of the elder artist? Or, as I would prefer to think, a manifestation of solidarity from the Master saddened by the brevity of the pupil's creativity? It is for you to decide.

A similar example of the juxtaposition of two diverse styles and a considerable lapse of time within a single artistic context is to be found in the Capella Nuova of Orvieto Cathedral. Here part of the vault was decorated by Fra Angelico during his extremely brief stay (no more than a couple of

A Perugino Madonna and Child

months), with the rest of the decorative scheme—a startling illustration of prophecies in the Book of Revelation together with a Last Judgement, which would inspire Michelangelo himself—completed by Luca Signorelli fifty years later. The debt owed by the younger artist to his "spiritual" master (and his own pride in being ranked alongside him) is made explicit by Signorelli by his inclusion of full-length portraits of himself and *il Beato Angelico* within the fresco. Some commentators would claim that the decoration of this chapel in all its bold novelty is of even more significance for Umbria than the decorative scheme of the Basilica of St. Francis at Assisi, especially as regards its influence on Michelangelo. I suppose it remains a matter of taste, and so I confess that I find Signorelli eccentric and flashy. He remains, however, a master not to be ignored.

Perugino did not stop working till his own death, in his mid-seventies, from plague which he contracted in 1523 whilst staying in Fontignano, a small town on the road between Perugia and Città della Pieve. His last work still to be found there is, suitably enough, a Madonna of gracious sweetness.

MASTERS AND MYSTERIES

If Perugino is the most obviously iconic of Umbria's true native artistic geniuses, he is far from being the first. Unnamed masters such as those of the St. Francis Cycle on the walls of the nave of the lower church in Assisi and the Triumph of St. Francis in its vault are generally thought to have been local, influenced variously by the "incomers" Cimabue and Lorenzetti. The full-blown International Gothic Style (1350-1420), too, is well represented throughout the region, with a particularly rich strain to be found in and around Gubbio. Ottaviano Nelli and his children were prolific in their provision of life cycles of saints (St. Francis and St. Augustine in Gubbio itself) and Madonnas with Child, notably in Umbria's northern quarter (Santa Maria delle Grazie in Città di Castello and the *Pala,* altarpiece, originally from Pietralunga now in Perugia's Umbrian National Gallery). Another less masterly, though perfectly competent, hand, that of Ugolino di Prete Ilario, completed a major cycle of the Life of the Blessed Virgin in the sanctuary of Orvieto Cathedral between 1370 and 1380, and followed it up with the official account of the Miracle of Bolsena in the cathedral's Corporal Chapel. These images would be the base of the spectacular scenes in enamel on the sumptuous reliquary for the

"Umbrian" land- and cityscapes around Bethlehem

corporal, subject of Chapter Seven, still housed in the same chapel. Gentile di Fabriano, though born just over the border in the Marches, is well represented in the region, and especially so in the National Gallery. Here too in this marvellous gallery of treasures is to be found the finest examples of the first major Umbrian artist of the Renaissance, Benedetto Bonfigli (c. 1420-96), a native of Perugia. The fresco cycles of San Ludovico da Tolosa and San Ercolano (two of the city's patrons) are witnesses to what has been termed a distinct "Perugian Humanism", which emerged in the 1450s. Bonfigli was partnered in a lively local artistic scene by Bartolomeo Caporali and Fiorenzo di Lorenzo, whose collective groundwork was then reinforced by Perugino and his school in the second half of the fifteenth century.

In contrast with his master Perugino, Bernardino di Betto (1453-1513), known it seems for self-evident reasons to his contemporaries as *il Pinturicchio* (the "Pocket Painter"), though born in Perugia left the majority and most celebrated of his works in places other than Umbria, principally Rome and Siena. With one wonderful altarpiece in Perugia's National Museum, the previously described Baglioni chapel in Spello and a chapel in Spoletto's *duomo* for Bishop Ercoli, these are the major evidences of his artistic talent designed for his native territory. He was more obviously influenced by the modern craze for *groteschi*, fanciful, classically inspired decorative borders and painted frames, than Perugino, and he also displays a unique interest in perspective grouping of figures and composition in general lacking in the flat plains of his teacher. Not as daring as Raphael would become in the wake of his exposure to Michelangelo's mastery of foreshortening, Pinturicchio's genial figure groups cannot fail to captivate the modern observer representing as they seem to the real people who made up the papal, episcopal and signorial courts for which he worked. If his religious works are hardly spiritual (the so called Infant Jesus of the five hands has recently been identified as a fragment of a scandalous work in which the Madonna is a portrait of Giulia Farnese, the Borgia Pope Alexander VI's young mistress, presenting the Christ child to her pontifical lover in the guise of the Blessed Virgin), he does succeed in summoning up the flashy stylishness of the age.

Other local Umbrian centres also produced their own expert Renaissance painters. Foligno and the towns around (to a distance of no more than ten miles with the single exception of Narni's Franciscan church) was the workplace of the minor but technically assured fresco painter, Pieran-tonio Mezzastris (c. 1450-c. 1506). His oeuvre is best appreciated by a visit to Foligno's town museum in the Palazzo Trinci, but can be appreci-ated elsewhere especially in Trevi, Montefalco and Assisi. He ought not to be confused with the third-rate sixteenth-century Mannerist Bernadino Mezzastris, who worked in the same area and may well be the better artist's son.

Of all "visitors" to Umbria among the best represented is the first-rate Mannerist Nicolò Circignani, known as Pomarancio (1517-96). Born in the western Tuscan town of Pomerance, near Pisa, works attributed to him on board and canvas as well as frescoes are scattered liberally across the region from end to end: from southern Amelia's cathedral, to the eastern Church of San Francesco in Cascia, through Perugia, Umbertide and Città di Castello to the tiny hill-top village of Citerna in the far north-west. His legacy is also to be found in the area from Perugia again to Santa Maria degli Angeli below Assisi, from Mongiovino in the commune of Panicale to the western Cathedral of Città della Pieve. This ubiquity is perhaps due to the fact that in his long life he was assisted by his son Antonio and a student Cristoforo Roncalli, both of whom went by the same, rather par-ticular "surname", leading scholars to propose that they were all born in the same small town—a local family affair that became "internationally" famous across the complicated puzzle of states that was sixteenth-century central Italy. It is claimed that the elder Pomarancio has left his own me-morial with a self-portrait in the Deposition of Citerna's San Francesco Church. From behind the cross a round-faced man, distinctively charac-terized with heavy spectacles, could have the particularity of a portrait, es-pecially since glasses seem to have been known as a "painter's tool" in this period. Or any period, one might add, for the short-sighted.

No account of painting in Umbria if not Umbrian painting can ignore the unique example of Fra Filippo Lippi's (1406-69) work found in Spoleto. With his masterful fresco cycle in the Cathedral of Prato com-pleted, the Florentine master travelled south in 1466 for the first time in his career to take up the commission for Spoleto's duomo, the apse and choir. Among the most adventurous and downright scandalous of Vasari's subjects in *Lives of the Great Painters* (captured by pirates and freed from his Carmelite vows to marry his nun-mistress), Lippi's work has a dream-like fantasy quality which derives mainly from his experience of Massaccio,

Filippo Lippi's apse in Spello's cathedral

the first Florentine master of a fluid placing of figures within an accurate perspective, and was inherited by his student Sandro Botticelli. More interested in landscape than in architectural forms, an idealist rather than a student of anatomical realism, we see all this in his Nativity scenes and giant images of the Madonna which seem to flood the apse end of the great church with a roseate glow. He was assisted by a friar colleague Fra Diamante who would go on to finish the work after the master's death while working here. Prato petitioned to have Lippi's body brought back to Tuscany, but it was kept by the Spoletans and interred in the cathedral which he had done so much to beautify. To this extent, then, by right of burial, he really can be claimed for Umbria.

Among those who assisted Lippi and Fra Diamante in Spoleto was an apprentice, Piermatteo d'Amelia. We know this from the lists of those who received wages for the work. Behind this figure lay for centuries a fascinating mystery. Something had long been known of his career because of other documentary evidence of his contracts for a range of interesting jobs that included the original painting of the Sistine Chapel's ceiling with a starry sky and the attempt to commission him to complete the San Brizio Chapel in Orvieto's duomo, before this job finally landed with Luca Signorelli. It was not until well into the twentieth century, however, that a speculative art history theory proved well-founded, that the works attributed to the so-called Master of the Gardner Altarpiece were in fact his. This much esteemed, but up until then anonymous, master earned his soubriquet from the work originally painted for the Church of the Holy Annunciation in Amelia, which then was passed to the Porziuncola of Santa Maria degli Angeli before being purchased in 1880 by the fabulously wealthy collector, Isabella Stewart Gardner, in whose Boston museum it is to this day.

Less ethereal than Lippi or Perugino, more fleshy than Piero, he handles both figures and architectural setting with a confidence that is overwhelming. Happily you can still see another masterwork of this painter, and the one which clinched his identity as Piermatteo d'Amelia, in Umbria, at the Terni Art Museum. This is another altarpiece that he originally painted in 1483 for the town's Franciscan church and for which the officially registered contract was rediscovered in 1985, following the detective work of the indefatigable true believer in the theory, Federico Zeri. With the emergence of this legal document from the high Renaissance the unmistakable hand of the Master of the Gardner Altarpiece was finally securely given a body and a name, that of Piermatteo from Amelia. His home town has just one surviving work of its lately-come master, a panel of St. Anthony Abbot now housed in the town's gallery, but others are spread across Umbria in Orvieto, Narni and Avigiano Umbro. It was with considerable civic pride that an exhibition celebrating this addition to the glories of Umbrian art was organized in 2009 from his home town with the obligatory itinerary to the other towns holding his works.

SERIOUS ABOUT ART

Centuries pass between the high Renaissance and the next occasion on which Umbria would truly rejoin the cutting-edge of artistic endeavour. The eighteenth century saw distinguished if ultimately uninspiring work of Roman Academicians throughout the region, work which has left its mark disproportionately on such important churches as San Florido, the duomo of Città di Castello, with its presbytery cycle by Marco Benefial

(1747-49) and late seventeenth-century decoration of the cupola by Tomaso Conca. The most extraordinary works which were once in this church are now to be found in the adjoining museum: a Madonna and child by Pinturicchio and the spectacular Transfiguration of Christ by Rosso Fiorentino, reckoned among the most representative of his sparse oeuvre.

Late 2006 saw the brave attempt to celebrate the role of nineteenth-century Umbria as an artistic crossroads with a major exhibition (Umbria Nell'800) sponsored by the region's Casse di Risparmio, the banks which were founded with a local "savings" mentality during the same period. With stages of the whole show in six important centres (Città di Castello, Foligno, Orvieto, Perugia, Spoleto and Terni) and curated by two of the leading art experts in contemporary Umbria, Francesco Frederico Mancini and Caterina Zappia, both professors at Perugia University, it made the best case possible for assessing the impact on the region of visiting foreign artists (particularly Germans) in search of "sublime" subjects, a local artisan tradition excelling in *objets de virtù*, and derivative neoclassical sculptural and neo-Gothic fresco work to church commissions. Honestly, it would be difficult to assess this worthy show or its period of interest as "important". Thank goodness, then, that Umbria finally returned to greatness in the person of Alberto Burri (1915-95).

Burri is Umbrian because he was born in Città di Castello during the First World War, and because in 1981 he helped establish a foundation in the same town to immortalize his artistic legacy. He scarcely lived in Italy between the discovery of his special artistic gift while held in a Texan concentration camp after the Allied invasion of Mussolini's Italy during the Second World War and his death in Nice aged eighty. Burnt, stained plastic, old sacking with printed figures and letters, textures in synthetics which resemble the peaking of a slowly frying omelette—it is a dark world view, using discarded materials to "make" something out of the dislocation and waste of the nuclear age. I noticed one of his works, a detail of pitted red plastic with an uneven hole burnt through it, used as the cover for the latest book written by Roberto Saviano. He came to prominence in 2006 as the author of *Gomorrah*, the dangerously truthful and shocking account of the *comorra,* the Neapolitan mafia. Burri's bleak but at the same time sophisticatedly imaginative world strikes just the right note to illustrate this most poignant of contemporary Italian voices.

Città di Castello, acknowledging Burri's home-grown genius, has not been sparing in its efforts to preserve his legacy with its two massive exhibition spaces (Palazzo Albizzini, with 32 works donated by Burri, and the former industrial-scale Tobacco Drying Sheds, designed to take his large painting cycles). He is easily shown to be the most influential Italian artist working in the post-war period with historic shows at the Venice Biennale of 1951 and in New York and Chicago in 1953 establishing beyond question his international status.

So how is it that this seriousness about art persists in Umbria, making it possible for an occasional genius to emerge? I would argue that it persists in the persons of individual artists, who may never aspire to much more than a show in a local, hired space, but who themselves take up causes to preserve the artistic heritage of the places in which they live and who contribute in small but still significant ways to new public expressions of a collective artistic sensibility. One such is Giancarlo Vicchi of Morra, a small village on the road between Città di Castello and Castel Fiorentino, immortalized in Lisa St. Aubin de Terán's *A Valley in Umbria*. Growing up there at the end of the Second World War, Giancarlo served as an altar-boy in the two churches, the little twelfth-century *pieve* of Santa Maria della Neve and the Oratory of San Crescentino. The former is largely undecorated but with an imposing architectural solidity which cannot fail to impress. The latter has some little-known frescoes of Luca Signorelli, depicting Christ's passion, and some striking naive images of the local patron dating from the medieval plague years (mid-fourteenth century). Alberto Burri himself can be thanked for the preservation of these rare and important works, since he dedicated his prize money from the Venice Biennale to the restoration of the oratory's roof.

This environment, already steeped in the cherishing of a tradition, led Giancarlo to cultivate an interest in art as a student and then to preserve it during his working years with the Italian military (parachute regiment) and secular employment with Alitalia. In his free time from work and now in retirement he follows the example of Burri in utilizing discarded materials to create geometric abstracts which rarely veer in the direction of figurative subjects—this in spite of his closeness to the local church which earned him some commissions, for a Via Crucis and a war memorial.

At times, perhaps, Giancarlo can be a bit over-enthusiastic, but never small minded. He is a dapper man with a small grey pencil-moustache, well into his sixties, his spare but muscled frame still hinting at the energetic military career he followed in his youth. He lives in the same house where he was born and in which recently his 88-year-old mother died. She was a formidable old crone, her hair done up in a kerchief and her bird-like frame wrapped around with a floral housecoat for the daily chores. His restoration of some antique articles in his parish church's possession is arguably a little heavy-handed—could the reliquary of the Fragment of the True Cross really have been intended to have such very scarlet padding to protect its precious contents? (It looks as though it might have been designed by Vivienne Westwood.) Even if this is re-interpretative rather than restoration, his concern for objects which otherwise would be mouldering away in some sacristy cupboard exactly illustrates what I have wanted to say about the sharing of a common taste and attention to art throughout the region. Giancarlo Vicchi may not be among the ranks of the greatest artists, but he is a local one and that makes all the difference. Perhaps there really is Umbrian art, then, its definition simply hard to pinpoint. There never will be a Vicchi trail for aspiring art lovers to drive, but without him and people like him the care expended on the conservation of what has survived from the great periods would be a much costlier and riskier business. Long may local artists flourish in Umbria and long may the trails be followed.

Chapter Ten

THE PALACE

THE AGE OF THE *SIGNORI*

Warlike, yes; sometimes pious; indolent, provincial, maybe even second-rate; such might be your take on the Umbrian aristocracy as I have represented it to this point in the book. Their castles and churches still dominate the landscape; the odd individual emerges from the mass, such as Braccio Fortebraccio, but confronted with the powerful sanctity of local saints and the subtle genius of Umbria's artists they fade into the background. We have noted the tussle that emerged between aristocrats and a flourishing mercantile/artisan middle class in the Middle Ages, and, as we have seen, the townscapes of the region are still dominated by the civic architecture which speaks of the uneasy truce of a government held in common between these factions. Thus the emergence of *signorie*, "lordships" (rule by members of a single local family), as the next form of government to predominate in Umbria from the middle of the fifteenth century through the seventeenth, seen first in Orvieto (see Chapter Seven), is something of a turn around. Lords needed palaces from which to rule, and therefore the crop of Renaissance noble piles is equivalently bountiful and unsurprising. We are first going to focus on one palace and one family, but will visit others and "get to know" the families. Obviously in a book which seeks to celebrate an area, I intend to accentuate the positive—so please may I introduce you to Federico Cesi (the Third), and welcome you to Palazzo Cesi at Acquasparta.

Pacific, liberal (as far as religion is concerned), gifted, international and first-rate. So stands the co-founder and leader of the Accademia dei Lincei (the Academy of Lynxes or Lynx-Eyed—ever watchful for developments in scientific knowledge) and one of the first and most important of Italy's experimental scientists. The Accademia (1603), Europe's earliest scientific society, was the dream-child of Federico together with his friends and relations Johannes van Heeck, Anastasio de Filiis and Francesco Stelluti. It is still in existence more than 400 years later with its present seat in Rome in the beautiful Tiber-side Villa Farnesina. Its stated aims were expressed thus:

> The worship of God best and greatest through his works. The constant study of the universal machine of the world. The mind forever fed by the writings and sayings of the wise, fully satisfied by what it possesses and never pushed to envy of what belongs to others, put in motion instead by a desire to help and support.

Federico's ancestors as a whole might not live up to such dizzy heights; they were conventional Umbrian nobles pursuing careers in the Church, or consolidating their land-holdings and extending their wealth, power and influence with strategic marriages. A charming chapel in the Basilica of Santa Maria Maggiore and the façade of the Chiesa Nuova, both in Rome, celebrate the relative ecclesiastical successes of the family, for generations Bishops of Todi. Yet from this unexceptional stock came a flowering of genius and much valuable fruit from the middle of the sixteenth to the end of the seventeenth centuries.

The country north of Terni and south of Perugia had been a traditional sphere of influence for the Farnese family (holding the papacy under Paul III during the mid years of the sixteenth century). It was from Pier Luigi Farnese that Isabella di Alviano, wife of one Gian Giacomo Cesi, purchased the lordship of Acquasparta in 1540, and it was here in the following years that the couple, and Gian Giacomo's brother Cardinal Federico Cesi, the first in the family to be bishop of nearby Todi, laboured to transform the old "manor house" into an imposing palace reflecting their growing prestige and aspirations. The Florentine architect Guidetto Guidetti designed and supervised the building work from 1561 until his death three years later, and then the project was adopted by the Milan-born Giovan Domenico Bianchi. It was finished around 1579, ready to welcome the newly wedded heir of Gian Giacomo, yet another Federico (the father of the scientist), with his bride, the wealthy Olimpia Orsini. The matriarch Isabella, outliving both husband and son, was the one to continue to supervise Bianchi in the completion of the architectural plans with the laying out of a spacious piazza before the main entrance to the palace. She also constructed or restored the paving of the streets and repaired the town walls.

Palazzo Cesi, Acquasparta

Reflecting on the legacy of this enlightened clan on the built environment and culture of their surroundings Jonathan Keates writes that they "created what was essentially a little renaissance paradise, where the learned men and women of Italy might come and converse in the tranquillity of the Umbrian countryside."

If perhaps a little idealized in its expression, such a thought is easy to substantiate. Galileo Galilei, undeniably among the most creative of minds not only of his own but of every age and yet the subject of an investigation for heresy, was a guest here in 1624 as he journeyed from his Florentine home to the seat of the Roman Inquisition. He was found guilty, forced to recant notions such as the sun-centred solar system, and confined to house arrest until his death. Federico had known the scientific master for years. His personal contact with the Roman house and schools of the Padri Scolopi (the Poor Teaching Fathers), founded by San Giuseppe Calasanz during the last years of the sixteenth century to offer general education with an emphasis on modern mathematics and science, ensured that he moved in Galileo's circle. The order's Florentine house provided the genius scientist with a highly expert, mathematically experimental research facility, one that fascinatingly would continue after his "theological" condemnation. Ten years before the fateful "Processo di Galileo" in 1614, Federico had written to his mentor: "After some entertaining but brief holidays I have settled for a while at Acquasparta, as much to please my tenants as to escape Roman preoccupations and enjoy a philosophical and healthy rest..."

Federico had first taken refuge at the palace in Acquasparta immediately following the Accademia's foundation in Rome, when its activities and ideas had provoked negative criticism from his relatively unimaginative and decidedly unscientific father. His collaborators would join him there over the years and the house was finally legitimized as a fixed centre for their activities since it became his own property on the death of the elder Federico in 1618.

The house is much influenced in style and decoration by Roman models of a similar period: a double loggia opens on to a broad staircase carrying the visitor to the *piano nobile,* with a vast and imposing *salone* and other rooms intended for public events and large-scale entertaining. The frescoes celebrate the origins and warlike feats of the Cesi ancestors and are the works of Gian Battista Lombardelli. Particularly fine are the wooden coffered ceilings in the salone centred upon a massive carved Cesi coat-of-arms. In the lower floor, which seems to have been reserved for the occupation by the family itself, there are many examples of the symbol of the Accademia, a lynx surrounded by wreaths of laurel, and the other frescoes elaborate themes taken from Ovid's *Metamorphoses*. All in all, the palace might be considered one of the best examples of Roman Renaissance taste to be found in Umbria.

Francesco was buried in the late sixteenth-century chapel built in the nearby Church of Santa Cecilia for his great-grandmother Isabella. So he was to enjoy the eternal rest which Umbria offers, as he and his studies had enjoyed it during life.

GUBBIO

The single most famous feature from any Umbrian palace is also connected to intellectual pursuits. It is the *studiolo* ("private study") of another intelligent aristocrat, Federico, Duke of Montefeltro, which was installed in his Gubbio residence after it had been remodelled in Renaissance style in the years following 1476. This small room, just like its equivalent in the better-known ducal residence at Urbino (now the National Gallery of Le Marche), was entirely lined with intarsia woodwork creating the *trompe-l'oeil* illusion of shelves and cupboards filled with astronomical, musical and mathematical instruments. It was bought by and removed at the end of the nineteenth century to the Metropolitan Museum of Art in New York, where it is viewed by millions of visitors who can scarcely have any sense of its original location or significance.

For the entire twentieth century all that was left in the palace in Gubbio to hint at this rich interior were some of the original doors and one particularly fine ceiling. And sadly it was not much visited. At the highest point of the city, you have to feel fit to venture up the steep Via del Duca leading from the Palazzo dei Consoli to both the palace and cathedral. Or you have to be resourceful—there is a lift, not well sign-posted, rising from the level of Piazza della Signoria down a passage in the classically faced building which closes the long side of the piazza. This then gives direct access to the Museo del Duomo, and the neighbouring ducal palace. And both were well worth the effort even without the interior of the studiolo. But in this still relatively new century local ingenuity and skill have been employed to pay tribute to the dignity of the building and increase its attractiveness as a tourist destination. Gubbio's artisans have made a recreation of the studiolo now installed in the original space, and to a plan which is thought to be more accurate than the display in the Metropolitan. Dr. Francesco Scoppola, director of Umbria's Beni Culturale (Heritage Preservation), cites this (as we will see in Chapter Fourteen) as one of the best examples of the way in which the region is a model for how artistic conservation is resourced and sustained by local skill and initiative.

Gubbio remained a free *commune* until 1384 when the citizens voluntarily handed over rule to the Montefeltro family, lords of Urbino in Le Marche. A local family, the Gabrielli, had attempted to establish a *signoria* in the town, but this was obviously a case of better the devil you do not know. The Montefeltro remained in power until their dynasty died out in 1508 to be replaced by the delle Rovere. Like the Cesi's Federico III, the Montefeltro Federico (1422-82) was a genius; but even if his interests were learned in both artistic and scientific terms, it was in the fields of generalship and diplomacy that he showed his real brilliance. Born at the Castello di Petroia in Gubbian territory, and therefore one might claim an

Umbrian, his legitimacy was contested as a child. However, this did not prevent him inheriting the duchy on the death by assassination of his half-brother. Used as a general variously by the popes, the Republic of Venice and the Kingdom of Naples, Federico relaxed by building up a refined court, commissioning art, whilst in manners he was cited as paragon of well-polished behaviour in Baldassare Castiglione's book, *Il Cortegiano*, *The Book of the Courtier,* based upon experiences of ducal Urbino. For Montefeltro and any other well-bred Renaissance aristocrat the key concept of behaviour is *sprezzatura*, a "certain nonchalance". The character based upon the duke expresses his belief in this principle: "Accordingly we may affirm that to be true art must not appear to be art; nor to anything must we give greater care than to conceal art, for if it is discovered, it quite destroys our credit and brings us into small esteem."

Although it was only the second seat of the court, the ducal palace in Gubbio does not fail to impress, especially as it represents a feat of engineering ingenuity, transforming an earlier Gothic *castello* into a refined Renaissance residence. Truly a fine example of art concealing art. The architect was most probably the Siena-born Francesco Giorgio Martini, following the example of Luciano Laurana who was responsible for the stunning classicism of the ducal palace at Urbino, and the courtyard in particular echoes the proportions of that earlier work, though robbed of its perfect symmetry based as it is on an adaptation of an earlier pre-determined space. The chambers circle the central court, varying in size according to purpose—a grand hall with views over a sunken garden, to function as ducal throne room, smaller rooms in which to dine or take council, and finally the smallest to provide a bedroom and the celebrated study for the duke. Unlike the palace at Urbino there is not an entirely separate wing for the duchess and her attendants, but the additional floors must have provided more than adequate accommodation for the reduced court which accompanied the duke on progress. Over each doorway finished in *pietra serena* you might well be surprised to see carved in low relief the symbol of the Order of the Garter. It was awarded to Federico by King Edward IV of England, and it was a distinction of which he was inordinately proud.

In the celebrated double portrait of Federico and his duchess Battista Sforza by his preferred court painter, Piero della Francesca, now in the Uffizi of Florence, we see the weather-beaten, hook-nosed old soldier in

The Montefeltros by Piero della Francesca

profile facing the pale anonymous features of the perfect Italian noble woman. It was for the exhibition of these serious, refined and wealthy aristocrats and the exercise of their power and patronage that the spacious interiors of Gubbio's ducal palace were created.

NOBLESSE OBLIGE

The Italian Republic abolished titles and lordships at its foundation in 1946 but that does not mean to say that they are not still current, even if registry for census purposes awards everyone the straightforward *signore* and *signora*. You can meet *baroni* and *marchesi* socially, at the bar having a coffee, eating in modest restaurants, going to church, joining in local life, though you might never know it. They are most obvious as the owners of traditional properties which they have to maintain, a burden of *noblesse oblige* no less onerous than that shared by their British equivalents forced to open up their stately homes, to diversify with safari or theme parks, or to win highly remunerative film contracts for location shooting. In Umbria the most obvious form of diversification is to convert some part of the property into an *agriturismo*, a bed and breakfast with an element of a working farm. Castles and palaces and their chapels or local churches can also be used for hosting weddings in which everything is provided, from a master-bedroom suite with baronial four-poster bed to the flowers from the renovated formal gardens, from the locally produced cheeses at the buffet to the services of a priest still cast in the role of a private chaplain. In a society as "traditional" as the one we find in Umbria it is inevitable that the old families have maintained a profile despite the currents of political correctness.

But it is important, too, to remember that Umbria is part of the "red belt" of north-central Italy (most notably exemplified by the Emilia Romagna region centred on Bologna) where the post-war "modern" communism, unique to Italian politics, flourished until very recently. It is still common to see public notices on myriad hoardings around the region advertising August's Festa della Libertà (a "Freedom Party" organized by the local *party*) taking pride of place as summer begins to fade. I once attended a local version of this event with an Anglican priestly Umbrian neighbour, Fr. Paul Butler (followable on Twitter as RedRector). He and his wife, Lindsey Barker, a thoracic surgeon at one of north London's larger hospitals, have holidayed in the region around Assisi for as long as I have— getting on for twenty years. They finally took the plunge and purchased their own property in 2007, a charming town-house in Città di Castello, after a search which covered more than half of the region. Paul, one of the rare examples of a traditional type of Anglican cleric, the "Red Priest", was vicar of a neighbouring parish when I worked in south London. He was famous for his greetings (even on the answer-phone) "Eh up, comrade" and his refusal to stand up at the playing of the British national anthem at parish events (not only "red" but also anti-monarchist).

The said communist get-together was advertised as starting at 8.30 p.m.: we were at the public gardens where it was scheduled to be held by 8.45 p.m. only to find we were the sole merrymakers together with a small team of elderly women preparing the food. "Oh yes, this is the place and 8.30 p.m. is the time: it's just that everyone else will come at about ten." So they opened a huge straw-covered demijohn just to placate these strangely punctual British lefties. By the time the lads began to assemble we were well and truly oiled—it led to a lively evening. No hesitation in joining in the dancing and singing, tongues freed from their embarrassment of not speaking sufficiently good Italian (or Umbrian—dialect was much in evidence), uninhibited toasts to the various fragments of a surviving leftist movement in our respective home countries. And the food—well, left or right, young or old, north or south, Umbrians know what you should eat outside on a late summer night: *bruschette* (toast) smothered with porcini mushrooms, olive spread or truffle condiment, grilled lamb chops and sirloin steaks, salad vegetables fresh from *orti* (garden plots), fresh fruit. And to drink the local red from the straw-covered demijohns—until, that is, we got to the *liquori* stage, when various versions of grappa made from walnuts were tabled. The rendition of *The Red Flag* and *L'Internazionale* were appropriately fiery and wholehearted.

Paul and Lyndsey's house in Città di Castello is only blocks away from the family palazzo of the marchesi Lignani Marchesani, home of the local right-wing politician, Andrea L-M, whom we met in Chapter Six, and who would rather be dead than seen at a *festa della libertà*. Steps away from the principal piazza of the town you enter the fourteenth-century complex from the pedestrianized street leading down to the town's Rome Gate. It looks very much like the rest of the façades fronting the street, but when inside the broad stairs immediately lead you to the first floor where the main entrance to the house is to be found. The present family, comprising Andrea, his mother and sister, lives in a couple of (relatively) small apartments across a mezzanine courtyard with an exquisite well-head at its centre. But through the grand double doors we enter the "public" *stanze di representanza* (formal reception rooms) of an Umbrian middle-ranking noble family. Each room gives on to the next in a natural progression of formality, from the hall of entrance decorated with suits of armour to a room with an adjoining chapel and access to a hanging garden planted with vines and fruit trees and with a small central fountain, through a small chamber decorated with family portraits variously in eighteenth-century oil or early twentieth-century photography, to a salon decorated in empire style with frescoes inspired by Napoleon's Egyptian adventures, and finally the family "wedding" bedroom. Yes, a bed crowned with a canopy with ostrich feathers at the corners, and a tiny *en suite* bathroom. The frescoes were painted by Marco Benefial, the same artist who decorated the apse of the nearby Cathedral of San Florido during its nineteenth-century makeover. Virile rather than subtle, they make a fascinating contribution to the craze for all things Egyptian even beyond any Masonic connections (hotly denied by the piously conventional present owner). This palazzo is not open to the public, but it still has its public role to play. Andrea can do political work here, hosting receptions for his party workers, business people or even local dignitaries of opposing political loyalty. And one day he might well marry and the state bedroom serve its purpose for the benefit of the family.

A major ancient palazzo in the heart of the same town, however, is very much open to the public. It is that of the Vitelli alla Cannoniera (the family built five extensive palaces in the city during their rule) who held the signoria of Città di Castello through two centuries from the mid-fifteenth. It is now home to an art gallery, probably the most important in Umbria after Perugia's National Gallery. This building, too, over and above its collection that includes a major depiction of the martyrdom of St. Sebastian by Luca Signorelli, is a fascinating example of what it meant to have noble privileges and obligations in the Renaissance period. Built for Alessandro Vitelli between 1521 and 1532 by Antonio da Sangallo the Younger and Pier Francesco da Viterbo, it is decorated inside and out by Vasari (most celebrated for his account of the lives of better, and better-known, contemporary artists); the stenciling in the garden courtyard is especially interesting. Much of the historically themed fresco work of the *piano nobile* has had to be extensively conserved due to a failure in technique at the moment of execution—not something we see in Vasari's works in oil, an exceptional example of which can be seen as the altar piece in the Vitelli chapel of the town's Franciscan church. On the staircase there is a

Vasari's stencilling

series of frescoes in the lunettes of the vault by an unknown hand: depictions of encounters between the philosophers and various women, most notably Socrates and his wife Xanthippe, and a wonderful allegory of a woman riding a gagged and blindfolded male. The idea is that whatever pretentions male culture and learning might claim, the role of women to engender heirs for noble lines is essential. Painted, it is thought, to celebrate the marriage of one of the Vitelli (literally the veal calves) with a woman from the other leading Castellan family, the Buffalotti (literally the little buffaloes), we can only speculate on the happiness of the match though there is no doubt as to the strengthening of the herd.

Successful signori established their families for centuries. The Medici of Florence married into all the royal houses of what would become Catholic Europe, and established their own Grand Duchy of the whole of Tuscany which lasted until the family merged in the female line with the Hapsburgs. We have seen that the Montefeltro had some limited success in establishing themselves in one small corner of Umbria. The family which probably had the best chance of truly making it to the big time in and around Perugia during the Renaissance were the Fortebraccio of Montone, had not the exertions of the warring city factions brought the great Braccio Fortebraccio to an early grave. Thus his offspring had to continue to make their mark by acting as *condottiere* in other parts of Italy and beyond, and the creation of a true new duchy in our region had to wait until Pope Julius III alienated papal lands and added them in 1550 to those of his Perugian family, the della Corgna, to create the tiny "state" based upon Castiglione del Lago on the Tuscan side of Lake Trasimene. The transformation from a village to a ducal capital was similar to the process that the Cesi worked on Acquasparta, a medieval castello or manor house had to be reworked in true Renaissance style and its interior decoration completed with the obligatory fresco cycle celebrating the history, achievements and virtues of the family. Though the result is elegant what remains truly impressive at Castiglione is the real defensive castle linked to the palace by a covered walk-way. The walls are strong and the promontory upon which it was built uniquely strategic, but the della Corgna were unable to hold on to their little handkerchief of sovereignty after 1643, through the failure of the male succession.

Another Perugian family which managed to carve out a tiny state was that of the Bourbon del Monte. Apparently distantly related to the family which has provided monarchs for France and then Spain, they exercised the marquisate of Monte Santa Maria in Tiberina from 1355, when the village (there have never been many more than a couple of hundred inhabitants) was given its independence by the ruling Holy Roman Emperor. Occupying an enormously strategic position on a high hill on the west side of the upper Tiber Valley it had been fought over repeatedly throughout antiquity and the Middle Ages. It maintained its tenuous claim to autonomy right into the nineteenth century where it was the last place in Italy where a duel might legally be fought—attracting therefore a rather specialized form of tourist. The massive and rather gloomy castle of the marquises stopped being their principal residence before the end of the Renaissance period, and they can now be found in a rather comfortable Tiber-side manor house surrounded by many well-cultivated acres at Montecastelli a mile or so north of Umbertide.

The Italian noble family which really won the jackpot was the Savoia, who maintaining a duchy on both the French and Italian sides of the south-west Alps from the fifteenth century onwards were able to transform themselves successively into Kings of Piedmont, Sardinia and finally a united Italy. But this national signoria was to prove as fleeting as so many of its Renaissance prototypes. Four kings reigned—one of them, Umberto I (1878-1901), lending his name to the apparently hyper-patriotic Umbrian town Fratta, ever after known as Umbertide. Umberto II had to go into exile after the winning of a plebiscite by republicans in 1945. It is near Umbertide that the present heir apparent to the family's titles and pretension to the empty throne, Emmanuele Filiberto, grandson of the last king, has built a large country house. Excluded for years from residing in Italy by a constitutional clause, he married a French actress, Clothilde Coureau, at Rome's Church of Santa Maria degli Angeli in 2004, almost as soon as it was possible to retake up residence. He has recently cut a fine figure taking part in the Italian version of the reality show, *Strictly Come Dancing* (*Ballando con le Stelle*—literally, Dancing with the Stars), actually winning the contest. He was not by any means hampered by the charming boyish smile he has kept since jet-set childhood, a smile much in evidence in the framed silver photo (aged about five) with his parents on Andrea Lignani Marchesani's piano. Undeniably first rate in its own particular way, it may not be the Accademia dei Lincei, but it is certainly the sign of the permanence of the Umbrian aristocracy.

Chapter Eleven

THE CASA COLONICA

FARMING AND THE AGE OF THE PAPAL STATE

As I have already recounted in my tale of banking woe and my revenge on the manager, my house is reached by a stony track which winds uphill two miles in distance and a thousand feet in altitude. It is very steep. For the first few hundred yards where it leaves the main road between Umbertide and Città di Castello it is in fact metalled, and that is where the houses of the sensible locals cluster, those who want a mains water supply, direct gas and regular visits from the postman or, as in our local case, postwoman (*postinola*). But as the road sweeps with a sharp right-hand bend past the wood-store of the last such residents it becomes one of the ubiquitous *strade bianche*, the white roads, of Umbria. Requiring properly a four-wheel-drive vehicle, or a horse-drawn cart, to traverse them, these are the capillaries of the region, carrying humanity into the wild hills from the settled valleys to engage in their time-honoured pursuits: hunting and gathering, roaming free from parental control when young, and perhaps most surprising, small-scale but elaborately developed farming. The kind of farming you find up on the hills is traditional and family-managed—a plot for an *orto*, or kitchen garden, some bee hives, a stand of chestnut or walnut trees, some gnarled olives, a few rows of ancient vines, a small greenhouse or shed, a well-head with some rusty pumping equipment.

Over the years that I have had my house the number of cleared plots along the stony road has increased dramatically. We seem to be experiencing a veritable return to the land. These plots "stay active" for a long stretch of the year, producing *fave*, broad beans, asparagus and *carciofi*, artichokes, at the end of spring; the rich crop of a variety of tomatoes (those for bottling, those for salads, those for making *passata*, the basis of most pasta and pizza sauces) and salad leaves in high summer; nuts and maize in early September, the wine harvest in full autumn and the olives at its end as the first bite of winter suggests itself. Then come the brassicas: cabbage, Brussels sprouts and broccoli, dependent upon the coming frost.

Those who work these plots are the wiry, grizzled and bronzed locals well into the third age who have retired from full-time paid employment, if they ever really had it, perhaps always having constructed a living from the variety of activities which go up to making a *contadino,* a smallholder. Seemingly ancient women and men weed and hoe, drive small tractors and sit at the end of a long day in the shade to survey their empires of order and fruitfulness. I once pulled over on the road up to the house mesmerized by the ruby-fruit glow of ripe tomatoes. The gnarled owner hailed me with his usual affability and I strolled over to the heart of his plot muttering compliments about his productivity. Then to business: would it be possible for me to buy some of his super-abundant crop? His face fell; no, he was very sorry, he had a family of seven children, thirteen grandchildren and six great-grandchildren all of them crazy for tomatoes by the kilo in this weather and at this time of year. Then there was all the bottling that had to take place to provide pasta sauces for this ravenous horde throughout the winter. This fruit was already well and truly booked.

Farming is at the heart of Umbrian society. I suppose it always has been, the myriad valleys lending themselves to human subsistence since the time Paleolithic settlers made their offerings of grain to the Green Venus of the Devil's Lair caves. During the height of the Roman Empire no taxes were levied on the crops of the Italian "home" provinces, allowing rich and less rich landowners alike to enjoy the fruit of their (or others') labours in their entirety. Only towards the end of the classical period with the need to defend the empire's borders more strenuously with larger, costly armies did this tax break come to an end. We have seen that later administrations such as that of the Ostrogothic Kingdom tried once again to stimulate productivity in the region by reducing the tax burden, but this may reflect the real difficulty faced by the inhabitants, caught between swamp, forest and bare mountainside, as much as any planned economic policy. The medieval period of the *communes* undoubtedly saw the flourishing of their individual *contade* with some concerted attempts to return to the engineering projects of the ancients, both as far as drainage and water-supply, to render more land useful for cultivation, and it is from this period that we begin to find the traditional division of the hillsides into olive groves, vineyards and smaller garden plots, like those I still encounter today.

The two high plains in the region, those of Colfiorito and Castelluccio, had always been suitable for the cultivation of lentils and other

The high plain of Castelluccio

legumes, and with the arrival of the potato from the New World at the end of the fifteenth century another bumper crop was added to their stock-in-trade. It is also important to remember that tomatoes only appeared at the same time and for the same reason. Yet despite such advantages the region was known, especially in the period of government by the Church State, as an impoverished one. The landowners were either aristocrats who lived most of the time in Rome or the religious orders governed from afar, the estates were enormous, and the system of cultivation employed was that of *mezzadria* in which gangs of landless peasants lived in squalid barracks far from their villages for long periods of the agricultural year. A very high proportion of what was produced went directly for sale to enrich the landowner, and each labourer earned a tiny subsistence portion. Inevitably, the system did not lend itself to the most efficient practices.

If the Stato Pontificio, the Papal State, despite its claims to legitimacy stretching back to the Emperor Constantine, had really only been founded with the military operations of Cardinal Albornoz in the fourteenth century, it was towards the end of the Age of the Signorie late in the sixteenth century and early in the seventeenth that the state acquired its distinctive administrative structure and its regime began, as it were, to bite. The last ruling aristocratic families gave way to ordained legates from Rome who would exercise hard-line repressive policies intended to keep Umbria and the rest of the Papal States distant from the philosophical and political speculations of the Enlightenment. There was no free press, very little possibility of social advancement without the sacrifice of entering the ranks of the celibate clergy, and virtually no access to industrial developments taking hold of production across the rest of Western Europe. Labouring under these conditions it is hardly surprising that the workforce lacked motivation or ingenuity. Backwardness bred devious and corrupt behaviours in both rulers and ruled, and it can come as no revelation that this period exhibits the least commitment to caring for or extending the cultural heritage of the region. A broken-down and wild zone in stark contrast to the orderliness of its neighbour, Hapsburg Tuscany, Umbria earns nothing but horrified condescension from its foreign visitors in this period. Luckily the Umbrian spirit itself was ultimately shown to be indomitable.

A by-product of mezzadria, and a much happier one than the starvation wages and state sanctioned exploitation of the official version, was in effect to make every householder, and every member of their family, kitchen gardeners. The identity of the contadino, sometimes translated as "farmer" but better as "smallholder", has established itself indelibly on the Umbrian psyche since the period of the Church State. Everyone, like my producer/consumer of tomatoes, wants his or her own vegetable plot, everyone has a few domestic animals, at least hens, everyone harvests what the hills, woods and streams offer. It is for this reason that it is sometimes hard to find fresh vegetables in the region's smaller shops and supermarkets— there is literally such a small market for such produce that it is not worth stocking. Everyone has their own fresh greens, tomatoes, eggs and fruit. Better, look for an old woman on a local market day who might be found in the midst of the countless stalls plying the rag-trade, with their often North African proprietors. She might be sitting on an upturned crate with an ancient hand-held pair of copper scales nearby. Her produce is what was in her garden this morning: salad greens, chicory, spinach; some onions, maybe zucchini, some small, sweet apples, a few big brown eggs. She cannot earn much from it, but apparently she cannot use the produce either. Almost uniquely she seems also to have no family with which to share her produce. A local tragedy, were she not so cheery and garrulous. So she is here as regularly as the town clock chimes in the market day, and somehow she seems as if she might have been here since the seventeenth century.

LOVE OF THE SOIL

In 1955 more than fifty per cent of Italy's population was engaged in agricultural work; in 2010 fewer than four per cent were so employed. The flight from the land may have been substantial but it is relatively recent, resulting in a residual love for the soil within most city dwellers' souls. This manifests itself in the abiding tradition of *villeggiatura* found in all strata of Italian society. Originally an aristocratic privilege, in its classical eighteenth-century form when it was immortalized in Carlo Goldoni's farce of the same name, this is a period of summer "country" living. Not for the many is the trip to a vast villa with attendant farm and an army of servants, but rather to a small village house probably last inhabited full-time by their grand- if not great-grandparents. It is from here that they revive the interests of the contadino, engaging in some hobby agriculture and thus explaining perhaps the expansion of smallholdings which I have noticed locally in the last fifteen years. The summer return of the ex-locals also gives them the chance of fully-fledged participation in *sagre*, a word that really defies translation.

Sagre are festivals dedicated to particular items of food, and they reflect the enormous increase in affluence enjoyed by Italians in general in these last fifty years. They are not directly connected with the Church calendar or even really the agricultural cycle itself. They are celebrations of the ability of modern Umbrians to feast, and to feast on food which would have been beyond the aspirations of most of their ancestors. Meat would have been rare on most Umbrian tables as a daily feature until relatively recently. And what meat there was would have been game, chicken or preserved pork of one sort or another. Umbria has never had a tradition of dairy farming and associated beef rearing, features which are particularly characteristic of its neighbouring regions of Emilia-Romagna and the Val di Chiana. The most traditional dishes were based on the use of bread/pasta made from wheat and/or maize flour, both when fresh and when stale. Overdependence upon *polenta*, the maize porridge which is an autumn staple, often led in the past to a high occurrence of the vitamin deficiency pellagra in the region. But such analysis of deprivation is far from the confident statement of plenty at the heart of a *sagra*.

Advertised with giant hoardings strung across the road or huge billboards by its side, these annual gatherings never fail to tell you how venerable they are. And as I have already indicated, that is not very venerable at all in this land of antiquity: 25 years of the mushroom festival at San Leo Bastia, seventeenth edition of the Beefsteak Binge at Todi, even three years of the Festival of Spare-ribs at Cornetto. As noted above these are summer events when the largest numbers of "locals" will be gathered, with the need for city dwellers to return to their roots in the country mainly to get away from the heat. Although they do not seem to have a direct link to its round of celebrations, I have sometimes mused on their appropriateness to the stories of the saints which the Catholic Church remembers at this time of the year. For example, St. Lawrence is kept on 10 August, and he is famous as a Roman martyr of the third century who met his end by being barbecued on a grid iron. Patron of chefs, his last words are reported to have been, "Will you turn me over? I'm done on this side." *Sagre di bistecche*, Steak Barbecues, abound around this date. Coincidence or pious commentary?

Then on 24 August there is St. Bartholomew. who was skinned alive—
and although, sadly, Umbrians do not eat snakes, whose casting of their
skins would have made a perfect parallel, they make up for it with a
plethora of mushroom sagre, with many of the *funghi* on offer being peeled
of their skins before cooking—imagination is beginning to run wild. Fish
festivals really ought to be limited to the towns around Lake Trasimene or
the high valleys from which river trout can be caught, but now they are
common throughout this uniquely land-locked region of Italy. Some villages opt for nothing more taxing than a beer festival, borrowing inspiration from visits made by Umbrians who have travelled north of the Alps.
But best (or should that be worst) of all was when I caught sight of an ad-
vertisement for an Ostrich Meat Feast; these antipodean birds have been
farmed commercially since the 1980s. It would be hard to make a connection between this variety of sagra and a local or well-known saint, none
I think being celebrated for their having hidden their heads in the sand.
However, in these events their aspirational character is underscored. If they
are "traditional" in any sense then it must be as an echo of a millionaire
antique Roman's banquet (*pace* Apicius' cookbook and Apuleius' Golden
Ass) rather than any kind of healthy return to the soil.

The degree to which the *cultura contadina* is not immediately accessible to the visitor or indeed the modern local can be gauged by the appearance in the 1960s and 1970s of institutions dedicated to its
preservation. At least two well-known "folk" museums are to be found in
the region. Until the late 1990s the Centro Documentazioni Delle
Tradizioni Populari, just south of Città di Castello, was a rather haphaz-
ardly organized museum open to the public in a large farmhouse, the
brainchild of a local philanthropic landowner. It then remained closed for
some years while remaining an institution for the preservation of documents relating to the life of the contadino. Happily for such a genial collection, its exhibits, eclectic enough to include a steam locomotive, are
now since April 2010 once again on public display.

Rather more "standard" and correspondingly more useful as an exhibition is the *casa contadina* beautifully kept in the centre of Corciano, the
small fortified hill-town above the main road between Perugia and Lake
Trasimene. Four spaces essential to the functioning of a traditional contadino's dwelling have been recreated in a medieval building: *la stalla,* the
animal stalls; *la cantina*, a store room; *la cucina*, a living room where

cooking and eating were central; and *la camera*, the bedroom, the only (partially) private space. Painstakingly adorned with furniture and tools largely in use until the 1960s but dating from over a hundred years before, a sense of the single-mindedness of the life of the smallholder and his family is wonderfully evoked.

Even the woodland itself is harvested. Umbrian trees outside the specially preserved forests of the national parks are relatively young and they are farmed every fifteen years or so. They cover the hillsides much more extensively than they would have done in antiquity and even the Middle Ages, entirely dependent as the people of those times were on the cultivation of these middle- to upland slopes, being deprived of the marshy or flooded valley bottoms and distant from other markets. During an Umbrian vacation twenty years ago I watched each day from the side of a September swimming pool, my holiday-home neighbour, Alberto, take his donkey down from his garden, across the stream in the valley below and up an almost hemispherical hill to gather the wood of the trees he had already felled in the last weeks of August, arranging it into neat, large piles. All this would have to be approved and would certainly have been under the scrutiny of a state institution, Il Corpo Forestale dello Stato, the State Forest Police Force.

Normally simply referred to as the *forestale,* it was founded in 1822 within the confines of the Kingdom of Sardinia (which included mainland Piedmont) by King Carlo Felice. Having been subsumed into a broader Fascist civil defence force in the 1920s and 1930s, it was re-established for the Italian Republic in 1948, and operates as a permanent official police force with the specific brief of protecting the environment and maintaining public safety within defined country areas. Such areas undoubtedly include the six designated national parks within Umbria: those of Colfiorito, Monte Subasio, Monte Cucco, the Valnerina, Lake Trasimene and the Tiber Park. There are more than 8,500 agents employed nationally, and their duties can vary from employing the extensive fleet of helicopters equipped with fire-fighting equipment when forest fires get out of control, to giving judgements about whether you can fell a tree in your garden. (It was in this last competence that I have encountered the forestale most directly.) Very recently they have also assumed responsibility for promoting and guaranteeing the safety of Italian food produce, and determining the ways in which organically produced foods can be marketed and advertised. Its agents wear a dress uniform of dove grey with green trimmings (which might easily be mistaken for that of the Guardia delle Finanze, the Fiscal Police) and practical camouflage fatigues for turns of duty, and they maintain all the elements which every self-respecting Italian force of law-and-order demands as a matter of pride: a mounted unit, an official band, sports facilities which have produced Olympic champions and an elaborate annual display *in piazza* on a Saturday near to the anniversary of its foundation, 15 October. Its heraldic device shows a golden eagle guarding a damaged but still living oak stump, surmounted by a band of acorns topped with a civic crown of watchful towers. Its motto, *pro natura opus et vigilantia,* has a neat double meaning, Labour and Watchfulness by/for Nature. The forestale even has its (obscure) patron saint and an official prayer. St. Giovanni Gualberto was the tenth-century founder of the beautiful forest Monastery of Vallombrosa not far from Florence, and it was Pope Pius XII who thought he would be particularly adapted to extend his patronage to the forestale, without, however, giving any particular explanation.

The prayer is moving and direct:

> O Lord, who with your grace illumines our hearts and minds, help us to grow in hope every day. You have given us life for the service of our country, in order to conserve, care for and protect the most beautiful things in creation: trees, animals, waters and mountains all of which you have given for our benefit. Make us more aware, O Lord, of this privileged duty and keep us fully committed to it.

It seems a good deal more Franciscan in the popular sense than the writings of St. Francis himself.

Alberto, the contadino I used to watch harvesting the wood of the forest, lived in what was part of a typical Umbrian country *casale* (large house), a former *casa colonica*, now broken up into a spacious holiday house owned by an Englishman who had done the conversion of the property himself, with Alberto and his wife in the lower more confined portion of the structure. Casa colonica is not an architectural term, though it is often used today as if it were. Instead it relates to the system of mezzadria alluded to earlier in this chapter. Originally these buildings were occupied by families or groups of relations not constituting anything like a nuclear family in the modern sense (*coloni*, literally colonies) who were themselves not the owners of the building. They occupied it under the terms of a *contratto di mezzadria,* an agreement with the owner that typically gave him the right to fifty per cent of their annual harvest (occasionally a different proportion was stipulated in the agreement). In return he was supposed to provide half of the expenses of production and the upkeep of the house. On the one hand this system seems to favour the *colono* at the *mezzadro's* expense, since the owner's share, in effect the rent, is proportionate to what can be produced in crisis years; however, the disadvantage to the *colono* of even having to produce double the amount necessary for subsistence in years of bad harvest soon becomes apparent.

The tenants in this system also had the weight of maintaining a logbook accounting for all expenses and items claimed for—a duty which surely must have involved third parties requiring a fee in a society where less than ten per cent of the population could read or write well into the

Casa colonica

twentieth century. This third person might be the *cataldo* or agent of the owner, which introduced a further conflict of interests and another level of "earner" from the already stretched system.

Typically *case coloniche* were painted red on the outside with a white patch upon which the name of the owner and the number of the colony was indicated. They are classically of three storeys with store rooms and animal stalls on the lowest level, and access to the first floor via an external covered staircase. Access to the third floor and attic spaces would probably have originally been by ladder, but subsequent adaptations have introduced internal stairs.

It is largely these structures which have provided the raw material for that new crop of modern, foreign settlement that Umbria has "farmed". Whether you are looking for a ruin to renovate or the "off the peg" luxury makeover already complete, you will still find plenty to choose from in planning and then realizing a holiday home in Umbria. Everyone's prayer, however, for their dream house ought to be to avoid getting involved with an unscrupulous expatriate "operator" such as Stan Blemish in Barry Unsworth's *After Hannibal*:

> (Blemish) was pleased with his morning's business and especially with the way he had handled the Greens. They were a promising couple, he had thought so from the start. He saw them now in his mind's eye, standing side by side at the top of the steps, grey-haired, blue-eyed and guileless, smiling in welcome. Once again it came to him that they were like a deserving couple in a folk tale, the ones who treat the mysterious guest kindly and get the magic goose. Only the simple-hearted could convey an impression like that. Fools, in other words. He felt renewed ill will towards them. He had gone there on business and they had tried to make him share in their life. Well, this time it would be the mysterious guest who got the golden eggs.

Blemish goes on to fleece his clients, the Greens, assisted by an incompetent and dishonest Italian builder leaving them with their casa colonica purchased for restoration in a dangerous state of near collapse. Even as the truth begins to dawn on his gullible victims Blemish continues his deceit.

A *casale* with sunflowers

"Everything will be all right in the end, of course. We have seen it happen again and again. The various pieces will fit into place, you will find yourself in possession of an extremely desirable country residence, all these teething pains will be forgotten." He packed all the sincerity he could into this assertion. A house was more than a simple acquisition, it was a dream of the future, he knew that; by pointing to the future you could generally persuade to put up with what was unsatisfactory in the present. Especially gulls like these two... "Elegant and spacious," he said, "standing in its own broad acreage, with extensive views across to the foothills of the Apennines."

Yes, surely that is the dream of those who come to buy in the property market of Umbria's rolling hills, and I am glad to relate that I have only ever found excellent working practices from native and expatriate professional alike. But be warned if your dream should take you there.

Mezzadria was, of course, dedicated to producing staple crops. Today the cash crops of a modern market have largely driven out the traditional produce. Thus throughout the region you will find sunflowers planted in the vast fields of the river bottoms, beautiful for about ten days in mid-July, and then a depressing skeletal expanse of thinning vegetation as they are left to dry out in the sun, until harvested in the early autumn. Once when sharing my enthusiasm for Umbria with a London-based friend, she thought for a moment before saying, "Hmm, Umbria—that's the place filled with fields and fields of blackened sunflowers, isn't it?" I could have jumped in by saying that there was tobacco as well, but on reflection that is not a particularly strong defence of the region. Green the tobacco plants may remain, but how many already blackened shrivelled lungs are they preparing to poison still further? There is a dark side, then, to Umbria, and it comes from that same ground which provides such a rich bounty of produce.

I once returned to my Umbrian house after a few months of being away in Rome and the UK to find that one of the windows of the wooden garden shed had been broken. On investigation inside, although there was a bit of confusion, I could not identify any major item as missing. Shrugging my shoulders I put it down to the occasional, probably childish and mindless vandalism which I had noted on my property. It was only weeks later on meeting a British acquaintance in the piazza of Umbertide on market day that I was fully filled in. A young man of twenty-two had driven up to my house one late May day, parked his car where I normally would and climbed into my garden. It seems that he bathed in the swimming pool, and then broke the window of the shed in search of a length of plastic tubing. He re-dressed (so the police believed) and returned to his car with the tubing, which he proceeded to attach to his exhaust pipe and insert through the window of the car. He turned the key in the ignition, and the motor started. Some minutes later he was dead. Needless to say I was extremely shocked and saddened, and surprised that the forces of law-and-order, neither *carabinieri* nor forestale, had actually contacted me to inform me of their investigation which centred on my property. I still pray annually for the repose of the soul of that youth, and try even harder to live well in this place of beauty which still remains far from paradise.

Chapter Twelve

FOOD

TIMELESS UMBRIA

An old man told me the story of the village dog, with no particular owner, which went to funerals. And not only funerals, but every sort of "celebration" imaginable—all those associated with individuals and individual families: weddings, baptisms, birthdays, *onomastiche* (name-days), first communions, as well as the communal ones: patron saint of town, national holidays, summer fetes and *sagre*, of course. The dog would inevitably go to church first, and then accompany the crowd to whichever house or public building was designated for the merry-making—because even funerals have to have food and wine. The time came when the dog became old and ill and had to be fetched to these events because his presence had become a symbol of well-being to all those present. And when he at last gave up the ghost and departed for heavenly *feste* a successor was elected from a large litter to become village dog, receiving the appropriate training to fulfil this role. And just to prove that this is not some one-off crazy fabrication that an Umbrian raconteur palmed off on me I want to assure readers that I have personally met Orvieto's city dog, Archimede (not his real name, for even dogs should enjoy a certain amount of privacy). I have seen him strolling down the main streets and into the most peopled of *piazze* of that jewel of a city, being greeted and petted by all the locals, waddling (he is a *bassoto* cross, a sausage-dog in UK English) into the bars and pastry shops to receive tit-bits. Solitary, but never alone, he typifies a general sense of well-being and security for beings far beyond the canine world.

Thus is created and confirmed a tradition of *cani beati*, happy dogs, which has, I am told, not been broken in the village of my informant since the self-election of the first public hound. And there is plenty to be happy about for his successors and indeed those who surely will also come after Archimede. In the rather amateurish frescoes of the side chapel of the Church of Santa Maria delle Grazie in Città di Castello, most noted by art historians for the altar piece of the Madonna by Agostino Nelli, the lesser, almost certainly local artist includes a dog in every single scene. He has also lavished more attention on the dogs in these representations of various biblical events than on their sanctified human participants. Be it the birth or marriage of the Virgin Mary, the wedding at Cana or the Last Supper, the dogs are having a better time than the people, and the artist also seems rather more familiar with dogs than with people, at least anatomically.

He is not the only Umbrian to be so dedicated to the canine. I will never forget a night in early October, the autumn already deepening in the direction of winter, when I heard a strange sound outside my house as I was collecting wood for the first indoor fire of the season. Someone was walking up the hill behind my garden and shouting—a long, high-pitched wail of pleading, a single word elongated way beyond its couple of syllables. It was a name, and not that of a human being—the name of a precious, beloved hound, perhaps also significantly valuable to the owner as a hunter, or a finder of truffles. A light flashed in the darkness as the solitary searcher continued to call more and more desperately as he continued to climb the hill. Who knows what had happened to the hapless "Lucky" whose luck it seems had finally run out. Victim of a viper's fang or a wild-boar tusk? Or simply lost in the dense woods? Happy, another *cane beato*, far away with new owners who had taken him/her in? Or searching as keenly for the master as the master was for the dog?

Umbrians love their pets and they love a party. We have already visited some of the annual summer *sagre* in the last chapter. But asking what might be on the menu for any get-together with the exception of these speciality food fests is the Umbrian equivalent of enquiring into the pope's religious convictions: he's a Catholic, hadn't you heard? What you will be served is Umbrian food, which communicates a sort of self-satisfaction of epic proportions. There is no better food than what we can offer and therefore that is what you will eat.

This is, of course, only a magnification of the general insularity of Italian cuisine. Dishes known and cherished in one area are entirely unknown, or often at least called something entirely different, in another. Foreigners inevitably identify Italian cooking with two 'basic' dishes: pasta and pizza, both Neapolitan in their modern classical versions, and of course ubiquitous today in every region. But this is not what we can identify as classical in our region.

Here as in nearby Tuscany more basic and even cheaper food for the peasant kitchen took the form of variations on the cooking of stale bread dressed with a little oil, onions, tomatoes or the very cheapest cuts of meat. This finds its way into the preparation of *ribollita*, twice boiled soups, which use any seasonal vegetables from broad beans to curly kale together with the necessary breadcrumbs to add body. More thoroughly Umbrian, however, are the admittedly far from alluring variants on *panzarella*, literally "fat tummy", a softening of bread crusts with the smallest amounts of oil and water and at best spiced up with a little tomato sauce or braised *coratelle*, sheep's offal. This is a *cucina povera* (peasant cooking) of a particularly extreme variety but surely must have formed the staple of many ordinary Umbrians for centuries, re-emphasizing the lesson of the last chapter that this region, especially in the early modern period during the misgovernment of the Church State, was far from affluent.

Forms of the simplest pasta made from flour and water and cut into ribbons, *papardelle*, or rhomboids, *maltagliati*, are of course also extremely cheap, as are the bullets or twirls of the same mixture which here are named *strozzapreti*, priest-stranglers. If the Church in some way was seen to keep the common people down and poor in the seventeenth and eighteenth centuries they could at least eat meals dedicated to revenge. (*Strangolapreti* is the name of a type of gnocchi in rural Lazio—the concept being naturally the same, only the weapon exemplifying local anticlerical refinements.)

Machine-produced, dried pasta, which gradually caught on throughout the peninsula during the nineteenth century, was originally known as *spaghetti napoletani*. Although an important manufacturer, Giobatta Buitoni, started mass producing pasta in San Sepulchro in the 1820s and quickly extended his business into Umbria with the opening of a shop in Città di Castello, it was always to be a visitor here. No modern family or communal celebration would be complete without home-made pasta, accompanied most typically with a *ragù* of wild boar, goose, or hare in the north and west, or cream and sausage in the south and east. This last sauce is called *alla norcina*, named after the Umbrian town of Norcia with its national celebrity for pork products, and thus establishes its local credentials in the most enduring way. The other sauce named in tribute to an Umbrian town (Terni) does not speak with the same distinctive voice: *alla ternana* is made of tomatoes, garlic and pecorino cheese, a variety of a recipe to be found throughout Italy. Lovers of rarities and something tasty can also occasionally still find *pasta alle rigaglie,* with a sauce based on chicken innards dressed with parsley, onions and herbs. Filled pasta is not so common as elsewhere in Italy, though Christmas and Easter dinners commonly include a version of *tortellini in brodo,* meat-filled twists of pasta served in chicken broth. A wonderful exception to the rule, however, are the *chicche al tartufo* served in the north of the region. These are fat pasta parcels stuffed with a nutty truffled filling, and slathered with a creamy sauce also flavoured with truffle. I hardly need say that this is by no means part of "Umbria-lite" nor an invention of cucina povera.

Pasta is essential to any meal worth its salt. Yet despite its designation within the category of *primo piatto,* first course, which would also include any kind of soup, *risotto* (an import from the rice-growing areas of Emilia Romagna across the Apennines) or polenta, it is not the thing you will eat first. So how does the meal start? With *crostini* certainly, little pieces of toasted bread spread thickly with pastes of various kinds: olive, mushroom, truffle, chicken-liver or simply goose-fat or lard. *Ciaccia,* a thin, salted flat-bread made on a heated stone and known more generally as *torta al testo,* is a favourite party food, or mid-morning snack, when stuffed with local cured ham or *salami.* Here is how it is made, at least by Signora Lanari, resident of Morra, who inducted me into the procedure one late summer afternoon.

Il testo is a round stone or specially manufactured piece of smooth concrete with a diameter of about fifteen inches which is also called a *panaro,* and Mrs. Lanari's is stamped with the date of its manufacture, 1974; not so old really, but still in some senses as long as a life-time. These simple griddles would originally have been put directly into a fire to heat. Now they are placed neatly over the circular aperture in the top of an old-fashioned wood burning range. Mrs. Lanari keeps just such a stove in an outhouse solely for this purpose. To make eight *ciaccie* she prepares a flexible dough made from two kilos of flour of the "OO" quality, four packets of dried yeast, a quarter of a litre of water or milk, or a mixture of the two. You can add an egg if you like. She separates the dough into eight equal portions and cooks the flat-breads, pressing them and flattening them down onto the hot stone for about five to six minutes, turning them three or four times. They are almost crisp and golden brown on the outside and chewy within. Simple food heaven.

Another and similar snack more properly belonging to Emilia Romagna but very common throughout Umbria is the *piadina*. It differs little from torta al testo as far as ingredients go but is not leavened and is prepared on a greased griddle or even sometimes deep-fried. You can buy them from road-side vans or special dedicated shops, which is the nearest thing to a British fish and chip shop that I have ever found in Italy, especially when one considers the deep-fat fryer much in evidence within. Piadine fillings can demonstrate the degree to which the extremely traditional is open to entertaining experiment. Sea-food (or at least *surimi)* stuffed is one variant I have seen, and for those with an irredeemably sweet tooth chocolate spread is ubiquitous if entirely post-war. At least to date I have yet to see ostrich proposed as a filling.

Umbrian ham is less refined than its relations from further north (Parma or San Daniele). Its strong taste perhaps can be explained by the preference locally for wild boar meat and sausages. Claims are also made that the domesticated pigs in Umbria all carry a strong genetic strain of their forest cousins, interbreeding (both planned and spontaneous) between them being extremely common. A subsequent robustness of flavour and texture therefore comes as no surprise. An Umbrian speciality in preparing the curing of pork is *cappocollo,* a cut from high on the ham, which is then rolled and covered in pepper corns before being hung. It is the tradition to eat this meat on Easter day with hard-boiled eggs and bread made with cheese, *torta al formagio*, as I noted in Chapter Seven. This cut, if found in other parts of Italy, is known as *coppa,* which confusingly in Umbria is the name for a rich brawn (a force meat made from brains) flavoured with pine-nuts and fennel seeds.

Pig butchery is, interestingly enough, named throughout Italy after one of Umbria's towns, *norcineria* being the common name for cured pork products. At certain times walking down the main street of Norcia one can literally smell that peculiarly half-soapy, half-meaty odour emanating from the numerous shops dealing in these delicacies. Many of the best of the region's truffles are also found around Norcia, making it in some senses Umbria's gastronomic capital, the final touch being given by the spring-time harvest of saffron that it produces.

The husbandry of sheep also supplies an important traditional feature of the Umbrian diet. It has been Sardinian shepherds who have since the 1960s and the native depopulation of upland Umbria habitually spent the

Norcineria

summers in the high pastures of the Apennines, only descending to the valley bottoms as the winter began to bite. Sheep's milk cheese, *pecorino sardo locale*, is found almost as much as that of cows, and a crispy dish of *agnello alla scottadito*, grilled lamb chops with a healthy squeeze of fresh lemon juice on top, is found on many rustic eating-houses' menus. More traditional still are dishes made from sheep innards: *trecce* and *coratella*, both served spiced. But by straying from pigs to sheep I have rather jumped the gun by presenting these main courses before having finished with the *antipasti*.

A gargantuan spread of *antipasti* will certainly be a feature of any village festival, the type of occasion frequented by the lucky dog who opened this chapter. And where would this take place? In modern Umbria the most popular venue for big communal events and the bigger private ones is the *pro loco*, the social centre or village hall. These structures are far from attractive, often being nothing much more than a gigantic pre-fabricated shed, with perhaps an open veranda at one end. Often to be found next to the local sports ground, and with the kitchen usually in a rather more substantial structure also containing changing facilities for the village football team, the pro loco buzzes all the year round. New Year celebrations probably took place here; the spring brings a string of first communion parties; and some sort of harvest home/*vendemia* will make its bibulous mark upon the life of the villagers. It is also where the late summer sagre are held, or the newfangled German import, the Bierfest.

CULTURE OF EATING

If the antipasti and the home-made *primi piati* are imported from the cooks' home kitchens, the *secondi* will almost certainly be prepared on the spot. Barbecued meats are the staple of such village feasts, and it sometimes looks as though a whole Viking funeral pyre is prepared to furnish sufficient quantities of smouldering ash to grill the meat. Obviously the pleasure in eating such food comes from the quality of the meat and the sense of dining in community in an age-old fashion. There is nothing refined about this cuisine, and just like the sagre, what it seems to celebrate is a belief in plenty for plenty's sake, intelligible as a feature of a society which for centuries went hungry on a regular basis. That is not to say that there are no good places to eat offering refined and even innovative cuisine in Umbria. It is just that that is not the defining style of the popular culture, and certainly not that of the pro loco.

As if to challenge the gargantuan proportions of an Umbrian feast Gianfranco Vissani, perhaps the region's most celebrated contemporary chef, recently (2009) had this to say on TV about cooking: "One must always make savings in the kitchen, not only in a time of economic crisis."

Born at Civitella del Lago near Orvieto in 1951, Vissani did his first training at Spoleto only to leave his native region to perfect his art from 1967 to 1973 in restaurants in the chief tourist locations of Italy: Venice, Florence, Cortina d'Ampezzo and Naples. He returned to the shores of Lake Corbara where his parents had owned a small *trattoria* for many years, and transformed its traditional simplicity into such a rarefied sophistication that his restaurant was awarded first place by the *Guida d'Italia dell'Espresso* for over twenty years, and *La Guide Michelin* confirmed an award of two stars in 2007. He is a public figure because of his frequent appearances on TV and radio (including a stint as judge on the daily cooking show *La Prova del Cuoco*) and because of his many books about cooking. I have never eaten in his restaurant, but have had an interesting conversation with him and his charming French wife about truffles while eating next to them at a well-known restaurant in Rome. Umbrian through and through, Vissani likens his talent to the artistic excellence of his native region, even if his examples of painters are rather *off piste*: "Great cooking comes from the heart, it produces feelings and emotions which can lift you into sometimes painting like Picasso, or sometimes creating a Rembrandt."

If there is an ingredient that you will find more used in Umbrian dishes than probably anywhere else in both home and restaurant cooking, it is the fungus variety termed "truffle". The white truffle (*tuber magnatum*), which is found only in autumn in the region, grows underground near oak, beech, poplar or hazel trees, and is incredibly highly prized, whereas the black, so-called Périgord truffle (*tuber melanosporum*) grows for a longer period of the year and only in the vicinity of the oak. There is also the less prized summer truffle (*tuber aestivum*), used mainly to lend its distinctly earthy flavour to oils and bottled sauces. If you want to see how well truffles can be used in an affordable way across the menu, you certainly could do worse than visit the family-run restaurant Da Lea in Via

Still life: pasta awaiting truffle, or vice versa

San Florido, Città di Castello. This is a decently, but not in any way fancily, decorated locale of three rooms, again furnished in the most straightforward of ways. You get a glimpse of the bustling kitchen as you enter the premises and there is a reassuring mix of genders and ages involved in getting the food to the diners. Many people, including the *tiferni*, the town's natives, come here specifically to eat dishes based on truffles. When the town holds its annual market dedicated to the luxury fungus simply walking into the main piazza can overpower you with their unmistakable earthy smell. Irresistible.

Grated directly on to an omelette or included in the making of a local cheese, you can also eat them as antipasto. Grated over buttered pasta they make a divine *primo*. Grated over rare cooked roast beef sprinkled with a good olive oil you simply cannot go wrong as far as *secondo*. I am sure some millionaire has made them into some kind of *dolce*, sweet, but let's not go there, since Da Lea has yet to include a truffle dolce in its menu, except for, that is, the mass-produced double ice-creams known as *Tartuffi*.

If you do have a sweet tooth Umbria can please even here, though as with most Italians, Umbrians tend to end meals more often with fruit than with puddings. However, Ian Campbell Ross, the gazetteer par excellence of the region, has a fine account of its *pasticcerie*:

> For special occasions… Umbria offers a remarkable range of characteristic breads and cakes some of which are now available… all year round, though often only in localized parts of the region. A typical autumn example from Perugia is *brustengolo,* based on maize flour combined with water to produce a kind of polenta which is then mixed with a little olive oil and sweetened with sliced apples, nuts, sultanas, and sugar and cooked in the oven.

He continues with descriptions of mainly Perugian sweets: *torciglione, torcolo di San Costanzo* and *fritelle di San Giuseppe.* It seems that even before the industrialization of sweets with the nineteenth-century arrival of *Perugino* chocolate the *capoluogho* (main town) of Umbria was providing plenty of work for dentists.

જી

My dogs are extremely lucky in having such a wonderful countryside to roam through, though I am carefully mindful of the tale of the desperate owner and the lost hound which opened this chapter to the extent that they do not roam unaccompanied. Our habitual walk is up the hill beyond our house as far as a large stand of sweet chestnut trees sloping gently away into the next valley. In the autumn when the chestnuts fall the dogs go sniffing around the prickly shells with their usual curiosity, and more often than not come away with sore noses. This might amount to being an unhappy dog, but only for as long as it takes to walk back down the hill and tuck into the dinner of cooked chicken/beef/lamb scraps which they more often than not have waiting at home. And so, in general, Umbrian life might well be that of a dog, which is no bad thing.

Chapter Thirteen

THE FACTORY

THE NINETEENTH AND TWENTIETH CENTURIES

Much of this book has focused upon the rural essence of Umbria, and the natural character of what this regions beats out into the body of Italy from a green heart; the water of the Tiber, cultural and artistic trends and activity associated with its spiritual past, and robust food traditions. It is time, however, to turn to a region that Jonathan Keates you remember could describe as having, in Terni, its own "Manchester". Umbria has traditionally been the second most industrialized area in the peninsula, after the Torino-Milano corridor, and although evidences of the fact are not as dominant as we would expect from a zone of heavy industry in a northern European country, they are far from being absent. As late as 1981 a census showed that up to fifteen per cent of the population of Umbria was employed in the industrial sector, and casual observation would argue that this percentage has not decreased. Following the *superstrada* route E45 over the hilly ridge which separates the Tiber Valley at Orte with the Nera's widening bowl, past Narni and its deep gorges, one could hardly fail to notice the veil of pollution which regularly hangs over Terni and its distant hollow. A hint has already been given, as one passes a big industrial plant sprawling across the broadening of the Nera Valley just as the lesser water joins the greater, right on the border between Umbria and northern Lazio. But the impression at this stage is still predominantly and reassuringly rural.

Orte is perched on its heights behind you, Amelia is to your far left and Narni Scalo ahead. The highway cuts through craggy outcrops crowned with villages dominated by their churches' ancient clock towers and otherwise clothed in thick woods. It would be easy to imagine that the factory, with its tall barley sugar-like red and white striped chimney belching out white smoke, although noteworthy, was still an aberration. But the Vale of Terni proper vanquishes any such delusions. On the lower slopes towards Narni, on the broad river plain around St. Valentine's city itself, and even high up behind you are the signs of this busy region's commitment to manufacture and the exploitation of natural resources. Later, looking back from Terni itself, the heights you have just crossed are in fact dominated by two striking edifices, alike in their solidity and blankness, but they could not be more distant from each other in design and purpose.

One is Cardinal Albornoz's fourteenth-century fortress dominating Narni, the other a huge open-cast gravel mine with its surrounding quarry and processing plant. Bigger factories and smaller industrial units are scattered along the Nera Valley, and the superstrada, groaning from the heavy traffic of vast wagons and articulated lorries, seems in perpetual evolution with new exits encircling Terni itself like medieval siege works. And at the heart of the industrial output is a vast steelworks on the north side of the town, the same company now, Thyssen-Krupp, as sixty years ago when the city was a focus for Allied bombing in the spring of 1944. The city was almost flattened and little of medieval Terni, let alone Interamnia Nahars of the Etruscans and Romans, survived. If much of this book has presented us with the rural idyll of an imagined and distant past as the controlling features of Umbria, the nineteenth and twentieth centuries bring us up sharply, changing our preconceptions, and not only in so much as heavy industry can be a blot on the landscape. Terni was not the only Umbrian community to witness the industrialization of war exemplified by the twentieth century following its mechanization in the nineteenth. Even though the early chapters of our historical consideration focused on the passage of armies through the region it is easy to underestimate the impact of the most recent hostilities to have afflicted Umbria. Following the aerial bombing of spring 1944, itself enabled by the Allies' capture of the Foggia airfields in their push up the peninsula, it was that same year's autumn that saw Umbria once again transformed into a theatre of war.

Although Italy herself had declared an armistice as early as 3 September 1943 as the Allies crossed from Sicily to the mainland, signalling Mussolini's fall and a change of government, the German forces were slow to yield. The four battles fought at Monte Cassino and the fiercely contested Allied landings at Anzio during the hard winter of 1943-44 meant that Rome was only liberated in June 1944. It is at this point that the Italian Campaign, though so costly in human life, was eclipsed by the D

Day landings and the opening of the Western Front. The second phase of the war in Italy is now termed by historians the "Forgotten Campaign", though 60,000 Allied troops were lost and a slightly larger number of Germans. British and Commonwealth War Grave cemeteries are still to be found tended to an exemplary degree at Orvieto and Assisi, marking the passage of the Allied push towards the Germans' last stand at the Gothic Line of the Appenine Range. And if it all seems so long ago as to rank with Witges or Narses, then think again.

Only a couple of years ago I was called upon to assist at the dedication of a new plaque affixed to the war memorial at Vaiano, a tiny Umbrian hamlet high up and looking across the Lago di Chiusi to Montepulciano in Tuscany. A British veteran of the action on that strategic ridge in August 1944 was present with me and recalled the assistance the local people gave to the Allies ("me and my pals") as the Germans pulled out, even at the risk of their own lives. The presence of many graves in the war cemeteries of Sikhs, Buddhists and Hindus also marks the vital contribution to the campaign of substantial elements of the Indian Army. And if Empire really is to be evoked for the last time in our Umbrian timeline, let it be in the review of Allied troops conducted by the King-Emperor George VI in the Morra Valley in September 1944. Elderly acquaintances from the area still treasure photos of the royal visit.

But if the high cost of this horror of modernity, total war, is to be fully understood let the last word be delivered in my own commune of Umbertide. On the night of 25 April 1944 Allied bombs aimed at the railway bridge across the Tiber in order to throw the German supply lines into disarray hit instead nearby Borgo San Giovanni resulting in seventy civilian deaths. It is with irony that a year later this date became the official day of Liberation for Italy and marks the formal close of hostilities. This day, even many decades later, still cannot be marked as a wholehearted festival, though always kept as a national holiday, and I myself have seen candles burning for family members lost in that tragedy in the windows of today's Piazza 25 Aprile.

Returning to Terni after her almost complete destruction, well she picked herself up, brushed herself down and started all over again—though with what has been a return to the heavy industrial base established in the nineteenth century it is difficult to imagine how it can really still be economically viable.

INDUSTRIAL LANDSCAPE

Terni may be the hub of industry in Umbria, but it is not the only focus. There are myriad small industrial estates, in effect on the outskirts of every settlement ranking above that of village—some related to the processing of agricultural products, such as tobacco and sunflower oil, and others more purely dedicated to the support of an industrialized society. Farming machinery, mining, processing plants, the bottling plants for local mineral waters: all are visible on the broader canvas of Green Umbria. Then there is the mining, a particular eyesore in the region of the Martani hills. The towns of Massa Martana, Gualdo Cataldo and Bastardo have a surprisingly downbeat and grimy feel for settlements in such picturesque surroundings.

But it really takes travel by train through the region to reveal the skeleton of the industrial identity which still exerts a claim on Umbria. Inevitably circumnavigating the *centri storici*, the iron road, so late an arrival here through the obscurantist opposition of such papal rulers as Gregory XVI, passes close to the warehouses and factories large and small which it was built to supply in the industrial explosion of post-Unified Italy. The view from Assisi's railway station is typical in this regard: a large colony of

Factory sheds near Terni

brick-built sheds with now cracked glass panels in their sloping roofs crowned with a couple of soaring smoke-stacks. It could be that these indicators of lives more gritty than prayerful strike a dissonant note being placed so close to the massive basilica of Santa Maria degli Angeli, were it not the case that even often in their abandonment they display a surprising elegance. Their mellow brick solidity recalls the terracotta churches of Umbrian towns like Città della Pieve, and even their slender chimneys—with a healthy dose of imagination—could be descendants of the medieval *torre*. Certainly they jar less in the romantic mind than the universally uninspired architecture of the McDonald's restaurant also visible from the train halted at Assisi.

Nor are these industrial premises always by any means in an advanced stage of decay as at Assisi, or outside Spoleto, or in the run in to the Ponte San Giovanni train junction outside Perugia: for example, there is a particularly well-kept chimney attached to a factory which abuts the E45 highway just north of Deruta. I do not think that it can have much direct connection with the industrial processes now followed within the Tecnotessile plant (producers of good quality floor coverings) to which it belongs, for it never seems to have smoke belching out of its top. But it chimes well with the distant view that one begins to get at precisely this point of the spires of Perugia's great churches away on their hill top. (Oh dear, I really must stop slipping back into my natural art-historic register and write something about industry.)

Replacing the brick-built mills, now mainly in decay, are acres of low-level light industrial developments which continue to follow the rail tracks and the main highways of the region. Never intended to be structures of beauty, they do however from time to time sport features of interest and whimsy: towering glass atriums, porticoed façades or crenellated gables, not making any conscious decision about whether Guelph or Ghibelline. I am not sure whether such embellishment makes them more acceptable or less so. However, I have to "come out" as someone who does not object strenuously to the intrusion of industrial elements in a landscape; in fact, it falls into the category of "moderation and intelligibility" which I cited in the Introduction as one of Umbria's main attractions for me. I prefer a lived in and worked upon environment to one without any sign of human activity, including the most modern and technological. The compilers of the Umbria volume in *Le Guide di Dove* agree with me:

From Città di Castello to Terni, from the Trasimene Lake to Norcia, Umbria enchants because of its countryside, but also because of the fragility of an environment which is at perpetual war with industrialization and the dissonances of progress.

Scale is, as ever, perhaps the chief consideration as a criterion of what is and what is not acceptable. Thus the ugly sprawl north of Città di Castello, which extends across almost the whole of the Tiber Valley at this, one of its narrowest points, breaks through the ceiling of acceptable development, as does the gravel mine just south of Acquasparta. The widespread use of concrete posts as opposed to the traditional wooden supports for industrially cultivated vines is something that can jar if they come to dominate a hillside, as does the laying out of photo-cell solar panels across entire riverside fields. As for the cement works just outside Gubbio, one might be led to think it is a kind of surreal joke, so monumental, so dominant is it, in a rather Gothic way, on its otherwise uniformly medieval suburban context. But while we note that art tourism is undoubtedly a local and valued industry, other forms of wealth production are needed to sustain the Umbrian economy. And it is to something (almost) entirely natural, the Marbled Cascades, Le Cascate delle Marmore, of the River Velino, which has been tamed, indeed harnessed to an industrial process, that we next turn. It was presumably alluding to this feature of Terni's environs that the eighteenth-century Viennese playwright and poet, Franz Grillparzer, proclaimed that "here he could live and die", rather than its proto-Mancunian industrialization. And he was not the only one to be won over thus.

Taming the Falls
The ancient Roman mythological and aetiological legend concerning the falls relates (Ovid's *Metamorphoses*) that a nymph called Nera was in love with a shepherd, Velino. Their true love aroused the envy of Juno, who also desired the youth but was too aware of her own dignity to pursue him. She therefore transformed the nymph into a river, the Nera, out of spite and the shepherd cast himself from the cliffs above the river's gorge into her waters, an action he was to perform repeatedly for all eternity until he too was transformed into the river that makes the same leap over the falls.

Cascate delle Marmore

These falls are among the highest in Europe, with a total descent over three different "drops" amounting to almost 550 feet, and deriving their name from the deposits of calcium salts which are visible upon the rocks, giving a marbled effect. Marmore is also the name of the village at the head of the falls. Since 1929 the careful controlling of the flow of the water of the River Velino over the falls from its "holding tank", Lago di Piediluco, into the gorge of the Nera, has meant that up to 530 Megawatts of electricity can be generated from the station at the village of Galleto below. This industrial harnessing of the water's power means that the flow over the falls is far from being constant. In fact, the falls are "switched on and off", reducing the flow to a trickle, a feature of their lost grandeur which inevitably disappoints. A timetable of when you can observe the falls at their best is available even on the visitors' centre website and notice is given by the sounding of a siren as the sluices are opened, with the full force of the falls achieved in just a few minutes after this operation. Normally the falls are "on" for about two hours each day but this is increased in holiday seasons. To get to the best spots to view the waters you now have to pay for an entrance ticket.

The history of the human intervention in this story of nature tamed is fascinating and long. By the mid-third century BC a noxious swamp had gathered on either side of the natural bed of the Velino in the Valley of Rieti, and the Roman consul, Manius Curius Denatus, decreed the construction of a canal in the year 271 BC (il Cavo Curiano) to carry the stagnant waters in the direction of the already existing point of escape into the gorge of the Nera at Marmore. Seasonally or with bad weather, however, this resulted in so much water entering the Nera system that ancient Terni (Interamnia Nahars) was repeatedly threatened by serious flooding. By 54 BC the arguments between Rieti and Terni were so fierce about the respective benefits or dangers of the canal that a lawsuit was brought before the senate, with none other than Marcus Tullius Cicero acting for Rieti. Terni had to do with Aulus Pompeius. Despite the advocacy of the most famous brief of any Roman day, neither Rieti nor Terni scored a victory. Perhaps Pompeius was not such a bad brief after all. Through time, however, the Roman canal became less effective and Terni lived in less fear of flood.

By the end of the Middle Ages more work was needed to drain the swamps and this was first tried in 1422, but completed definitively about a century and a half later after Pope Paul III commissioned his favourite architect and engineer Antonio da Sangallo the Younger to improve the original canal (1545) and then Giovanni Fontana (brother of the more famous Roman architect Domenico) constructed a simple sluice system to regulate the channel's flow; it was completed in 1598. Further engineering works were carried out at the behest of Pope Pius VI in 1787 under the supervision of the architect Andrea Vici, and it is to this restructuring of the channels and their flow that we owe the present organization of this "natural" feature.

Despite their grandeur being the less for not yet having been artificially enhanced, or being of public utility, the falls were well known and a popular natural wonder in antiquity, second only in Umbria to the Fonte del Clitunno in their attractiveness to ancient Roman naturalists and writers. Pliny the Elder includes them in his *Natural History*, and Cicero writes of having visited them in his fact-finding trip for the lawsuit of 54 BC. It was thought that Virgil's account of Lake Amsanctus in Book VII of *The Aeneid*, is based on a visit to Piediluco and the falls.

There's a place in Italy, at the foot of high mountains,
famous, and mentioned by tradition, in many lands,
the valley of Amsanctus: woods thick with leaves hem it in,
darkly, on both sides, and in the centre a roaring torrent
makes the rocks echo, and coils in whirlpools.
There a fearful cavern, a breathing-hole for cruel Dis,
is shown, and a vast abyss, out of which Acheron bursts,
holds open its baleful jaws, into which the Fury,
that hated goddess, plunged, freeing earth and sky.

(Translated by A. S. Kline, 2002)

This literary tradition (almost certainly false) and the sublime feelings of
a real encounter with the falls led James Boswell to note in his *Journal* on
14 February 1765 that he read the quoted passage three times before pro-
nouncing them "prodigious wild". He does not, despite the date of writing,
note a visit to the nearby Basilica of St. Valentine—a missed opportunity,
surely?

Galileo Galilei visited the falls a number of times both while staying
with the noble Federico at Acquasparta or at one of the other family
palaces at the town of Cesi itself, situated very close to the natural wonder.
It seems he also passed that way while journeying to and from his trial at
Rome. By the mid-nineteenth century *le cascate* had become a fixed feature
on the itinerary of the foreign grand tourist's *giro d'Italia*. They are most
notably celebrated by Lord Byron, as he previously had lauded the Fount
of Clitumno. But France and Germany get their classical commentaries
from the pens of Corot and Goethe respectively.

"Horribly beautiful", Byron has it—a change in terminology, then,
since the 1820s, but these stanzas from Canto IV of *Childe Harold's Pilgrimage* have their continuing instant appeal and communicative power.

LXIX

The roar of waters!—from the headlong height
Velino cleaves the wave-worn precipice;
The fall of waters! rapid as the light
The flashing mass foams shaking the abyss;
The hell of waters! where they howl and hiss,

And boil in endless torture; while the sweat
Of their great agony, wrung out from this
Their Phlegethon, curls round the rocks of jet
That gird the gulf around, in pitiless horror set,

LXXII

Horribly beautiful! but on the verge,
From side to side, beneath the glittering morn,
An Iris sits, amidst the infernal surge,
Like Hope upon a deathbed, and, unworn
Its steady dyes, while all around is torn
By the distracted waters, bears serene
Its brilliant hues with all their beams unshorn:
Resembling, mid the torture of the scene,
Love watching Madness with unalterable mien.

A modern sculpture by Peppe di Giuli, a marble bench with a bronze of a nineteenth-century travelling cloak flung over it, stands now in the little terraced garden from where one gets one of the best views of the falls. It carries the inscription of an Italian translation of the most famous of Byron's lines concerning the falls: "*impareggiabil cateratta, orribilmente bella*". It is more than can be said for the sculpture.

CHOCOLATE, WATER AND WINE

If an impressive cascade, perhaps even "horribly beautiful" depending on taste, is what you are seeking, then every October some of Perugia's fountains flow with liquid chocolate for a weekend. It is not an occurrence to which I personally look forward with any pleasure, not liking my chocolate melted. But these are the showpieces for the mammoth Euro-chocolate event staged by the Perugina confectionery brand, which now forms part of the Nestlé group. Founded in 1908 as Perugina-Buitoni, it kept its local management until the last years of the twentieth century. *Baci*, literally "kisses", are the most recognizable of the confections produced here; darkish chocolate truffles crowned with a hazelnut and individually wrapped in distinctive silver and blue foil, they also contain, hidden in the wrapping, a printed message, fortune cookie-like, of a sweetness even more cloying than the chocolate. All sorts of high cocoa content bars have recently been added to the product range, appealing undoubtedly to the more refined palate. A visit to the chocolate factory is occasionally on offer but it has yet to be developed into the tourist attraction on the scale of Cadbury World at Bourneville near Birmingham, that is with the exception of the Euro-chocolate weekend.

If, alternatively, it is a theme park on a modern, industrial scale appealing to all the family that you are looking for, Umbria and the environs of Perugia have at least il Parco del Sole on offer. Based at Collazone between Deruta and Todi, Sun Park is a miniature safari park covering about 1.5 square miles, which tries to recreate a suitable habitat for various (formerly) wild animals from around the world. One of its founding principles is to provide local children with the opportunity to study a range of wild animals close up. The range of wildlife includes deer, goats, oxen and boar from among the local fauna, and zebra, camels, lamas and red pandas from foreign species. The lake is furnished with over thirty species of migratory wild birds. Fortunately, the Umbrian mania for hunting is not encouraged within its gates. There are no fully-fledged fairground rides *à la* Bush Gardens in Florida, but the park boasts a bar, a play area for children and even a football field—and all this for only €7 for adults and €5 for children under twelve.

Deruta, a stone's throw from Sun Park, is, after Assisi, one of Umbria's small towns most visited by bussed-in tourists. Here is found the highest

Deruta ceramics

concentration of outlets for one of Umbria's most distinctive consumer products: the painted ceramics known as majolica, *maiolica*. More properly typical of the area around Gualdo Tadino (and with some excellent smaller workshops still functioning in that town), these brightly coloured pottery pieces include items as diverse as a simple salt cellar to a huge table top. Vast showrooms are directly accessible from the E45 superstrada carrying the shoppers to Deruta from north or south. Further exploration of the pretty *centro storico* reveal a beautiful church with a fine Perugino, and more to our point, an excellent regional museum dedicated to the development of the majolica industry from its simpler craft origins.

Making the most of what nature has given you can have no better example than the industrial treatment and direct sale of a local mineral water, and here Umbria is foremost in Italian regions. Joining Rocchetta as some of the most successfully marketed Italian mineral waters are those of San Gémini and San Faustino, with both their sources just north of Terni, and Nocera lower down the Toppino Valley than the source of Rocchetta at Gualdo Tadino. These sources are found along the geological fault which has also been responsible over the centuries for the destructive seismic activity seen in Umbria. To keep everybody calm, however, there is usually a spa hotel in park surroundings outside the industrial plants which control the mineralogical blueprint of these products (how much sodium, iodine and other minerals are present) before the bottling process itself. Thus the elegant, almost *belle-époque* image of these waters goes beyond the retro feel of the packaging—San Gémini in particular. Even though the bottles are now produced in plastic, their green colour and complex curvature recall the blown glass originals, not to mention the highly conservative typography of the labels. Water is clearly a serious business which demands the confidence of producer and client in a perfect equilibrium. And the product undoubtedly appeals to the Umbrian, and indeed Italian, natural conservatism when it comes to matters of health and nutrition. It would take a miracle to change the habits of even just a few generations.

And if it is a miracle that we are looking for, can we do better than that which transforms Umbrian water into wine? Wine has been produced in the region since pre-Roman times, as is evident from the complex wine-drinking paraphernalia found in Etruscan tombs and the scenes of feasting depicted on their walls. Pliny the Younger also describes the vineyards which clothed the slopes of the hills around his villa, although none of the wines prized by the Romans such as Falernian came from here; south Italian vintages were on the whole preferred. Until modern times commentators have noted that viticulture was pretty haphazard throughout the region, vines being kept but jumbled up in both fields and garden plots together with other crops. The exception to this rule is the wine that was produced in Orvieto's immediate hinterland, which for centuries has earned a significant reputation, especially in the variety of dry whites which are still well-known today. The semi-sweet *abboccato* and even Orvietan red wines were both also historically celebrated in the nearby urban centres, and some reds are again being produced here with success.

The grape varieties which abound are the rough and ready, bumper fruiting *sangiovese* and *trebbiano*, though from very ancient times the *greco* grape (thought to have been introduced as its name implies by Greek immigrants) was very common. Only around twenty per cent of Umbrian wine production is classified as DOC, Denominazione di Origine Controllata (Declared to be of Assessed Origin): this is a far smaller proportion than, say, the wines of Tuscany. Orvieto Classico still represents the best-known of the better wines, though the Vale of Umbria vintages from around Torgiano and the red wines, especially the *sagrantino* of Montefalco, and more widely the whole of the Martani hills producers, have a growing following from wine lovers. Both Orvieto Classico and Sagrantino di Montefalco include wines which fall into the highest category of all, that termed DOCG, Denominazione di Origine Controllata e Garantita, Declared to be of Assessed and Guaranteed Origin. (Add an extra word and everything is changed.)

The name sagrantino comes from our old friend the *sagra*, the summer food festival, since in its origin this grape variety was typically semi-dried and used to create a *passito,* a fortified wine regularly served at these village festivals. It is a fairly recent development to employ this grape in the production of a dry red, of considerable strength and body.

The wine producer Lungarotti, based in Torgiano, is the best-known name in the region, and it has almost cornered the market in the Perugia area, and perhaps won the war when it comes to aggressive marketing throughout the rest of Italy and beyond. Many smaller wineries abound in the area, however, and produce worthy products. Ian Campbell Ross is particularly acute in his consideration of what is on offer:

Such wines do not come cheaply, of course, but Umbria still offers superb value in wines that are not yet as well known as they deserve to be. The wines of Montefalco, for instance are excellent—particularly from the top makers, who include Adanti, Benincasa, Arnaldo Caprai, Decio Fongoli, Rocca di Fabbri and the Tenuta Val di Maggio. Adanti, in particular, offer a *rosso d'Arquata* which remains among the best value wine of the entire region.

He sounds like he knows what he is talking about.

Visits to these producers not only offer the opportunity to taste the contents of the *cantina*, but also to see the industrial process involved in wine production. Typically the harvested grapes are brought by tractor to an open concrete floor built into the slope of a hill, beneath which to a depth of up to three storeys is the processing plant. Thus the grapes can be passed through pipes set into the concrete directly into the fermentation vats beneath. This is done with as little human handling as possible, avoiding the removal of the bacteria necessary for natural fermentation. The vats themselves are now huge steel cylinders with all the complexity of modern control of pressure, sugar content and temperature strung about them. Previously concrete vats were used, but, of course, the role of oak casks to age and give character is still essential to the process.

Other areas which produce DOC-grade wines are to be found in the upper Valley of the Tiber, around Lake Trasimene, and the Amerini hills around the southern town of Amelia. But countless other producers such as my own favourite, Donini in Verna, continue to make wine which never achieves or indeed aspires to this accolade. It is still very much worth drinking.

To have found so much that is watery and more than a little inebriating in our consideration of industrial Umbria may have come as something of a surprise. It is not quite the steel-making myth of Terni's dark satanic mills, and I have yet to drink a dry white from Manchester. But to treat a natural product with a seriousness which maintains and promotes its enjoyment, which skillfully transforms it from being a luxury into a daily pleasure, is another element of the Umbrian character as far as I have been able to identify it. And it is undoubtedly one to which I am more than willing to drink.

Chapter Fourteen

THE MUSIC FESTIVAL

CONTEMPORARY UMBRIA I

It all started with a long held musical chord. The six instrumentalists bent into their bows, drawing them expertly across their viols' strings, and a feeling of intense pleasure, not far removed from pain, welled up inside me, the physical reaction to the magic of this music. I could do nothing about the tears rolling down my cheeks except screw up my eyes ever tighter. As I was in the front row of the audience only the players themselves might have registered the effect their music was having on me, and they surely were far too involved to notice or indeed to care. Here I was, on a warm, late summer evening, sitting in the exquisite Oratorio di San Crescentino decorated with frescoes by Luca Signorelli. Here almost outrageously, as it seemed to me, I was just outside the village of Morra, listening to the world-renowned viol consort, Fretwork, play a piece written by William Lawes, a seventeenth-century English composer hitherto unknown to me. The church was full, and the whole audience seemed acutely aware that it was witnessing something out of the ordinary.

The recital was part of the 2009 Festival Delle Nazioni, the 42nd edition of this north Umbrian concert series. I had already, a couple of days before, attended the opening concert in the Church of San Domenico at Città di Castello. Then it had been an Italian string orchestra directed by an English conductor in a programme of serenades by Elgar, Britten and Holst. Each year a different nation was picked as the partner with Italy to make a theme for the festival—this year the lot had fallen on Great Britain. Bizarrely I found myself representing the British Embassy at the opening concert and thus received special-guest treatment, including an invitation to comment on the accuracy of a Union flag made entirely from dried flowers. With some difficulty I dredged up from my memory the correct arrangement of thinner and thicker diagonals and proclaimed definitively that the flag was not upside-down: *Bravissima, Signora, non è capovolta.*

The festival programme draws on a fairly narrow variety of musical styles, the folk group Fairport Convention providing the most substantial element of difference from a largely classical content in 2009. There was a production of Britten's children's opera *The Little Sweep* in Castello's charming little nineteenth-century theatre, and other venues for solo and duet recitals included some of the prettiest and most interesting churches in the upper Tiber Valley zone. The festival is largely funded from advertising and local generosity, with a small public subsidy. Its scale for an arts festival is therefore appropriately modest, but its artistic standards are disproportionately high.

The Festival delle Nazioni is probably the second most important Umbrian classical music festival, eclipsed only by the internationally renowned Festival dei Due Mondi, founded at Spoleto by the Italian composer Giancarlo Menotti. But the cumulative effect of the two three-week events, Spoleto in early, and delle Nazioni in late, summer, gives a distinct boost to Umbria's cultural credentials. Otherwise they might be considered undernourished in comparison with other Italian regions. There is no repertory opera house in Umbria, and although small-scale summer festivals present lyric theatre pieces all over the region (the Mozart Opera festival over *ferragosto*, for example, at tiny Preggio) and some touring companies visit local theatres, the genre depends on its outings at Spoleto to command an international reputation.

The Spoleto Festival (the name most commonly given to the Festival dei due Mondi) was established in 1958 after Menotti had toured a number of central Italian towns considering their suitability for his artistic plans, the creation of a meeting place for the performance worlds of America and Europe, the "two worlds" of the festival's official title. It was the presence of a couple of reasonably sized theatres in the town and the scenic possibilities of the Piazza del Duomo as the venue for gala occasions that settled his choice there. It was the maestro's intention that all art forms would be represented in the festival, which he personally oversaw with the help of artistic directors, latterly his adopted son Francis, for 49 years. He died just months before the opening of the 50th festival in 2007. However, and probably inevitably with the founder's reputation as one of the most prolific and performed opera composers of the second half of the twentieth century, it has been the musical and theatrical elements that have predominated. Menotti's aim at Spoleto was to showcase the avant-garde of both America and Europe within the context of a respect for the classical and the traditional. Predominantly the festival's weight has been placed in hosting international performers rather than providing opportunities for Italian artists.

A similar guiding principle of encouraging international artists informs the work of the Civitella Ranieri Association, housed in the splendidly restored medieval fortress of that name two miles east of Umbertide. Here, summer long, sculptors, graphic artists, poets, novelists and composers are given six week scholarships, with the provision of housing, studio space and wonderful food. The only return they have to make is to give a presentation of their work to their fellows and to members of the Friends of Civitella, a database of over five hundred local names considered proficient in English and of a sufficiently culture-vulture temperament to form a suitable audience. Recently I have attended the musical presentations of composers from India and Spain, readings by Argentinian and Sierra Leonian authors, and slide shows of works by German and British installation artists. It is all a bit unexpected in this quintessentially Umbrian architectural setting but undeniably enjoyable. For culture-vultures, that is.

The various architectural locales which have been used for festival performance in Spoleto's ancient heart have also maximized the impact of that beautiful, but relatively little-known and untouched, city centre. Thus il Teatro Nuovo, the New Theatre, has generally housed opera and theatre pieces and the Teatro Caio Melisso orchestral concerts. The remains of the Roman Theatre (see Chapter Three) play host to classical ballet whilst the tiny Teatrino delle Sei usually stages modern dance pieces. As well as the Piazza del Duomo the courtyard of Cardinal Albornoz's castle has also been used to stage outdoor concerts and plays. The Church of San Eufemia was the setting for sacred music, while the Auditorium della Stella and the San Nicolò complex of buildings have hosted conferences and readings.

Unfortunately, after a series of ground-breaking festivals in the first thirty or so years of its existence and the creation of parallel festivals in Charleston, USA from 1977 and Melbourne, Australia from 1986, the artistic direction lost some of its robustness, perhaps to be expected as the maestro's long life stretched into its ninth decade. Financial and administrative problems also surfaced in the early years of the new millennium. This led Francesco Rutelli, the Arts Minister in the left-of-centre and short-lived Prodi government, to intervene in the festival's affairs in the autumn of 2007. He appointed as director Giorgio Ferrara, who has subsequently presented scaled-down but critically acclaimed festivals 51 to 53. Personally, I recall even as late as 1997 the thrill of attending a wonderful production of Prokofiev's epic opera based on Tolstoy's even more epic novel, *War and Peace,* under the baton of the late and much lamented British conductor, Richard Hickox. Yet it cannot be denied that the reputation of the Spoleto Festival was in doubt and that now, following unusually decisive state intervention, it seems assured. Umbria still retains its artistic jewel-in-the-crown.

Umbria Jazz

The other seam of musical celebrity which Umbria mined in the second part of the twentieth century was undoubtedly the festival known as Umbria Jazz (UJ). It was born on 23 August 1973 and proved enormously popular in the early years of its existence—in fact too popular. The concerts were free, and attracted huge numbers of jazz enthusiasts from around

Umbria blows its own horn

the world, often momentarily doubling the population of the series of Umbrian towns which took it in turns to present the concerts. The venues included Piazza del Popolo in Todi, Piazza IV Novembre in Perugia, Gubbio's Roman theatre and the Albornoz fortress at Spoleto, and often the vast numbers of spectators camped out in each of these small towns' public spaces created difficulties of access even for the performers. Count Basie's orchestra was notoriously marooned in a sea of sleeping bags at its Todi appearance.

The crisis came in 1976 as UJ became highly politicized. Local critics abhorred the destruction of Umbria's famed peace and quiet, a religious procession was disrupted in Todi, white musicians perceived as middle-class were booed by left-wing fans, and the presence of large numbers of police officers raised the tension to such an extent that what should have been a holiday atmosphere was transformed into the juxtaposition of armed camps. The 1977 festival was subsequently cancelled.

The following year saw the return of a modified festival which sought to resolve the overcrowding issues by programming two concerts in different towns on each night. However, the ensuing complexity of organization and a loss of regional support for the initiative saw the closure of the festival in its original form that year.

With the retreat of the public regional authorities and tourist agency from their involvement in UJ it took until 1982 for the festival to re-emerge under private voluntary direction, which gradually grew into the charity L'Associazone Umbria Jazz, ultimately becoming La Fondazione UJ, which re-established some public funding for the event. In these years of consolidation the moving forces were the organizing genius of Renzo Arbore and the artistic direction of Carlo Pagnotta. Although the festival had undoubtedly lost some of its initial freshness by being reduced in scale, restricting its performances to venues in Perugia and charging for entrance, these developments enabled it to continue in the last twenty and more years. It has also widened its appeal by broadening its repertoire to include not only classic jazz but other elements from "black music" (gospel, soul, rhythm and blues) and the occasional sally into the more general field of pop-rock. Thus such world renowned performers and bands as Elton John, Carlos Santana, James Brown, Donna Summer, Eric Clapton, Earth Wind and Fire and Simply Red have shared the bill with Miles Davis, Oscar Peterson, Wynton Marsalis and Dizzie Gillespie.

If these festivals contribute to music-making on a world scale, what of Umbria's native musical and artistic talent which while acknowledging itself as more modest still holds its head up? Well, two years ago a gifted young rock singer, Annalisa Baldi, from Tuoro, overlooking Lake Trasimene, got to the finals of the Italian X Factor talent show, since when national appearances, and a recording contract, have supplemented her already regular local gigs. Annalisa made it to television, the current global criterion for celebrity and success, whereas thousands of other performers maintain an artistic life with appearances limited to small venues scattered throughout the region. Posters abound along the winding roads inviting you to Enzo's accordion concert at the *locale*, nightspot, or other similarly unappealing sounding events. I have a sneaking suspicion that attending one such event might be more exciting than I fear. But I will leave it to you to fill me in on this one.

International visitors, too, have enjoyed contributing to the patchwork quilt variety (and quality) of Umbria's particularly summer artistic offerings. While resident in the Morra Valley, Lisa St. Aubin de Terán founded a cinema festival at little Montone, together with filmmaker and "ex-Python" Terry Gilliam—himself a regular visitor to the area. This more than simply worthy event (though it cannot be denied with some less than professional standards—time-keeping above all) ran for a number of years during the late 1990s and early 2000s, and brought a great deal of pleasure to and support from both a native and expatriate audience. It continues spasmodically and on a much reduced scale now that the "names" have moved on.

MUSICAL CULTURE

Considering the proliferation of such localizing of music and drama and wanting to draw some general conclusions about the Umbrian state of affairs in this field, I turned to an old friend, Colin Baldy. A British musician who has spent a lot of time in Italy over the past fifteen or so years, Colin finally bought a pretty town house in the Nera Valley *commune* of Scheggino. Although a performer himself (singing and directing for Handmade Opera), he has spent most of his professional career as a choir director, singing teacher and coach, work that with his appropriate language skills he has been able to extend easily into the Italian and even Umbrian context. Engaged by such major towns as Terni to "fix" various musical events for them (a 2004 visit of Canterbury Cathedral Choir, for example), Colin has also had a profound effect on the musical culture of his adopted town. There are only 300 people living in the centre of this commune, best known to history as the place defended by its women folk during a surprise thirteenth-century attack from a neighbouring hostile community. Even adding all the outlying farms and *case sparse* the total population scarcely rises beyond 500 souls.

And yet it is from this community, or more directly from its sympathetic mayor, that Colin has been able to attract (admittedly only small) sums of money to invest in musical projects that otherwise would have been undreamed of here—performances of foreign choral classics such as Handel's *Messiah* and Bach's *Easter Oratorio*, and a 300th anniversary performance of Handel's early Roman piece, *La Resurrezione*. And these have been consistently well-supported and patronized by all the commune's inhabitants.

But why in this country famed globally for its musical lyricism and in this region where small, gem-like theatres abound, and internationally known festivals maintain a strong profile, does it take an incomer to transform local musical life? Our conversation turned to the operation of the well-regarded music conservatories found in Perugia and Terni. Colin's experience of these centres for musical training was that they provided little more than the county musical services to be found in the United Kingdom, and other similar schemes in countries with dominant Anglo-Saxon cultures; that although graduates from this system all earned the designation *maestro*, "master", such universal acclaim and easy dignity led to low levels of aspiration and expectation; that customarily all classical musicians with ambition had to leave Italy to "make it". What is more, the teaching involved in these music schools was purposefully "narrow", focusing on a single discipline study, i.e. just one musical instrument and that exhaustively, whereas typically in German, British and North American musical contexts, instrumentalists would be expected to sing in the conservatoire choir and play in its orchestra rather than simply concentrate on becoming soloists. This creation of solo performers results in a gap between high and low cultures with the most profound negative effects manifesting themselves at the good amateur level. Similarly, the death of a church music tradition once prevalent, and particularly the playing of the organ in church, seems to have led to a steep decline in the general musical culture of the region and indeed the whole country.

Together we observed that in Umbria the energy and attention to detail lavished on the genre of *corteo storico* (such as those described in Chapters Five, Six and Seven), with their beautiful pageantry and superb costuming, significantly dominate the same market which amateur dramatics integrated with local music making do in other European and North American cultures. Such factors (like Scheggino's own Festa delle Donne, an annual historical re-enactment of its thirteenth-century female bellicosity mentioned above) do not rule out enthusiastic support when opportunities for good music to be cherished appear, such as the abundance of regional festivals and in Colin's own work. However, the regional lack of direction, or more to the point funding, with the exception of lending its "distinguished support" (*alto padronato*) guarantees this general denigration of standards. Despite much of the gloom which this account suggests, it is perhaps even because of these conditions that Colin Baldy is excited and engaged by the opportunities that Umbria offers as a place for music making both by visitors and locals. He has even revived the church choir in his tiny town, to much grass-roots acclaim.

Colin has yet to try to revive the *banda*, the town brass band, another tradition once prized in Scheggino, and indeed universally through Umbria, and yet which has dwindled dramatically in recent years. Even so, the following claim can still be made by Beatrice Monacelli in a recent academic study of this musical phenomenon:

> The Town Band today then is not simply a cultural phenomenon which is lost in the past, or in other words, on the way to dying out. Social and economic changes in the immediate post-war period and then the economic revival of the 1960s have brought about deep changes in the organization of minor Italian centres and the town band in many cases has been "remodeled" according to these circumstances and has assumed new roles and modern forms.

The classical formalization of the town band was in fact only a recent twentieth-century development, previously having represented an enormous range of local diversity. It was only when Colonel Vassella, director of the Royal Italian Army's wide variety of musical services, laid down in

Italian town band

1911 exactly which elements a band should contain (including the new fangled sousaphone) that the "ideal" configuration of instruments emerged. It then became standard and ubiquitous in the Fascist period. Laid down were other principles such as the expectation that instruments should belong to the commune, but be lent to aspirant players during an "apprenticeship". This consisted of the period during which the players would receive instruction by the local senior "incumbent" of the flute, trombone or trumpet. Such a structure is easily recognizable as establishing a craftsman philosophy for this music making rather than that of the developed romantic, artistic ideal of the musician in eighteenth- or nineteenth-century terms. So popular *was* this form of music that a regular weekly hour-long show dedicated to a different band on the national radio station Rai 3 even today maintains a rather precarious toehold in the scheduling. The programme is reminiscent of the slot on BBC Radio 4 called *Bells on Sunday*, during which peals of church bells from across the UK are broadcast; a slot which has got shorter and shorter, and earlier and earlier in the Sunday morning schedules over the years. For bandsman in Italy, we could read British bell-ringer, or should that be *vice versa*.

I have to admit having enjoyed the town band performances which I have attended. Wearing their far-from Ruritanian uniforms—the bandsfolk resembling at most local post-office officials—they collect in some peripheral square from where they are to process while sounding their instruments on the occasion of the religious or seasonal festivity. They are to be found across the region, if still more common in the north: Umbertide, for example, sports quite a well-known ensemble considering the town's small size and limited cultural aspirations. One has a feeling that the marching tunes which they blast out were all composed by their various leaders across the century or so of their formal existence. And it is this home-grown, rough-and-ready quality which provides their principal charm. Long may it survive to keep challenging the Umbrian tradition (and especially its financial patronage bodies) which has lost too much of its musical heritage already.

I asked Colin Baldy to tell me what he considered the best and worst things about the musical climate in Umbria. The first is easy: the wonderfully appreciative audience that any music making attracts. The second: a lack of appreciation of what it really takes to stage an event, concert or festival; the easy words are there, the good intentions abound but are not then translated into action. Asked for an anecdote describing both good and bad, Colin remembers a concert mounted by the commune of Campanello, the small Vale of Umbria town just south of Trevi. Following meetings with the town council's sponsored committee six months earlier Colin fixed the singers and musicians. They subsequently and dutifully gathered at the beautiful parish church in Campanello *in alto*, the upper town, an hour before the concert was due to start, only to find that contrary to agreement there was no piano in the venue. Pointing this out to the organizers led to them simply asking whether the show could not go on without a piano? When answered with a firm negative they shrugged their shoulders and said that they would organize the delivery of a piano— this now minutes before the scheduled start of the concert. An hour later, true to their word, and only minutes before the departure of the exasperated performers, an open-back pick-up arrived bearing a piano from who knows where. The show went on, rather inelegantly (you try moving an upright piano in evening dress), and more than an hour late—but as Colin notes wryly, it was still a fantastic concert.

Chapter Fifteen
MODERNITY AND TRADITION
CONTEMPORARY UMBRIA II

Arriving by train in Perugia on a cold and snowy March lunchtime would not be my recommended experience for accessing Umbria's most modern face. First of all there is no fast train to the region's capital; a choice awaits the traveller from Rome of taking the express to Foligno (comfortable and just one stop at Terni) and then changing to the *regionale*, which chugs its way past Assisi, waiting for an age at Perugia Ponte San Giovanni, before finally climbing up the gentle but relentless spur to Perugia Centrale. Or you could take the (slowest) train from Rome to Florence, get out after more than two hours at Terontola on the shore of Lake Trasimene, and wait for a connection "backwards" as it were to the metropolis' main station. The fastest you could perform these procedures would be a few minutes short of four hours, and this in a country with a train service that now boasts a three-hour link between Milan and Rome, more than three times the distance. And yet it was from Perugia that Benito Mussolini arrived in Rome by train to complete his famous "march" on the nation's capital in 1922, and the occasion on which he declared his aim that the trains would run on time during his regime. "On time", perhaps, but not necessarily speedily—and the same is true some ninety years later.

I had an hour to wait before I needed to be at yet another of the town's rail stations, Perugia Sant'Anna, terminus of the North Tiber Line, which runs between Perugia and San Sepulchro, to continue my journey north. With time to kill, then, I thought to treat myself to a diversionary hyper-modern experience: a spin on the Minimetrò, the city's latest addition to an integrated public transport system. But the first thing to do was to find it.

The official in Perugia Centrale's information office, with a grizzled beard and short of breath, denied all knowledge of the shuttle's existence, let alone the location of its stations, but recommended that I try the information kiosk for buses on the station's forecourt. I explained to the young woman there that I needed to transfer stations and had about an hour to do it and wondered whether it might be possible to do that and ride the Minimetrò at the same time. She regarded me, through the slight mist formed by my freezing breath and the drizzly snowflakes swirling around her cosy green booth, as if I were mad. There was a perfectly good bus that passed the station every twenty minutes and would carry me directly to the Sant'Anna terminus in a quarter of an hour at the cost of €1, she explained, as if to an idiot child. In any case, the Minimetrò went nowhere near Sant'Anna and there was not a station nearby from which to take it in any case. I thanked her, bought my bus ticket, located the stop where it would pass, and hit upon the wheeze of spending my few minutes of modernity in the nearby McDonald's. The bus, when taken, was fine but extremely crowded with kids breaking from school and heading for the same station as me. I promised myself a return visit, perhaps in better weather, to locate the fabled *mezzo*, means of transport.

Keeping my promise on a pleasant April morning (the snow thankfully now retreated to the Alps), and after a preparatory visit to the system's website and to one of the city's tourist information offices, I cannot really say that I was surprised to find that the Minimetrò in fact passes within a minute's walk of Perugia Centrale and indeed terminates at a station no more than three minutes' downhill stroll to Sant'Anna. The truth is that no one from Perugia actually seems to use it. Not *cattiveria*, malice, then, on the part of my informants, just straightforward ignorance.

As I have had reason to explain elsewhere Perugia is among the most spectacular of Italian cities, and certainly of Umbria, as well as being one of the most disorientating, simply because of its location—spread across three spurs of a high hill. Only careful study of a map, or an aerial view, can really fix the city in the mind and prepare one for passing from one part of it to another. And when walkers finally do venture forth to explore in the increasingly pedestrian-only city centre they soon encounter the hills. Listen to what Henry James has to say in describing it:

> From the hill on which the town is planted radiate a dozen ravines, down whose sides the houses slide and scramble with an alarming indifference to the cohesion of their little rugged blocks of flinty red stone. You ramble really nowhither without emerging on some small court or terrace that throws your view across a gulf of tangled gardens or vine-

yards and over to a cluster of serried black dwellings which have to hollow in their backs to keep their balance on the opposite ledge.

Today, however, some 150 years on, in confronting this daunting terrain you are helped almost everywhere by the construction of moving stairways or even elevators, which take the pain out of a steep ascent. These were built in a specific programme in the 1970s and 1980s to replace the tramways which had not long survived the end of the Second World War. Motor traffic had traditionally used a series of road tunnels which cut beneath the peaks and so avoided the necessity of hairpin, inner-city ascents, while few streets of the true intramural *centro storico* would ever have been suitable for cars. Designated car parking outside the city walls came to Perugia early in town planning terms and the variety of responses of how to get people from the lower zones to the high centre included small shuttle buses and an amplification and integration of the moving stairways and elevators. Perugia has thus for some time claimed the right to be considered modern in its public amenity response to the given terrain. Only the very recent addition of an elevator connecting Spoleto's Piazza del Duomo with the Rocca Albornoz comes close elsewhere in Umbria to matching the inventive thoroughness of Perugia's attempts to assist the pedestrian.

James noted this thoroughness in the 1870s.

> Even Perugia is going the way of all Italy—straightening out her streets, preparing her ruins, laying her venerable ghosts. The castle is being completely "remis à neuf"—a Massachusetts schoolhouse couldn't cultivate a "smarter" ideal. There are shops in the basement and fresh putty on all the windows; so that the only thing proper to a castle it has kept is its magnificent position and range, which you may enjoy from the broad platform where the Perugini assemble at eventide.

Earlier, the ancient Romans' re-founding of the Etruscan city employed the cutting-edge town planning of the *coloniae* by managing to devise the intersection at right angles of its two main streets, as noted in Chapter One, the *cardo* (Corso Vanucci) and *decumanus* (Via dei Priori)—the extreme gradient of the latter dictated by their meeting near the location of the *forum*, at the summit of the hill, in the vicinity of today's Piazza

IV Novembre. Urban planning here, then, seems always to have been an example of the ideal triumphing over truly testing conditions. And so to the Minimetrò (pronounced, you will note, with the accent on the final syllable—very useful for British readers who might otherwise be tempted to mix it up with a popular small car of the 1980s).

I finally encountered it by making my way to its inner city terminus, the so-called Fermata Pincetto. This pleasant terracing planted with pine trees and looking more or less due east is immediately next to the only general covered market in the centre of the city, itself quite difficult to locate for non-locals. You gain access through a narrow passage close to the excellent Risorante del Sole, itself boasting spectacular panoramic views (as well as superb *cotoletta alla bolognese*), and the atrium leading from the spacious, elegantly planted terrace is all rust-red brick, terracotta tiles and high arching steel and glass—the perfect marriage between new and Umbrian old. From this ticket hall (a ticket to ride for 75 minutes across the whole range of integrated transport services costs €1.50) you take either an elevator or escalator to the lower level from which the carriages depart, or rather pass, for they literally are individual carriages (rather than

A *minimetrò* carriage

trains) in a kind of perpetual fairground motion. And they are driverless: a series of people-carriers on a funicular railway model, traveling at a steady fifteen miles an hour. Seating only eight persons and with further capacity for twelve standing, these circulating bubble-like containers seem both in some way comical and at the same time reassuringly well-designed. What to call them? "Pods"? Too techno. "Capsules"? Overly space-age. I am going to stick with carriages, since there is in fact something twee, even retro about them for all their modernity. Various instructions in a trio of languages amplified by neat graphics explain the prohibited forms of behaviour (not much more than no smoking or jumping out of the moving conveyance) and those not permitted to ride (dogs—shame—and unaccompanied infants—understood).

The first part of the journey (with just me and an old lady who has been to the general market) is a steep, underground descent passing through an illuminated and coffered tunnel reminiscent of countless sci-fi fantasy sequences. One is tempted to believe that we are on the verge of achieving escape velocity. However, when the carriage emerges into the open air after its first two stations it is the atmosphere of the fairground that returns. Sliding down the terraced hillside, passing pleasantly constructed, park-like walks which follow the contours of the hill and gaudily painted children's play areas, there is something almost Swiss in its neat, miniature scale. And I might add, something verging on the creepy in its apparent commitment to public utility and moderate pleasure, tidying up the chaotic tumble of downhill construction as described by Henry James in the passage cited above. After a few stops we return to something more like Umbrian normality as we near the late twentieth-century urban sprawl and modest high rises of the business district around the Stazione Centrale. It would have been from this elevated station and section of track that I would have taken the Minimetrò the first time that I enquired of it had anyone actually known of its whereabouts.

On the dinky carriage sweeps, following a broad curve and now a far gentler decline through some well-designed and well-kept modern housing blocks used both by the students of the Perugia University and also providing low-cost public accommodation. The buildings thin out as we reach a large sports complex and then there is just one more stop to go before the shopping centre and acres of parking provided at the Minimetrò's out-of-town terminus, Pian di Massiano. The whole journey, passing through the seven stations, has lasted just eighteen minutes and I have been transported just over two and a half miles. I alight, visit the shiny public conveniences of the terminal, and then spring on to a returning carriage, this time joined by some Japanese youngsters for the ascent back to my point of departure. A strangely, even puzzlingly, gratifying experience.

The Minimetrò Spa (equivalent of Co. Ltd.) is so modern and up-to-date that it has a mission statement (of predictable blandness):

> The purpose of Minimetrò Spa is clear and important: to bring into effect a form of mass public transportation which is an alternative to that provided by cars and buses with a particularly innovative technology (Underground Lite), which will speedily connect strategic parts of the city (from Pian di Massiano to Monteluce).
>
> It is an important public work for Perugia, which, thirty years after the creation of the moving staircases, can now become again a point of reference both in Italy and throughout Europe for solutions to be adopted in the field of alternative transportation. Minimetrò Spa is the company which will achieve all this.

The Minimetrò was first mooted in 1998 in the Regional Council. It received a *nulla osta* legal go-ahead (literally "no objection" stemming from the terminology of the old papal government) in 2001 when the cost was projected at €60,716,516.77. (Don't you just love those seventy-seven euro cents?) How many times would it have to be revisited? Seven times? Or seventy times seven? In fact, by the beginning of the work on 4 November 2002 the budget had risen to a somewhat rounder €71,006,000.00. The project was entrusted to the over-all oversight of the French architect Jean Nouvel, who would design each of the seven stations and integrate the engineering with the design concept as a whole. The system finished and ready to run was inaugurated on 29 January 2008, the feast day of San Costanzo, one of the city's three patron saints. I wish I had been there to see the civic junketing, for surely there would have been some distinct discomfort in the mixture of tradition and innovation.

Let me give you an example, in miniature, of what it might have been like. Trestina, a hamlet which has recently quadrupled in size with the boom in the tobacco market, had until recently a rather congested centre. By taking the route via the industrial estate, a few yards nearer to the course of the Tiber than Trestina's main drag, you could always escape the cluster of bars, post office, video rental store and ironmongers and the central crossroads perpetually subject to small-scale traffic jams. But you no longer need to do this. That is since the opening of *the* "roundabout". This extraordinary civic engineering feat, a six-foot diameter circle in *pietra serena*, the local friable grey granite, filled in with brick work and deposited in the middle of a relatively busy and just conceivably marginally dangerous road junction, was solemnly opened by the mayor, with his tricolour sash, attended by representatives of the *vigili urbani* and *carabinieri*, and about four other people.

I happen to know this because I passed in my car at precisely the moment the elected representative of the people was reading his speech on the pavement facing the roundabout. It only wanted the parish priest with a bucket of holy water to bless it to augment the level of absurdity to the maximum. I imagine the opening of the Minimetrò was something similar but obviously scaled up from Trestina size to that of regional capital—and I doubt that we were wanting the presence of the archbishop, or indeed holy water, in Perugia.

A Modern Saint

Though very much present for his community, albeit in the rather etiolated form of an exposed holy mummy-like relic, and thus not up to wielding a holy water sprinkler, my favourite Umbrian bishop, St. Ubaldo of Gubbio, has recently been subjected to a series of extraordinarily modern scientific procedures. The guidebook on sale about his life at the hilltop shrine high above his city is fulsome (and not at all squeamish) in its explanation and even illustration of the medical tests to which his remains have been subject since the dawn of our intrusively inquisitive era. I have always been fascinated by relics when they are visibly whole bodies, and whole Ubaldo most definitely is—one imagines that he has been in small demand elsewhere and therefore escaped holy dismembering. He could hardly be called "incorrupt", however, a description generally awarded to the most popular saints, since he has shrivelled somewhat over the centuries—or at least I hope he has. You would have to be remarkably unfortunate to look like that in life.

The saint is on display above the high altar of the church dedicated to his memory and which forms the finishing post of the Corsa dei Ceri described in Chapter Six. If you are not inclined to emulate the muscular Christianity, or downright madness, of the *ceri* teams by running up Monte Ingino you can use one of Umbria's other ingenious and (relatively) modern forms of public transport: the *funivia,* cable car. I have to admit that it was this wonderful conveyance as much as the charm of the local saint which first truly endeared Gubbio to me. You depart from a cute little station at the far end of town, more or less where the old defensive walls begin their effortful climb up the lower slopes of the mountain. And at first the prospect of the trip seems like something out of Disneyworld. Not for long. The cabins do not really deserve that determination, resembling more the cages in which brutal early Renaissance *signori* might have suspended their enemies to die a slow death; and the first time that I ventured to leap aboard one of its ever-circling "cars" (a snug fit for two standing), it was with some considerable trepidation. There is a good deal of creaking, even swaying in the wind, as the cable clunks its way over the carrying wheels and Perugia's Minimetrò seems considerably more than just decades into the future. You pull higher and higher, with the distance trav-

Disneyworld or gruesome death? Gubbio's *funivia*

elled further up the mountain necessitating an ever widening drop below what seems to be an increasingly fragile cage. I really could not bear to look out over the expansive countryside pulling into view, keeping my eyes fixed on the approach of the mountain's brow where once again the ground beneath would mean that a sudden fall need not be fatal. Jumping down with the summit achieved I was far more than ready to offer up my prayers of thanks for deliverance to the saint we had come to see. Now, perversely, I just cannot wait to do the ride on every visit to Gubbio.

Trains chug through Umbria on the whole quite slowly, as the connections for Perugia which opened this chapter typify. And it seems that the region is visited by all travellers through Italy at some point, being the *ombilico*, or belly-button, of the country. For example the Eurostar service, known as Freccia Rossa or Argento, Red or Silver Arrow, links Rome with Ancona, the major port on the Adriatic, by means of a journey through quite a good deal of Umbrian territory. But these almost "bullet" trains seem to have met their match here; just consider the stretch between Spoleto and Terni, passing through a series of nineteenth-century cuttings in the buttery yellow limestone, and still for quite a good part of its length single-track. This means that should any regional train be late or suffer a breakdown in the ascent, the express *in discesa,* coming down, has to wait at the top of the pass turning over its engines in frustration.

MANAGING THE PAST

So much of what is new in Umbria seems to have to confront the past in far from straightforward ways. Reflecting on this, I wished to speak directly with someone who more than most has had to articulate the modern expectations of national and even international legislation and planning with the immemorial treasury of Umbria's past. Who better than the Sovrintendente dei Belli Culturale for the region, Dr. Francesco Scoppola?

When I suggested to Dr. Scoppola that the post he holds represents a relatively modern development in human culture, judging that "conservation" is a substantially recent concept, he was quick to put me right:

> I trace the origin of my duties to Law XII of the ancient Roman law code we call the *Lex Tabularium*, known only through the survival of fragmentary inscriptions. It is called *de tigno iuncto ne solvito,* which we might translate as "On not untying joined beams", or perhaps more el-

egantly if somewhat more freely, "On preserving what has already been built." Add to this the role of the *aediles curales* from their institution in 367 BC, with their particular care for civic buildings and roads in Rome and nearby towns, and we already see a very ancient sense of continuous care for the built environment. Later came the expanded powers of the various offices of *curatores*, public curators of common property. Even when we imagine that there might have been a less cultural conceptual concern for heritage during the decline of classical civilization, we find the Law *de urbis ruinis deformetur*, specifically protecting the ancient structures of the Empire. And then after the fall of the last emperor in the West, Theodoric, Gothic King of Italy, appointed an official known as the *comes nitentium rerum,* the Count of the Care of Things. This leads us almost seamlessly to the civic achievements of the medieval *communes*, the Renaissance, and the Age of Enlightenment, and here we are today.

Francesco Scoppola is an impressive figure, but not in stature or the way he presents himself. He is of average build, in his late forties or early fifties, with curly dark hair flecked with the same grey even more prominent in his beard. He dresses in the sort of tweedy style that I associate with British schoolteachers and university lecturers—and like the best of them it is the animation of his face and particularly his eyes that convince you of his intellect and seriousness. He is the son of a very well-known journalist, recently deceased, who while remaining a convinced Catholic never flinched from subjecting his Church and the Italian society which it overwhelmingly influenced to a penetrating critique of truthfulness and self-examination. This moral earnestness seems to have been passed on to his son, as it was with a real zeal that he speaks about the duty of care given to those who inherit such a rich treasury of art and architecture. It is rumoured that he has also had serious clashes in the past of his professional life with organized business and the administrations which it perhaps too easily influences. This, however, thank goodness, has not prevented him from arriving at what surely must be one of the most prestigious positions that his calling affords; the care of the cultural heritage of Umbria.

"Umbria is a landscape of peaks and troughs, highs and lows—and this is mirrored in the behaviour and practice of its inhabitants. You can find the best possible methods and intentions here: for example, the laboratories of the Protezione Civile at Foligno, and the special centre for restoration at Santa Chiode, which were developed after the 1998 earthquake, are superb, and their work in restoring items and buildings of all kinds following the devastation was just short of miraculous. It was substantially complete by 2000—something that we have yet to see happening in a neighbouring region following the 2009 earthquake centred on L'Aquila in Abruzzo. But unfortunately Umbria is exemplary also in its abuses of development without consultation or permission and in the attitudes of some of its officials—obviously it is more difficult to cite direct examples of this," he adds, with a wry smile and infectious chuckle.

For Dr. Scoppola the heights of Umbria's cultural heritage can be summed up with a couple of notable individual examples, even if you have to travel far from Umbria to make the connections:

> Talking of highlights, the *biga* of Monteleone di Spoleto would be one of my choices, even though what we can see now in the local museum is just a copy of the original held at the New York Metropolitan Museum. This ceremonial chariot in wood and bronze from the sixth century BC really shows us how even in a relatively wild and isolated place, surrounded by high mountains, through artistic excellence, and a skilled manipulation of luxury materials, early Etruscan culture flowered to a degree that remains surprising. And whilst on the subject of the Metropolitan, take the case of the *studiolo* of the Palazzo Ducale at Gubbio; after this Renaissance masterwork of paneling had been taken to the United States the space which had once housed it stood bare for over a hundred years. Now modern *artigani*, craftsmen, have recreated the marquetry work precisely, using the same skills of their predecessors—and scholars have suggested a disposition of the pieces more true to the original plan than that recreated in New York. An example, then, of a situation which could be at first assessed as a cultural gap into space for the re-acquisition of age-old skills.

It is clear that Francesco Scoppola sees the Umbrian cultural glass half full, while being fully aware of the room for improvement. His appreciation of the special considerations which the past imposes upon the modern environment and a canny eye for the resources needed in restoration makes him the very model of the modern curator which he has been called to be. Long may he fulfill this role, and long may individuals of like mind and the same education follow him in it. In this way ancient Umbria will be for ever made new.

Epilogue

I had planned that my leave taking of you in this attempt to describe my beloved Umbria would be on the plain, as opposed to the heights where we started from, and, as elsewhere in this volume, I hope to be as good as my word. So where are we? Walking along what I can only describe as the promenade at Pasignano one late spring afternoon. The sun is dipping in the sky towards Castiglione del Lago, and the waters of Lake Trasimene are shimmering as waters will shimmer when all is well with the world, an ice cream has recently been eaten and a (couple of) *negroni* drunk. I am with my friends, Alessandro, Ulrika and Philippe and we are watching yachts flit across the relatively still waters in the direction of Isola Maggiore. It is a moment of unheeded and almost certainly undeserved happiness.

I have fifteen-year-old memories of coming to the beach here before my own house had a swimming pool; of my friend Atticus losing his spectacles after a spontaneous dive into the lake's relatively murky depths; of taking the tiny ferry over to Isola Polvese to walk around its nature trail, explore its ruined church and watch the autumn cyclamens cluster off the late September path. Bakingly hot Sunday afternoons give way to those days that can surprise with their breaking of all weather rules: the late August Bank Holiday weekend delivering a kind of Arctic storm of hail, bitter wind and freezing rain—the only refuge to go into one of the lakeside restaurants and binge on the delicate lake fish, *persico*, perch. Nicer than you might think.

And talking of a summer squall, one of the things about Umbria that perhaps I ought to have come cleaner about earlier is that it can have long periods of rather disappointing weather. Gloomy Novembers can give directly on to Decembers characterized by freezing fogs. Spring comes late, Easter almost always having its sprinkling of snow and the summer usually breaks on the feast of *Ferragosto*, 15 August. Umbria's is typical mountain weather, hence my desire to linger here on the lakeside this May evening soaking up the sun.

Despite this tranquil moment I cannot leave Umbria or indeed this lake without remembering once more a human "storm", the distant past and Rome's great defeat at the hands of the Carthaginian Hannibal.

Lake Trasimene

Byron's *Childe Harold* inevitably had the same thought, in Canto IV 62-5 of the *Pilgrimage*:

> Is of another temper, and I roam
> By Thrasimene's lake, in the defiles
> Fatal to Roman rashness, more at home;
> For there the Carthaginian's warlike wiles
> Come back before me, as his skill beguiles
> The host between the mountains and the shore,
> Where Courage falls in her despairing files,
> And torrents, swoll'n to rivers with their gore,
> Reek through the sultry plain, with legions scattered o'er,
>
> Like to a forest felled by mountain winds;
> And such the storm of battle on this day,
> And such the frenzy, whose convulsion blinds
> To all save carnage, that, beneath the fray,
> An earthquake reeled unheededly away!
> None felt stern Nature rocking at his feet,
> And yawning forth a grave for those who lay
> Upon their bucklers for a winding-sheet;
> Such is the absorbing hate when warring nations meet...
>
> Far other scene is Thrasimene now;
> Her lake a sheet of silver, and her plain
> Rent by no ravage save the gentle plough;
> Her aged trees rise thick as once the slain
> Lay where their roots are; but a brook hath ta'en -
> A little rill of scanty stream and bed -
> A name of blood from that day's sanguine rain;
> And Sanguinetto tells ye where the dead
> Made the earth wet, and turned the unwilling waters red.

From the hamlet of Sanguineto, as from all the lakeside settlements, the view and indeed all the roads lead you naturally towards that bigger, better known neighbouring Italian region, Tuscany. Even driving around the lake on the main road, right over Hannibal's battlefield, will take you in and out of both Umbria and Tuscany a couple of times, and the horizon is always dominated by Monte Amiata, southern Tuscany's Mount Fuji equivalent. And there is no getting around it that Cortona, of *Under the Tuscan Sun* fame, is the town in the vicinity of the lake with the most compelling allure, though personally I have always thought Frances Mayes rather to have overstated her Tuscan credentials when the border with *little* Umbria is so near, less than a couple of miles in fact. I once encountered an elderly English man who lived at Città della Pieve on Cortona's station; he possessed a very place-specific licence to conduct certain Anglican religious services in Umbria, but here he was, *post cultum*, travelling home. He also clearly thought the boundary between the two regions to be fluid at precisely this point. After all, it is the *same* sun that shines on both Tuscany and Umbria here.

And yes, it is to general well-being that I turn again as my final explanation of all this—the idea that somehow in spite of the vagaries of the weather, the bloody history and the bloody annoying modern bureaucracy the quality of the sunlight just somehow is better here than elsewhere. There must be many places in the world that offer an equal peace to that which I and so many others find in Umbria, in all its seasons, but none could offer it to quite the same recipe of historical and artistic richness melded with timeless attractions. Have I finally become Umbrian, then, along the way? A Eugubine by virtue of my mad, joyous streak? A Perugian in my down and bitter moods? From Assisi when my spiritual antennae are at their most sensitive? Of course not. There is still a long way to go, as the omissions and shortcomings of this book make all too evident. But I hope that there will also be a long time yet in which to travel these hills, follow these rivers, walk through these woods and stand before these paintings. But the point is that "being at home" here is still the thing I crave for, and I hope that my writing of it might just make it a craving that you can not only share but, better still, satisfy. Welcome to Umbria!

Further Reading

Addison, Joseph, *Remarks on Several Parts of Italy*. London: 1705

Boardman, John (ed.), *The Oxford History of the Classical World*. Oxford: OUP, 1986

Campbell Ross, Ian, *Umbria*. London: Viking, 1996

Carpenetto, Dino, *Italy in the Age of Reason 1685-1789*. London: Longman, 1987

Ginsborg, Paul, *A History of Contemporary Italy: Society and Politics 1943-68*. Harmondsworth: Penguin, 1990

Giorgetti, Dario, *Umbria: Itinerari archeologici*. Rome: Newton Compton, 1986

Gordon, George, Lord Byron, *Complete Poetical Works*. Oxford: OUP, 1970

Guida d'Italia: Umbria. 6th edn., Milan: Touring Club Italiano, 1999

Harris, W. V., *Rome in Etruria and Umbria*. Oxford: Clarendon Press, 1971

Hay, Denys, *Italy in the Age of the Renaissance*. London: Longman, 1989

Hearder, Harry, *Italy in the Age of the Risorgimento 1790-1870*. London: Longman, 1983

Hutton, Edward, *Cities of Umbria*. London: Methuen, 1905

James, Henry, *Italian Hours*. (1909) London: Century, 1986

Keates, Jonathan, *Umbria*. London: George Philip, 1991

Larner, John, *Italy in the Age of Dante and Petrarch*. London: Longman, 1980

Livius, Titus (Livy), *The War with Hannibal*. Harmondsworth: Penguin Classics, 1965

Le Guide di DOVE: Umbria. Milan: Corriere della Sera, 2005

McIntyre, Anthony, *Medieval Tuscany and Umbria*. London: Viking, 1992

Macadam, Alta, *Blue Guide, Umbria*. London and New York: A. & C. Black and W. W. Norton, 1993

Mack Smith, Denis, *Italy: a Modern History*. Ann Arbor: University of Michigan Press, 1959

Murray, Peter, *The Art of the Renaissance*. London: Thames and Hudson, 1963

Owenson, Sydney, Lady Morgan, *Italy*. London: 1821

Procopius, *History of the Wars*. London: Heinemann, 1979

Propertius, Sextus, *The Poems*. Oxford. OUP, 2009

Plinius, Gaius Caecilius Secundus (Pliny the Younger), *Letters*. Harmondsworth: Penguin Classics, 1963

Ricci, Corrado, *Umbria Santa*, trans. H. C. Stewart. London: Faber and Gwyer, 1927

Sorbini, Alberto, *Perugia: nei libri di viaggio dal Settecento all'unità d'Italia*. Foligno: Editoriale Umbra, 1994

Sabatier, Paul, *Vie de Saint François d'Assise*. Strasbourg: 1893

Smollett, Tobias, *Travels through France and Italy* (ed. Frank Felsenstein). Oxford: OUP, 1979

Southern, Richard William, *Western Society and the Church in the Middle Ages*.
Harmondsworth: Penguin, 1970
Spivey, Nigel, *Etruscan Italy*. London: Batsford, 1990
St. Aubin de Teran, Lisa, *A Valley in Italy*. Toronto: Penguin, 1995
Unsworth, Barry, *After Hannibal*. London: Hamish Hamilton, 1996
Yoan, Niek, *Federico Cesi*. New York: Betascript, 2011

Some useful websites:

www.english.regioneumbria.eu
www.umbriaonline.com
www.perugiaonline.com
www.umbria.org

Index of Literary & Historical Names

Addison, Joseph 9
Aeneas 5
Aelianus 55
Aistulf, Duke 56
Albertino, St. 102
Albornoz, Gil Alvarez Calvillo de,
     Cardinal 26, 68-70, 96, 104, 152,
     174, 189
Alessi, Galeazzo 97
Alexander II (Anselmo da Baggio) 67
Alexander VI (Rodrigo Borgia) 130
Ancaiani family 31
Angelico, Fra/Beato (Guido di Pietro)
     92, 118, 127, 128
"Apicius" 155
Apuleius (Lucius Apuleius) 155
Aquinas, Thomas St. 90, 100, 115
Arbore, Renzo 191
Arnth Velimnia 22
Augustus (Caius Octavianus), Emperor
     1, 5, 9, 12, 35, 36, 41,
Aule Mettele 34
Aulus Pompeius 180

Baglioni family 24, 25, 125
Baldi, Annalisa 192
Baldy, Colin 192-96
Bellucci, Monica 44
Benigni, Roberto 43
Belisarius 7, 55
Benedict, St. 8, 15, 109-111, 116
Benedict XI (Nicola Boccasini) 67
Benefial, Marco 133, 145
Bernadino of Siena, St. (Bernado
     Albizzeschi) 98, 101, 119, 120
Berlusconi, Silvio 50
Betti, Bernardino (Pinturicchio) 12, 25,
     120, 121, 122, 124, 126, 130, 134
Bianchi, Giovan Domenico 138
Bonfigli, Benedetto 130
Boniface VIII (Benedetto Gaetani) 27,

101, 119
Boswell, James 9, 181
Botticelli, Sandro 122, 132
Bourbon-Sorbello family 63, 147
Brodsky, Joseph 35
Buffalotti family 147
Buonarroti, Michelangelo 98, 123, 128,
     130
Burri, Alberto 134-136
Buzzi, Tomasso 42
Byron, George (Lord Rochdale) 4, 52,
     181-182, 210

Caesar (Caius Julius) 7
Calasanz, St. Joseph 139
Calzoni, Umberto 17
Caprarola, Cola da 98
Campbell Ross, Ian 3, 34, 96, 122,
     171, 185-86
Campello della Spina, Paolo 52
Cancian, Domenico (Mgr.) 104
Caporali, Bartolomeo 130
Carducci, Giosuè 3, 52
Carlo Felice, King 156
Castiglione, Baldassare 142
Catherine of Siena, St. (Caterin
     Benincasa) 68
Celestine V (Pietro Angelerio da
     Morrone) 100, 118
Cesi, Federico (Cardinal) 138
Cesi, Federico II 138
Cesi, Federico III 101, 137-141, 147,
     181
Cesi, Gian Giacomo 138
Chamberlain, Richard 44
Charlemagne, Emperor 58
Charles of Anjou, King 95
Chiabotto, Cristina 66
Cicero (Marcus Tullius) 180
Cimabue (Cenno di Pepo) 112-114,
     128

Circignani, Antonio and Nicolò (Pomarancio) 131
Clare of Assisi, St. (Chiara Offreduccio) 47, 93, 95, 108, 116, 117
Clare of Montefalco, St. 105, 118
Clark, Kenneth 121
Clement VII (Giulio de'Medici) 28
Conca, Tomaso 134
Constant, St. (Costanzo) 51, 202
Constantine, Emperor 6, 152
Corot, Jean-Baptiste-Camille 34, 181
Coureau, Clothilde 148
Crescentino (Crescenzio), St. 50, 51
Cynthia 35, 36

Dante, Alighieri 43, 116
Danti, Antonio and Ignazio 1
Decius, Emperor 51
De Filiis, Anastasio 137
Del Verrocchio, Andrea 123
Delon, Alain 44
Diamante, Fra 132
Dimmock, Charlie 59
Donini family 186
D'Amelia, Piermatteo (Master of the Gardner Altarpiece) 132, 133
D'Este family 96
Da Vinci, Leonardo 126
Da Viterbo, Pier Francesco 146
della Corgna family 63, 147
della Francesca, Piero 104, 121, 123, 133, 142
di Alviano, Isabella (Cesi) 138, 140
di Cambio, Arnolfo 82
di Fabriano, Gentile 130
di Jacopo, Giovan Battista (Rosso Fiorentino) 134
di Gigliaccio, Giovanni 81
di Giuli, Peppe 182
di Lorenzo, Fiorenzo 130
di Micheluccio, Tommaso 92
di Sangallo, Antonio the Younger 25, 146, 180

di Savoia, Emmanuele Filiberto 148
di Savoia family 148
di ser Giovanni di Mone Cassai, Tommaso (Massaccio) 131
Diocletian, Emperor 1, 51
Dominic, St. 109
Duccio, Agostino di 120

Edward IV, King 142
Elias, Brother 107
Elizabeth I, Queen 94
Ercolano I and II, Saints 51

Faobard II, Duke 58
Farnese, Giulia 130
Farnese, Pier Luigi 138
Felicianus, St. 51
Felicitas, St. 55
Fellini, Federico 43
Ferrara, Giorgio 190
Fini, Gianfranco 86
Flagellants 24
Flaminius, Consul (Gaius) 5, 39
Florenzi family 63
Florido (Florus), St. 55, 62, 73
Fontana, Giovanni and Domenico 180
Fortebraccio, Braccio 24, 101, 137, 147
Fortebraccio, Carlo 101, 103
Francis of Assisi, St. 8, 13, 15, 38, 42, 47, 48, 93, 95, 97, 100, 105, 107-120, 128, 157
Frederick I, Emperor (Barbarossa) 68
Frederick II, Emperor (Stupor Mundi) 68

Galilei, Galileo 101, 139, 181
Garibaldi, Anita 81
Garibaldi, Giuseppe 26, 102
George, St. 50
George VI, King 175
Germanicus (Claudius Drusus) 34
Ghibellines (faction) 67, 68, 69, 80, 85, 91, 177

Ghirlandaio, Domenico 122
Gilliam, Terry 192
Giotto (Ambrogio di Bondone) 112
Gnaeus Satrius Rufus 31
Goethe, Johann Wolfgang von 9, 106,
    181
Goldoni, Carlo 153
Gozzoli, Benozzo 118, 120
Gregory IX (Ugolino di Conti) 15, 109
Gregory XIII (Ugo Boncompagni) 1
Gregory XVI (Bartolomeo Alberto
    Cappellari) 176
Grillparzer, Franz 178
Gualberto, St. Giovanni 157
Guelphs (faction) 67, 69, 80, 85, 91,
    177
Guidalotti family 24
Guidetti, Guidetto 138

Hadrian, Emperor 5
Hannibal Barca 5, 38, 209-10
Hawkwood, Sir John (Giovanni Acuto)
    68 -72, 101
Henry IV, Emperor 58
Hickox, Richard 190
Hill, Terence (Mario Girotti) 43
Homer 36

Innocent III (Lotario dei Conti di
    Segni) 67, 109
Innocent IV (Sinibaldo Fieschi) 68, 117
Isaac, Master 114

Jacopo da Todi (Jacopone de'Benedetti)
    118, 119
James, Henry 2, 7, 23, 29, 33, 38, 107,
    109, 110, 198-99, 201
John Paul II (Karol Wojtyla) 99
Julius II (Giulio della Rovere) 125, 126
Julius III (Giovanni del Monte) 147

Keates, Jonathan 105, 139, 173

Lafuente, Julio 98
Laurana, Luciano 142
Lignani Marchesani, Andrea 86-87,
    145-46, 148
Lippi, Fra Filippo 131, 132, 133
Livy (Titus Livius) 2, 39, 40,
Lo Spagno 81
Lombardelli, Gian Battista 140
Lorenzetti, Pietro 112, 114, 128
Lucretia 20
Lungarotti family 185
Lupatelli, Domenico 102

Malatesta family 96
Mancini, Francesco Federico 134
Mandela, Nelson 59
Marc Antony (Marcus Antonius) 41
Marius Curius Denatus 180
Martini, Francesco Giorgio 142
Martini, Simone 112
Martin IV (Simon de Brion) 67
Massaccio, see di ser Giovanni di Mone
    Cassai, Tommaso
Mattiacci, Giovanni 73
Mazzini, Giuseppe 26
Maxentius, Emperor 6
Mayes, Frances 121, 211
Medici family 147
Medicus, St. 50
Menotti, Giancarlo 188-90
Mezzastris, Bernadino and Pierantonio
    131
Midler, Bette 59
Monaldeschi family 96
Monacelli, Beatrice 194
Monicelli, Mario 43
Montefeltro family 96, 147
Montefeltro, Federico 124, 140-143
Montemelini family 63
Morlacchi, Francesco 29
Mortimer, John 121
Morton, H.V. 23
Mussolini, Benito 174

Narses 7, 55, 175
Nelli, Agostino 128, 164
Nelli, Ottaviano 128
Nicholas IV (Girolamo Masci) 114
Nicholas V (Tommaso Parentucelli) 119
Nouvel, Jean 202

Oddi family 63
Orsini, Olimpia (Cesi) 138
Otto III, Emperor 58
Ovid (Ovidius Naso) 140, 178
Owenson, Sydney (Lady Morgan) 9, 27

Pagnotta, Carlo 190
Paul III (Alessandro Farnese) 26, 28,
    66, 123, 138, 180
Pedellaio, Rosso 83
Perugino, see Vanucci, Pietro
Pinturicchio, see Betti, Bernadino
Pisano, Giovanni and Niccolà 83
Pius V (Alessandro Alghieri) 97
Pius VI (Giovanni Braschi) 180
Pius XII (Eugenio Pacelli) 117, 157
Plautus (Titus Maccius) 30, 31
Pliny the Elder (Caius Plinius) 20, 23,
    180
Pliny the Younger (Caius Caecilius) 2,
    37, 38, 52, 184
Propertius (Sextus Propertius) 35, 36,
    106

Raphael, see Santi, Rafaelo
Remus 5
Ricci, Corrado 8
Rita, St, 8, 99
Ronchi, Tomaso (Mgr.) 74
Romulus 5
Romulus Agustulus, Emperor 54
Roncalli, Cristoforo (Pomarancio) 131
Rufino, St. 106
Rusuti, Filippo 114
Rutelli, Francesco 189

St. Aubin de Terán, Lisa 95, 135, 192
St. Francis, Master of 111
Sabatier, Paul 8
Santi, Giovanni 124, 126
Santi, Rafaelo (Raphael) 124, 125, 127,
    130
Sassolini, Cesare 87
Saviano, Roberto 134
Saylor, Stephen 30
Scacchi, Cesare 94
Scalza, Ippolito 98
Scholastica, St. 109, 116
Scoppola, Francesco 141, 205-8
Sforza, Battista (Montefeltro) 142
Signorelli, Luca 92-93, 122, 128, 133,
    146, 187
Sixtus IV (Francesco della Rovere) 123
Smollett, Tobias 9
Solari, Marco 42
Sordini, Giuseppe 56
Spencer, Bud 44
Speranza Alhama di Gesù, Mother 99
Stelluti, Francesco 137
Stewart Gardner, Isabella 133
Strabo 32

Tacitus (Publius Cornelius) 37
Terence (Terentius Lucanus) 31
Theodoric 54, 55, 206
Tiberius, Emperor 34
Titchmarsh, Alan 59
Toritti, Giacopo 114
Toscano, Bruno 54
Totila 7, 55, 56

Ubaldo, St. 68, 84-85, 203-4
Ugolini di Prete, Ilario 128
Umberto I, King 148
Unsworth, Barry 24, 40, 159-60
Urban IV (Jacques Pantaléon) 67, 90-92
Urban V (William de Grimoard) 69

Valentine, St. 9, 51

Van Heeck, Johannes 137
Vannucci, Pietro (Perugino) 8, 98, 121,
    122-127, 130, 133, 184
Vasari, Giorgio 131, 146
Vassella, Pietro 194
Veneziano, Boninsegna 82
Vicchi, Giancarlo 135-136
Vici, Andrea 180
Victor, St. 50
Vignola (Giacomo Barozzi da Vignola)
    66, 98
Virgil (Publius Vergilius Maro) 36, 51,
    180-181
Vissani, Gianfranco 169-170
Vitelli family 146-147

Walsh, Tommy 59
Witges 7, 55, 175

Zappia, Caterina 134
Zefferelli, Franco 49
Zeri, Federico 13

Index of Places & Landmarks

Accademia dei Lincei 13, 137, 148
Acquasparta 138-140, 147, 178, 181
  Palazzo Cesi 137-140
Abeto 19
Abruzzo 116, 120, 207
Amelia 34, 42, 133, 173, 186
Amerini hills 3, 186
Amiata, Monte 211
Amore Misericordioso, Santuario dell'
  (Collevalenza) 98-99
Arezzo 16, 112, 123
Arrone 43
Assisi 13-14, 15, 26, 47, 57, 66, 68-70,
  85, 100, 110, 115, 116, 131, 175,
  183, 197
  Basilica di Santa Chiara 108
  Basilica of St. Francis 105, 107,
    111-115, 122, 128
  Church of San Damiano 108, 116
  Church of Santa Maria degli Angeli
    15, 97, 115, 126, 131, 133, 177
  Church of Santa Maria sopra
    Minerva 58
  Eremo delle Carceri 13
  Piazza Mateotti 14
  Temple of Minerva 58, 105
Avigiano Umbro 133
Avignon 27, 68

Bastardo 4, 176
Bettona 126
Bevagna (Mevania) 6, 42, 70, 78
Bologna 2, 29, 144
Bolsena 41, 89-91, 92, 95
Bomarzo 42
Bourbons del Monte, Marquisate of 1
Bridge of Augustus, Narnia 9, 32

Campanello 196
Campania 48

Canoscio 55, 64
Carpina river/valley 101
Carsulae 6, 32, 57
Casa del Diavolo 15
Cascia 8, 99, 131
  Basilica of Santa Rita 99
Castel Fiorentino 135
Castel Rigone 98
Castello di Monestevole 64
Castello di Petroia 141
Castello di Reschio 67
Casteluccio, Plain of 4, 150
Castiglione del Lago 147, 209
Cerqueto 126
Cerreto di Spoleto 64, 94
Cesi 181
Chiano river/valley 17, 19, 154
Chiasco river/valley 4, 18
Chiusi (Chamars) 20
Chiusi, Lake 175
Chiesa Nuova (Church of St. Mary and
  St. Augustine, Rome) 138
Chienti river 4
Cinecittà, Rome 42
Citerna 38, 131
Città della Pieve 43, 122, 125, 126,
  128, 177, 211
Città di Castello (Tifernum Tiberinum)
  2, 15, 38, 44, 50, 55, 62, 64, 70-
  74, 78, 79, 86-87, 101, 128, 131,
  133, 134, 135, 144, 145, 146, 149,
  163, 165, 188
  Alberto Burri Museum 135
  Centro Documentazioni delle
    Tradizioni Popolari 155
  Chapel of Santa Maria dei Bianchi
    126
  Church of San Domenico 187
  Diocesan Museum 55-56, 134
  Museum of Fine Art 146

Palazzo Albizzini 135
Palazzo Vitelli alla Cannoniera 146
Piazza Gabriotti 79
Piazza Mateotti 79
Piazza Santa Maria Maggiore 71
Ristorante Da Lea 170-171
Teatro dei Illuminati 30
Via San Florido 170
Civitella del Lago 169
Civitella Raniera 64, 189
Clitunno river/springs 3, 4, 51-53, 180-81
Colfiorito, Plain of 4, 150, 156
Collazone 119, 183
Colle Plinio 37
Collevalenza 98
Como 37
Corbara, Lake 4, 169
Corciano 155
    Museum of the Casa Contadina 155-56
Cornetto 154
Cortona 38, 211
Cospaia, Republic of 1
Costacciaro 18
Cucco, Monte 18, 156

della Corgna, Duchy of the 1
Deruta 123, 177, 183-4
Devil's Lair Caves (Le Tane del Diavolo) 17, 18, 150
Dunaroba 19

Emilia-Romagna 2, 13, 144, 154, 166, 167
Etruria, see Tuscany

Fano (Fanum Fortunae) 7, 69
Ferentillo 43
Fonte Columba 105
Fontignano 128
Fossato di Vico 18
Flaminian Way (Via Flaminia) 2, 5, 18,

32, 53-57, 62, 79
Florence 122, 124, 147, 197
Foggia 174
Foligno 3, 6, 51, 56, 68 78, 126, 130, 134, 197, 207
Palazzo Trinci 131
Piazza della Republica 79

Giove 42
Grotta di Monte Cucco 18
Gualdo Cataldo 176
Gualdo Tadino (Tadinum) 6, 18, 19, 55, 58, 66, 78, 83-85, 184
    Rocca del Flea 58, 66
Gubbio (Eugubium) 18, 22, 23, 43, 68, 73, 78, 79, 101, 112, 128, 140-143, 178, 203-5
    Diocesan Museum 141
    Fontana dei Matti 83
    Palazzo dei Consoli 141
    Palazzo dei Priori 83
    Palazzo Ducale 142, 207
    Piazza Grande 78, 83, 84
    Teatro Romano 31, 191

Ingino, Monte 83, 204
Isola Maggiore, Lake Trasimene 15
Italy, Kingdom of 26
Italy, Republic of 143, 156

L'Aquila 120, 207
La Scarzuola, Città Ideale (Montegiove) 42
Lazio 2, 7, 42, 91, 116, 165

Macerata 4
Marbled Cascades (Cascata delle Marmore) 4, 9, 43, 178-182
Marches, The (Le Marche) 1, 4, 13, 116, 130, 141
Marsciano 19
Martani hills 3, 6, 66, 176
Massa Martana 6, 50, 176

Metauro river/valley 7
Metropolitan Museum, New York 123, 141, 207
Milan 10, 30, 69, 173, 197
Molisse 116
Mongiovino 131
Monte Cassino 109, 174
Monte Santa Maria in Tiberina 148
Montecastelli 64
Montecastello di Vibio 30
Montedoglio, Lake 4
Montefalco 68, 118, 120, 126, 131, 185, 186
Montefiascone 91
Montegiove 42
Monteleone d'Orvieto 30
Montepulciano 175
Montone 64, 74, 101-104, 147, 192
    Piazza Fortebraccio 102
Morra river/valley 50, 135, 166, 175, 187, 192

Naples 30
Narni (Narnia) 6, 9, 18, 26, 33, 34, 41, 69, 85, 130, 133, 173
    Church of Santa Maria 41
National Archaeological Museum of Umbria 17-19, 115
National Gallery of Le Marche 141
National Gallery of Umbria 82, 123, 128, 130, 146
Nequinium 41
Nera river/valley (Valnerina) 3, 4, 6, 32, 58, 64, 156, 173, 174, 178, 181, 192
Niccone river/valley 64, 67
Nocera Umbra (Nuceria) 6, 38, 68, 184
    Piazza Caprera 79
    Portico di San Filippo 38
Norcia (Nursia) 3, 8, 19, 29, 64, 94, 109, 165, 167
    Castellina 66
    Piazza San Benedetto 66

Orte 173
Orvieto (Volsinii) 3, 17, 18, 20, 21, 28, 41, 69, 89-93, 96, 100-101, 105, 133, 134, 137, 163, 169, 175, 185
    Capella Nuova 127, 128
    Crocifisso del Tufo 21
    Duomo (Cathedral) 89-93, 127, 128, 133
    Pozzo di San Patrizio (St. Patrick's Well) 28
Ossaia 40
Otricoli (Otriculum) 2, 6,

Pacciano, Monte 82
Paglia river/valley 4, 66
Panicale 125, 131
    Church of San Sebastiano 125
Pantanelli 118
Papal State 1, 26, 69, 93, 95, 101, 152-153, 165
Parco del Sole 183
Parrano 17
Passignano 98, 209
Perugia (Perusia) 1, 2, 7, 9, 10, 13, 15, 20-28, 29, 34, 38, 41, 44, 49, 64, 67, 69, 78, 80, 83, 85, 86, 91, 94, 101, 105, 115, 120, 122, 125, 128, 130, 131, 134, 138, 147, 155, 177, 182, 183, 193, 197-203
    Carducci Gardens 25
    Church of San Domenico 26, 115
    Church of San Severo 127
    Collegio del Cambio 125
    Corso Vanucci 23
    Duomo (Cathedral) 23, 26
    Fontana Maggiore 82-83
    Ipogeo dei Volumni 21, 22
    Palazzo dei Priori 81, 83
    Piazza IV Novembre 83, 191
    Porta Marzia 25
    Ristorante del Sole 200
    Rocca Paolina 26, 67

Torre degli Sciri 64, 65
Università degli Stranieri 27
Via dei Priori 23, 64
Piediluco, Lake 179, 181
Pietralunga 128
Poggio Aquilone 19
Pomerance 131
Ponte 64
Ponte San Giovanni 22, 49, 177, 197
Prato 131, 132
Preci 94
Preggio 102, 188
Puglia 116
Puglia river 4

Ravenna 54-56
Rieti 3, 107, 181
Rocca di Orvieto 28
Rome 20, 30, 41, 51, 54, 57, 68, 86,
   91, 120, 122, 130, 138, 152, 174,
   181, 197
Basilica of Santa Maria Maggiore
   138
Church of Santa Maria degli Angeli
   148
Church of Santa Maria in Aracoeli
   120

San Crescentino, Oratory of (Morra)
   187
San Faustino 50, 184
San Gémini 184
San Giustino 74
San Leo Bastia 154
San Pietro in Valle, Abbey of 58, 122
San Sepolchro, Borgo di 4, 123, 165,
   197
Sanguineto 40, 210
Sarsina 30
Sant'Andrea di Sorbello 67
Sant'Eutizio, Abbey of 94
Santa Chiode 207
Santa Maria in Pantano, Church of 57

Scheggia, Town 18
Scheggia, Pass 6
Scheggino 192-93
Selci-Lama 37
Sibiline mountains 13
Sicily 19, 20, 91, 95, 101
Siena 68, 130
Sigilo 18
Sistine Chapel 123, 126, 133
Spello (Hispellium) 10-14, 25, 41, 78,
   80, 85, 90, 126, 130
Capella Baglioni 12, 130
Enoteco Properzio 13
Palazzo Bocci 10
Ristorante La Bastiglia 13
Spoleto (Spoletum) 1, 2, 6, 13, 26, 41,
   51, 56, 64, 66, 68, 69, 78, 105,
   134, 177, 188-90, 191, 205
Basilica of San Salvatore 56, 122
Church of St. Agata 31
Duomo (Cathedral) 131, 132, 190
Piazza del Duomo 79
Teatro Romano 31, 190
Subasio, Monte 3, 10, 13, 156
Subiaco 15, 109, 110
Syracuse (Siracusa) 20

Tempietto (Clitunno) 53-57, 122
Terni (Interamnia Nahars) 4, 6, 7, 9,
   10, 42, 51, 58, 64, 66, 68, 85, 105,
   118, 134, 138, 165, 173-76, 181,
   184, 186, 193, 205
Basilica of San Valentino 181
Museum of Art 133
Tiber (Tevere) river/valley 1-6, 13, 16,
   19, 33, 38, 51, 62, 64, 101, 102,
   148, 156, 173, 178, 186, 188, 203
Tivoli (Tibur) 35, 42
Todi (Tuder) 19, 21, 23, 57, 80, 98,
   119, 138, 154, 183
Church of San Fortunato 115
Church of Santa Maria della
   Consolazione 98

Palazzo dei Priori 81
Palazzo del Capitano 81
Palazzo del Podestà 81
Piazza del Popolo 80-82, 191
Topino river 3, 51, 66
Torgiano 185
Trasimene, Lake (Trasimeno) 5, 9, 15,
    38, 63, 102, 125, 155, 156, 186,
    192, 197, 209, 210
Trestina 64, 202-3
Casteluccio 64
Trevi 51, 70, 85, 98, 125, 131, 196
Tuoro 192
Turin 10, 173
Tuscany 1, 7, 13, 19, 48, 49, 74, 116,
    147, 152, 165, 175, 185, 210-11
Tyrennian Sea 4

Umbertide 30, 64, 131, 148, 149, 175,
    196
Umbria, Vale of 2, 13, 26, 51, 66, 70,
    118, 196
Urbino 1, 96, 124, 141, 142

Vaiano 175
Vatican 1, 21, 46
Veii 20
Velino river 178-80
Verna 64, 186
Verna, Monte 38
Viterbo 91